A BIT OF MYSELF

A Bit of Myself

Filomena Abys-Smith

To order additional copies of this book, contact:
Xlibris Corporation
1-888-795-4274
www.Xlibris.com
Orders@Xlibris.com
599793

Contents

This memoir is dedicated to my parents,
Fortuna Melise Abys and Ugo Abys.

I am forever grateful to them for having had the courage to leave behind a country that they loved with only the hope for a better future. I have tried in this memoir to give them a voice.

To my husband, Peter Thomas Smith,
Thank you for your never-ending encouragement and support.
Thank you for all the laughter and tears.
Most important, thank you for James and Nicole; they have given meaning to my life.
To James and Nicole, you both are the love of my life and the joy of my soul. Thank you for fulfilling my American Dream.

Special thanks to my cousin Ana Maria Catapano of Naples, Italy for taking the time to help me translate and spell out Neapolitan expressions, this simple act of kindness brought us closer and I'm forever grateful.

Foreword

by Peter Thomas Smith

I knew from the very moment I met my wife, Filomena, in the summer of 1986 that she was a special person; I was drawn to her by her straightforward, clean lifestyle. No drinking, no drugs, no gambling, not even a cigarette. I was the complete opposite. I had delved into drinking and drugs from a very young age, constantly hanging out with the wrong crowd.

I was clueless as how to live a sober, drug-free life until I met her. As much as I wanted to be with her, I hesitated, fearing rejection, asking myself why such a clean-cut person would want to be with a madman like me.

You will read in her memoir the struggle with my drug addiction; she calls them my inner demons. It was never her intent to publish this book; I, after reading each chapter and contemplating on her struggles as well as my own, encouraged her to do so, hoping that the message she tries to convey will inspire others to live a better life.

Names have been changed in order to protect the privacy of those individuals.

A Memoir of Passion

This memoir is written with deep affection for my children and all my descendants so that they may better understand their ancestors and the passion for life that helped us become an American family.

Through this journal, I share not only my most cherished and intimate memories but also memories of great struggle and heartbreak, hoping to reveal to the reader a bit of myself.

To the reader who does not know me well, please understand that I wrote this memoir with the intent of only sharing it with my family and then placing it in the old steamer trunk, which we arrived to the USA with, in the hope that my descendants would eventually read it and understand who I was; a kind of time capsule.

After many heartfelt conversations with my husband, Peter, he encouraged me to have it published, feeling that the message of determination to reach the American Dream will inspire others. We both hope you will enjoy reading and putting into practice the message I try to convey.

PART 1

Chapter 1

Bagnoli Remembered, 1955-1961

Bagnoli is a simple town near the coast of Naples, not far from the bustle of the heart of the city but far enough to maintain a more serene, more peaceful soul within a vibrant city that has been a cultural center for thousands of years. It is in the town of Bagnoli where I was born and have my fondest memories of family ties, savory food, and geographic beauty.

My earliest memories of life in Bagnoli are of simple pleasures enjoyed by happy people who took great care and pride in the smallest details of daily life but especially in preparing and serving meals.

The home I recall most vividly from the six years I lived in Bagnoli was a one-bedroom cold-water flat, which I shared with my older brother, Peppino, and our parents. The main focal point of this home was a large kitchen with a pilot-ignited, two-burner gas stove, a marble sink with an attached marble washboard, and a few cabinets on the wall with a small grey icebox. In a corner stood a tin bathtub where we took our baths. During the warm summer months, my mom (Nonna Fortuna) carried the tub outside to the back of the house, where there was a small patch of dirt. She would fill the tub with cold water using very large pots and allow the water to be heated by the hot Neapolitan sun. I have such vivid happy memories of enjoying this simple playtime with my brother that all the splash parks I've visited cannot replace this childish joy.

Beyond this small patch of dirt was a grassy area that overlooked the train tracks; we occasionally walked along the trains' tracks toward the NATO base. It was on those walks that I recall seeing rusted leftover American jeeps from the war that eventually changed all our lives. To the front of our home was a paved street, and across from the street was a grassy field where we spent most of our playtime. It still amazes me that such tasty meals were prepared on a two-burner stove and that we managed to stay clean and well dressed.

Everyone in Bagnoli seemed to take great care in housekeeping and preparing daily meals. Bright wash was always on everyone's clothing line, and there was a daily ritual of sweeping, mopping, and polishing; but the daily ritual I enjoyed the most was walking to the local food market. The market was filled with a variety of fresh fruits and vegetables. I was thrilled whenever my mom stopped to buy a cactus pear, carefully showing me how to hold and peel open this prickly fruit without getting the thorns stuck in my fingers.

I walked around holding and eating the pear, dripping red juice down my arm, feeling very loved and special. Each vendor's stall had a colorful display of bright purple eggplants, shiny red tomatoes, and cantaloupe-size lemons that are meant to be sliced and eaten. I can close my eyes and still see the mounds of fruits, smell the citrusy aroma of oranges and lemons, and hear the vendors' shouts, urging us, "Venit a vere com e bell! (Come, take a look how beautiful!)" I can still feel the excitement from a vendor as he waved a live octopus at my mother, telling her, "Uardate comme e frisc ro mare (Look, fresh from the sea)."

A trip to the market was a family event; we always met aunts and uncles, cousins, and grandparents. It seemed that we were in some way related to everyone in Bagnoli, and I was never lonely.

I don't think anyone in Bagnoli had a refrigerator, and all food items for the daily meals were freshly purchased. At times, we did buy ice from Signora Bettina, who had huge blocks of ice delivered to her home storefront, which she covered with burlap cloth to keep the ice from melting before she could sell smaller chunks to all her neighbors. On hot summer days, it was a thrill to run to Signora Bettina to buy a small chunk of ice and fight my brother for a few licks while we quickly walked home to place this prize in our icebox. It was pure joy when we were given a few extra cents to buy an ice slushy from Signora Bettina. She would scrape a metal plane over the block of ice to make ice shavings, and then pour the ice shavings into a paper cup, pouring flavored syrup over the top. Every mouthful of the cold, sweet ice brought a smile and an "ah, ah" to our lips.

Her next-door neighbor was Donna Rosa, who owned the local live-chicken market, and she sold not only chickens and eggs but hand-rolled cigarettes. On rare occasions when we did buy extra eggs, milk, or cheese, we placed the small block of ice in the old grey icebox and placed those food items on top. Like most Italians, we drank very little milk, which was always mixed with espresso coffee (caffe latte). Our breakfast usually consisted of a large bowl of caffe latte with bits of day-old bread soaked into it. This breakfast was eaten with a spoon, much like we eat cereal today.

Donna Rosa was very old, wrinkled, and almost completely blind. Whenever my dad bought fresh eggs from Donna Rosa, she placed her one good eye directly on top of the money to make sure it was the correct amount. When we started to laugh, she too would laugh out loud and, in a forceful Neapolitan dialect, ask, "I know you, little Ugo. You wouldn't cheat me, would you?" My dad made her laugh even louder by telling her that no one could get past her one good eye. He occasionally purchased a still-warm fresh egg and, with a stick, put a hole in the egg to suck out the inside.

I recall spending many of my lunchtime hours at Donna Rosa's while my mother fed me as much pasta with fresh tomato sauce as possible. Apparently, I had a poor appetite and ate better while watching the different-colored chickens. My mom carried a plate full of pasta with me in tow, asking Donna Rosa if I could watch the chickens while I ate. "Of course," Donna Rosa replied, "little Mena is much too thin. She needs to eat more." Looking back, I realize that they were trying to feed me enough pasta for a full-grown man. So there I stood among the straw and sawdust, eating my pasta, admiring the chickens' beautiful colors, and clinging to my mother if one got too close.

My memory is often sparked by simple daily events, and today, the sight of live chickens conjures up visions of walking home with my brother near Donna Rosa's home and finding a plump white chicken meandering about. We both looked at each other in amazement, and since we could not possibly know where the white chicken came from, a few words were exchanged between us as Peppino quickly scooped up the chicken, carrying our new pet home. We were instructed to put the chicken in the back of our home, where the small patch of dirt stood. Overjoyed by our pet, we both took very good care of Whitey and fed her the best of the leftovers for what seemed to me like a very long time. It seemed that my mom loved Whitey as much as we did; checking daily to make sure that our pet was in the best of health.

The sunny weather finally started to chill, and my mom asked us to step out of the home to play. As we played by the front door, we heard my mom yelling and crying. Quickly, we ran inside to find the chicken splashing about with a half-severed head, splattering blood all over the kitchen. I'm not sure if it was a dull blade or lack of skill, but my mom, attempting to cut the head off, missed and only partly severed the head. The chicken jumped out of my mother's grip, running a bloody muck while my mom yelled and cried. We stood in shock for a few seconds—my brother looking at me, I looking at my brother; but without hesitation, in unison, we both ran outside and started the clothesline connection, which was as quick as a phone call and in no time, Nonna Carmela arrived.

Nonna Carmela didn't blink an eye; she simply grabbed the chicken by its partially severed head, and that night, we had a warm bowl of Stracciatella soup. Grief counseling was not given, and we suffered no apparent emotional disorder.

We didn't have any heating unit in our home, and for the cold winter months, we kept warm with hot water bottles in bed or by adding extra clothing. I cannot remember ever being cold, and snow was unheard of.

My most vivid memories of Bagnoli are of sunny summer days spent at the beach, which was within walking distance of our home. Bagno Fortuna was the beach where my parents rented a small wooden cabana, and as soon as the weather got warm, we would head off early in the morning. My mother remained at home to clean up and prepare our lunch, which she delivered to us at noontime in a checkered black-and-white metal box.

My taste buds still dance to the memory of crispy pasta frittatas, lightly coated potato croquettes (*panzarotti*), creamy ricotta fritters, and mozzarella-filled rice croquettes. At the end of our meal, my dad purchased fresh melon and coconut slices from vendors walking the beach for us to snack on. I still have a great fondness for these fruits and indulge whenever possible.

Both of my parents were very fussy about washing our hands, brushing off all of the sand, and sitting down to have lunch as a family. The dining concept that was handed down to us by parents and grandparents is that people dine, animals eat. Regardless of how simple the meal is, it's how the food is prepared, served, and eaten that gives quality to our lives.

My memory is filled with simple pleasures of playing house in the wooden cabana with my female cousins. Crab hunting with my brother, which brings back this one particular comical memory. We were, as usual, waiting near the shore for incoming fishing boats that would leave tiny crabs behind. We gather them up in our buckets and bring our catch home for Mom to prepare a sauce. On that particular day, Peppino was not careful, and a crab bit him on the thumb. While I jumped and screamed, he shook the crab off, and stepping on it, he picked it up again and swore to have it for dinner that night. Of course, my mom made sauce for dinner, and until this day, Peppino insists that he ate that particular crab.

Rowboats at the beach were always available, and occasionally, my dad (Ugo) would rent one to take us on a short ride. I will forever remember the fright I gave him while we were on one of those trips going toward deep water with the boat filled with my cousins, all under the age of ten, without life jackets. As my dad rowed toward deep water, I noticed that a dirty object was in the boat. I guess I was a clean freak from an early age and decided to pick up the dirty object and toss it into the water.

Little did I know that it was the cork keeping the water from coming into the boat. I saw the panic on my father's face as he realized what was occurring; he frantically started to look around for the cork as he put his heel into the opening to prevent water from rushing in. I cried and confessed what I had done. It was by the grace of God that he managed to row back to shore without sinking. I don't remember receiving a shiny new butt for that folly, and in looking back, I realized how carefree we all were.

On warm summer evenings, like all Italians, we would take our stroll (passeggiata) near the waterfront and occasionally stop at one of the many stalls that sell lemonade, cold beer, and peppery *taralli*. I can still see myself munching on a *taralli* and sipping the foam off my father's beer while I watched the waves, smelled the fresh ocean breeze, and felt happy, safe, and loved.

For the residents of Bagnoli that were well off and had apartments on the second or third floor, some of the daily shopping could be done without leaving their apartments. They simply had to listen for the calls of the different vendors and lower a wicker basket on a long rope to the horse-driven carts and yell down what they needed. After the items were inspected, the money was placed in the same basket and lowered down to the vendor.

I can still hear the calls for fresh bread, potatoes, and onions; it's that familiar Neapolitan singsong sound that lingers in my heart and soul.

My very being is filled with the sight of endless clotheslines that are a Neapolitan trademark, but our Sunday walks to Nonna Carmela's home fills my heart with pure love of family.

The aroma of her sweet ragù sauce, which I could smell a block away, will be forever linked to who I am today. As Nonna Carmela greeted us with a smile and kisses, she quickly started to scoop out the inside of a crusty heel of bread, which she poured hot sauce into. I'm not sure if it was her technique in preparing the sauce or the quality of the ingredients, but we have not been able to duplicate the flavor.

Nonna Carmela lived in a one-room flat with Nonno Pasquale, and I will never understand how they managed to have and raise nine children in such a small place. The main room you walked into was a small kitchen with a coal-burning stove, which seemed to me that she was always fanning to maintain the proper temperature. This was the stove where she lovingly prepared our traditional Easter bread (*casatiello*), which she gave to each grandchild decorated with eggs on top holding crisscrossed strips of dough over each egg. The peppery salami and cheese *casatiello* has always been my favorite; the biting sharpness of each slice still brings me back to my early childhood and Nonna's kitchen.

Nonna Carmela made many tasty treats for all her grandchildren, but the most memorable is *sanguinaccio*, which was prepared during the carnival season. She prepared large pots of this chocolate pudding made with pigs' blood and spiced with candied fruits and pine nuts. During our carnival visits to her home, she had pots of this warm pudding on her stove, and as we walked into her tiny kitchen, she would scoop out bowls for us to eat. This recipe is lost to us in the United States, and even if we did have the recipe, I don't think we could purchase pigs' blood due to health concerns.

Carnival season was celebrated by all the children of Bagnoli, and we dressed up in our favorite papier-mâché costume. I along with my cousin Carmela, "the Redhead," always dressed as fairy godmothers with tall cone hats, holding a magic wand. Peppino dressed as Zorro, and Ana Maria as a Spanish lady. What fun we had having adult family members wrap papier-mâché around metal-framed hoops that when completed looked like expensive cloth costumes. To this day, I have not seen Halloween costumes that can outmatch these fanciful handmade ones.

During the feast of Saint Joseph, which falls on March 19, my grandmother and mother also prepared a fried potato doughnut to honor the saint and to celebrate my brother's name day, which in Italy is celebrated more so than a birthday. I can still hear my mother telling me to move away from the hot oil as she fried large batches, and I eagerly anticipated dipping one in table sugar and devouring it.

Playtime for us was completely by imagination. We spent most of our playtime in the open field in front of our home. There, we would gather sticks and stones to build the perimeter of our make-believe home. Within that home, we would each take on a different role and play different characters. I remember one incident when my brother refused to let me enter his make-believe home, and after many pretend knocks, hoping to be granted permission to enter, I became so frustrated that I picked up the sharpest rock I could find and threw it, hitting him square between the eyes on the bridge of his nose.

Peppino ran home crying and bleeding while I ran and hid in my *zia* Marittella's hallway; but nothing stayed a secret for long in Bagnoli, and I was quickly found. Zia Marittella, my mom's youngest sister, yelled from her balcony to my mom, informing her that I was sitting on the last step of her building's staircase. My mom yelled back, telling her what happened, and, using the Neapolitan expression "quand vena a cas che facco o cul nuov nuov," informing my aunt that when I got home, she would give me a brand-new butt. I sat on the last step inside her hallway until I got tired and hungry and, finally, decided to go home for my shiny new butt. Peppino, to this day, has a pinhole on the bridge of his nose, and he occasionally points to it to remind me of my folly.

Without the use of video games, the web, or Super Mario, we entertained ourselves in the most educational way children could at the time. Small lizards were plentiful, and we developed a strange ritual of catching them and cutting off the tail. While holding the wiggling tails in front of us, we would form a conga line and start to sing a song about the lizards' mother. I can still sing that jingle ("e Toj. eToj, e Toj. Mammt ball co cul stuort.") Often my brother would place a lizard on what we called "the sacrificial stone," cutting it open to see what was inside. I guess he was born to be a scientist, and all of us gathered around to inspect it and hear what he had to say. I prefer to think of this behavior as a thirst for knowledge and not as a disorder; as of yet, none of us has become a mass murderer.

Toys were very rare, and the only doll I recall playing with was a prized black doll at my *zia* Pina's home. I along with other female cousins sat on the sofa in her living room with the French doors open to the long balcony and took turns holding this prized doll. I now realize that Zia Pina was better off than we were; she lived on the second floor with a living room and a balcony, where she was kind enough to let all of her nieces hang out and play. I always felt loved and accepted among my family, and regardless of anyone's financial situation, we were never made to feel less than them.

At times, my memories of life in Bagnoli bring on bouts of great laughter or tears, but I cherish them all and recall them to my children with great pride. One of the most comical memories is that of every parent's nightmare. My dad (Nonno Ugo) had taken me and Peppino on an outing and was told by my mom (Nonna Fortuna) not to give us any junk food since we both had and still have very delicate stomachs. Of course, we wore my dad down, and he gave in, buying us each an ice pop. For some strange reason, Peppino started to cry; he had a terrible stomachache and needed to use the bathroom. Within seconds, he made a mess in his nice clean pants, and my dad started to swear in Neapolitan.

I smirked at Peppino, thinking, *oh! he's such a baby. I'll never make in my pants.* As the mess started to drip out of his pants, my belly started to hurt, and oh no, I needed to use the bathroom. I couldn't believe it. I started to make a mess in my nice new pants, and as the mess started to drip out of my pants, I started to cry. My dad swore some more, complaining, "Now I'll hear it from your mother," while dragging us both by the hand as fast as he could toward home. Until today, Peppino insists that I made in my pants first, but we both know that he shit in his pants first, and that's that.

Peppino, from a very young age, was intellectually brilliant but also prone to sickness and accidents. He can clearly recall the traumatic experience of having his tonsils removed without any anesthesia to the very last detail. He tells the story of how he was taken to the hospital in Naples at about the age of three and lined up with other small children. He recalls a nurse holding his hands behind his back, a clamp inserted in his mouth, a quick spray, and a quick *clipping* sound as he was told to spit out his tonsils into a white basin. Even today, he can clearly describe that basin to the very last detail of every chip and crack. I now understand why Peppino shit in his pants first!

There was also the time he came down with scarlet fever at the age of six, and I was removed from the home to stay with my paternal aunts, Zia Titina and Zia Vincenza. The choice was put to my parents to either have me removed from the home and put the rest of the household under quarantine or place Peppino in a hospital. The decision was made to keep him at home and have me stay with my aunts for forty days. For forty days, I was coddled and fussed over, treated like a princess. With all of their efforts, I still cried every day and begged to see my mother and brother. They patiently walked me to Mom's kitchen window, where I tapped on the pane and waved. My mom and Peppino waved back to me while I cried and begged to go home. I clearly recall falling asleep on my *zia* Titina's arm to the ticking sound of a large black clock that stood on her dresser, wondering when forty days would be over.

Can this compare to Peppino having his knee stitched together after a fall on a sharp can top? He was in the open field chasing butterflies that we later carefully pasted into a notebook with the wings open to show off the colors. We were both so fascinated by the colors that we spent many hours chasing them together, but on this day, I had gone to the market with my mother, and Peppino hunted alone.

I recall walking up the hill heading home when one of our cousins came rushing at us, announcing the news. Peppino had just gotten home from the hospital with a serious knee injury. My mom, almost nine months pregnant with my sister Paola, grabbed my hand hard, pulling me along as she ran as fast as possible with such a heavy load. By the time we got home, Peppino was already being attended to by other family members. There he sat with his bandaged leg up on a stool, munching on a few pieces of chocolate. The solution was made quickly at the hospital by the attending doctor—pour alcohol on the cut that went almost clear to the muscle and stitch. Who needed anesthesia when you could have chocolate? Do I still need to wonder why he shit in his pants first? I don't think so. I often wonder what happened to that butterfly collection. I can only assume that the butterfly he was after that day got away.

Paola, our baby sister, was born soon after that incident. The time came for us to spend a night at our Zia Vincenza and Zia Titina's house; at that time, most children were born at home with a midwife to assist. My mother's cousin was a midwife, and she assisted with all three of her deliveries.

My aunts asked us what we wanted for a sibling, a boy or girl. I was confused, not quite sure what to wish for, but Peppino, being older and sharp as a tack, loudly stated, "A girl. I want to be the only male king in the family." His wish was granted; Paola was born on July 1, 1960, only a few days before my fifth birthday. Early in the morning, Zia Titina woke us up with the news that we had a baby sister.

Peppino stood up on the bed, lifting his hands in victory, stating, "Yes, the sole king." We were both full of excitement as we quickly got dressed and ran home to see baby Paola. My mother was still in bed, being attended to by female family members. Paola, all bright-eyed with a full head of curly black hair, lay next to my mother, swaddled all in white. I was truly fascinated by this new person that had entered our lives. Nonna Carmela asked not to have another granddaughter named after her; she already had three.

Relatives in Bagnoli were not only our emotional support but provided practical support as well. The practical side of having many family members within walking distance was personified when we enlisted the help of Nonna Carmela to remove a cat-size rat that had taken residence in our kitchen. As you already know, Nonna Carmela was as tough as nails and was not easily frightened, but my mom had an unreasonable fear of small critters. The only practical solution was to enlist Nonna's help.

The rat proved to be a crafty critter and dodged every blow Nonna Carmela shelled out with heavy broom until it finally jumped onto the last shelf of a metal kitchen cabinet under a sack of oregano. Nonna Carmela ordered my mom to step on a chair and lift the sack with a stick so that she could get a good shot at the critter. Mom summed up her courage, releasing my grip from her dress, and stepped onto the chair, lifting the sack. The rat didn't hesitate, jumping on her head and onto the floor. I can still hear the yell of horror from my mom as she realized what had just happened. Nonna Carmela paid her no mind and kept chasing and swatting the rat. I don't recall if that crafty rat was ever caught, but the memory makes me howl with laughter.

As I write, I'm starting to realize that experiences and memories are not lost through time but become part of who we are. They mold and shape us, forever staying in our very being. Even a simple aroma can conjure up a strong emotion.

The aroma of frying hot peppers will forever remind me of Signora Sparagna. Signora Sparagna was not only our neighbor but also our teacher or, should I say, Peppino's teacher. From the early age of three, Peppino attended Signora Sparagna's home-based school and was always at the top of her class. He was such a gifted student that he was able to not only complete all of his class work but also that of all the older students. Signora Sparagna realized that he was a special student and started to give him private lessons.

Of course, my parents also tried sending me to her class, but I was a totally different type of student. I spent more time romping around her home that was filled with paintings and sculptures made by her very eccentric husband and her two brilliant sons that sitting at a table learning numbers and letters just didn't make sense to me. The painting I admired the most was of a young Signora Sparagna with an updo hairstyle in a low-cut gown, revealing a good portion of her breast. I spent a good amount of time staring at the painting, wondering how Signora had been placed there so still and forever so young.

That brings me back to the aroma of frying hot peppers. Signora Sparagna was always frying a large quantity of spicy hot peppers with potatoes for her sons before we started class; my first stop, of course, was to the kitchen for a taste. Who needed to sit still for hours learning from a book when I could spend hours admiring paintings and eating fried hot peppers with potatoes?

Signora Sparagna finally told my parents that I had pepper up my butt and that it was too early for a formal education. This was just fine with me since it gave me plenty of time to play with her daughter, Marica, and snoop around as much as I wanted.

Life seemed perfect, and the aroma of frying spicy peppers still brings me back to her home. Signora was a very forward-thinking person for that time period and enjoyed an occasional cigarette. During one of my play dates with Marica, we both noticed cigarette butts in an ashtray and decided to have a try. We each quickly picked up a butt and lit it with a match, pretending to be all grown up, puffing away, until we heard Signora's footsteps. Quickly, we put out the butts and play-acted at other games. We both thought we had gotten away with our crime until I went home, and my mom smelled my breath. She knew exactly what had occurred and didn't hesitate in giving me a shiny new red behind. I know today the parental trend is to give a time-out, but I never touched a cigarette again and thank my mom for that well-intentioned discipline.

As for Marica, I'm not sure if she received a time-out or a Neapolitan-style shiny new butt, but Signora turned one hundred in 2010; I guess she didn't inhale.

The only formal schooling I attended in Bagnoli was kindergarten. I went to school on a bus with my cousin Carmela, "the Redhead." We traveled a short distance to a garden-type location where the school stood. For the most part, I found school very boring; the large brown blocks didn't excite me after a few tries, and other school activities could not compare to snooping around Signora Sparagna's home. Admiring paintings and hanging out in the grassy fields cutting up lizards was far more interesting.

A very substantial lunch was provided by the school and was the highlight of the day. I was never able to finish the complete meal and passed the remaining portions to my cousin. Talking was not allowed at lunch, but of course, I was caught asking Carmela if she wanted more minestrone soup. The lunch ladies threatened me with the usual threat they made to other children—"Come up here. Let me cut out your tongue."

I noticed many times, as other children cried and begged not to have their tongues cut out, that in fact, tongues were never cut out. So I defiantly walked up, stuck out my tongue, and told them, "Go ahead. Cut out my tongue." The lunch ladies must have been in complete shock having a peanut-size rascal calling their bluff, so they told me to sit down. I was very proud of myself, and that threat was never made to anyone again.

It was in Signora Sparagna's home that I saw the first TV and was mesmerized by the tiny people in the box. How did they live in there? I would constantly try to figure out how they ate, slept, and performed other essentials in that small box. Her husband, Signor Sparagna, was a bit eccentric and did not approve of TV as he felt that it would somehow affect the intellect of his children and students. However, Signora Sparagna was a free spirit and paid him no attention, purchasing a TV, which we hid in an armoire. We huddled around the black box, which had two channels, completely amazed. Topo Gigio was a favorite character, and we laughed at every silly gesture. A singing carousel which was solely for an advertisement fascinated us. I can still sing the tune for Cinzano vermouth, "Ginji, Ginji Cinzano."

This very decadent form of entertainment was kept a secret for quite a long time until one day, unexpectedly, Signor Sparagna arrived home. Signora Sparagna shouted to us that her husband was on his way up the stairs, telling us to turn off the TV and close the armoire. We all quickly ran to do as we were told; the armoire was closed, but in the mayhem, we forgot to turn off the TV.

Signora Sparagna realized what had occurred and began to talk very loud to muffle the jingly sounds that were spilling out of the armoire. Her husband realized where the sounds were coming from and pulled open the door. All the children ran in different directions, hiding under beds and behind drapes. I recall peeking from behind the drape and seeing the shock on Signor Sparagna's face; maybe he expected a lover instead of a TV. As soon as the yelling started, I ran home as fast as I could and started telling my mom what had happened. Her hands immediately went into her hair in distress, and she started mumbling to herself. The TV was locked in the armoire until Signor went back to work teaching university students, but as soon as he left, Signora Sparagna unlocked Pandora's box.

We were so close to Signora Sparagna that she was good enough to dress up as Santa every Christmas. While all the other Italian children waited for La Befana, an old woman who flies on a broom and brings presents on January 6, we also had the pleasure of Signora Sparagna dressing up in a Santa suit on December 25. We were told by our parents that this Santa climbed into our street-level window for a visit.

On one of my snooping tours of Signora Sparagna's home, I opened a trunk, where I found the Santa suit and realized that she had been Santa all along. I recall telling my mom about this revelation, and she explained that Signora was just washing and storing the suit for Santa and that I should not snoop. Much to my disappointment, I never believed in Santa again.

The sounds of the Zampognari, the shepherds who came to Bagnoli from their mountaintop home to play the bagpipes for us, are imbedded in my very being and symbolize Christmas at its best for me. On their pilgrimage, they stop at every home and play Christmas tunes on their sheepskin pipes. My father always offered a drink of sweet liquor, and while they chitchatted for a few moments, memories of a lifetime were made. The essence of Christmas for us was not so much the giving of gifts but the unity of the family and the preparing of holiday meals.

This was a long complicated process as all food items were freshly purchased and prepared. A week before Christmas, baked goods such as struffoli and almond brittle were prepared, dried figs and dates which were stuffed with an assortment of nuts were set aside for Christmas Eve. A day or two before Christmas, seven different types of fish were purchased and prepared. The only food items that were store-bought were panettone, the traditional Christmas bread, and gingerbread cookies which were covered with dark chocolate, along with a few fancy pastries.

We didn't receive many gifts—mostly edible treats for the holidays as money was very scarce—but the memories are filled with the most precious gift of all, laughter and love.

My memory of life in Bagnoli has sparks of sounds, smells, laughter, and vivid colors. On New Year's Eve, Bagnoli would be dressed with tall poles holding wheels of brightly colored fireworks. At the midnight hour, the fire wheels were set off, sending bursts of colorful sparks into the midnight sky. I was delighted and frightened at the same time as all our neighbors came rushing out of their homes with pots and pans, making noise and shouting well-wishes.

What other shadows of memories lurk inside of me from my short time in Bagnoli? Short spurts of recall often enter my mind; a neighbor, a holiday, a taste, or an emotion enter my being like an old movie reel, replaying a long-ago scene. Flashes of an old lady that I was so frightened of, I would faint every time she came near to offer me a few of her prized hairpins. Today, we would just explain and ask her to keep away; in those days, that would be considered impolite. We had a great deal of respect for our older neighbors, and not much of a fuss was made when I pass out. A bottle of vinegar was put under my nose and a few pats on the face until I recovered.

I see myself holding hands with my cousins, making a circle while dancing around a blazing bonfire with a scarecrow in the middle, celebrating a harvest festival.

I see myself looking out of our neighbor's bathroom window as I and her son played with a toy boat. We had filled the tub with water and splashed the toy about for such a long time that both our mothers were hysterical looking for us. We heard the commotion outside; peeking out of the window we saw our mothers crying, talking to each other, saying that maybe gypsies had taken us.

The grandmothers came; both our aunts and uncles came; finally, the police came, but we just peeked out the window and continued to play. At one point, I realized we were in big trouble and decided all the more to stay inside and play.

Finally, Signora Fontnella became sick and came into the bathroom, and there we were found. Often, my mother reminds me how I nearly gave her a heart attack and what I put her through with those fainting spells. I call this Neapolitan mother's guilt control and inwardly smile to myself.

In the recesses of my mind, almost like watching an old-fashioned movie, I view episodes of my past. I'm with my cousins, running around Bagnoli without any fear or adult supervision. A Neapolitan *Little Rascals* scene, children looking for adventure. I feel the acid sting on my arms as we sit on Signora Sparagna's rooftop terrace jarring tomatoes. I see myself at our table, helping to roll out gnocchi on a fork as I watch my mother carry bowls full of this handmade pasta to dry on her tablecloth-lined bed, the only place with enough space to dry the gnocchi.

As a young child, my life in Bagnoli seemed perfect with all the comforts and joys of a loving family, caring neighbors, and beautiful landscapes; in actuality, the never-ending struggle that Neapolitans have been enduring for centuries against poverty and inequality was the reality for my family. We were swimming in a whirlpool of social injustices disguised by laughter and sunshine. Just like the Neapolitan mascot Pulcinello, a joker that laughs and sings, hiding behind his mask because there is not much else he can do. My father (Ugo) was determined to correct this injustice for his family and waited over fifteen years to be given permission to enter America. Over and over again, I remember the words "America, America" being uttered as if the word itself could magically improve the circumstances of one's life.

I don't remember the exact details of my father's departure, only a feeling of sadness and loss. We did give up our somewhat luxurious apartment which we were living in at that time. The most vivid memory of that apartment was that it had hot and cold running water. It was a spacious second-floor apartment with a water heating unit in the bathroom. That newfound luxury nearly took my life. Without anyone's knowledge, the gas leaked out of the heating unit while my mother gave Peppino and me a bath. My mother had placed me on the toilet seat, wrapped in a towel; as she dried me off, I went limp in her arms and fainted. She quickly yelled out the bathroom window for help, and within seconds, family and neighbors came to assist.

I recall awaking in my parents' bed, being checked by a doctor, and as I turned my head, I saw my brother in his birthday suit with his kibble and bits bouncing up and down, crying and asking if I was dead. In front of me, the entire bedroom was filled with family ready to help. That luxurious apartment was quickly given up when my father received his visa. Of course, that was to save money while my father settled into the land of opportunity. We again moved into a cold-water flat that my paternal aunts had vacated; they too were leaving for America.

My father left the only place he had ever called home with a heavy heart—not only was he leaving behind his family, but his country and culture, which he cherished. With him, he took what all immigrants bring with them, great hope and a fierce determination to acquire the American Dream. I don't recall much of the time we spent apart, only the occasional care package with some photos of my father on American soil.

It was while I sat on the street-level windowsill staring at those photos that I wept and anticipated our reunion. My favorite gift from America came on my sixth birthday with a beautiful white frilly dress and candy. I immediately started to feel rich and very American. That was the last birthday I celebrated with my Neapolitan family until my fifty-fifth birthday.

It seemed to come in a flash after that sixth birthday. My mother received very important papers from America and, with that, the turmoil of packing. She seemed in a frenzy, trying to decide what to take with us and what to leave behind.

Into the storage trunk went the linens that my grandmother Carmela had given to my mother for her wedding, along with good china, pots, and pans. All those special items we were sure would be needed for a fancy new American home.

We had medical appointments made so that our visa would be issued, and then the unthinkable happened—my brother and I came down with the mumps. My mother was in a panic. Would we be allowed to leave, or would we need to delay our departure? Thankfully, we both passed our medical exams, and all was in order for us to leave.

These were, for me, the saddest days of my young life. We were scheduled to leave in October, and all of my cousins started school in September. My mom didn't even bother to enroll us; what was the point? I was in tears watching my cousins head off to school without me. I started to feel so alone and forgotten. The only saving grace was that I was excited about seeing my dad again and going to America. I was certain I would find gold coins scattered in the streets.

I don't recall saying my good-byes; I don't recall any tears from family members. I guess they felt no need for tears since we were going to a far better place, a special land of easy opportunity and wealth.

I do recall my Nonna Carmela and Nonno Pasquale not wanting to travel with us to the port, and we said our last good-byes in their small home. That was the last time I saw both of them. The one clear good-bye memory I have is from Signora Sparagna's oldest son, Francesco, who asked us to pose for a sketch.

I recall having a beaded necklace on, my hair in its usual braids and standing very still. He seemed to work very quickly and magically handed us the sketch, telling us that he hoped it would help us remember. I safely kept that sketch for many years in my room—often staring at it, wondering who that person was—until one day, I became so filled with anger, lashing out and ripping the sketch to shreds. As a young child, I could never have imagined the incident that would cause me to shred that prized sketch.

Signora Sparagna accompanied us to the port with her daughter, Marica, and I clearly recall her talking to me with comforting words and reminding me not to forget about them. She asked me to look for her from the ship's deck—that she would wave her white hanky, which she always kept in her coat sleeve—and say her final good-byes.

Before I could truly comprehend what was happening—that I was leaving the land of my birth, the land of my culture, and just about everyone that I loved—I was standing near the ship's rail with hundreds of others waving to the people below. It was by a miracle that I somehow clearly saw Signora Sparagna waving her hanky and wiping tears away.

I share these special recipes with you because, out of all my food memories, these bring me back to my happy childhood days in Bagnoli.

Casatiello di Nonna Carmela

Preparing *sugna con cicoli*, "pork lard"—this can be prepared weeks ahead of baking the bread as it stays very fresh if kept in the refrigerator in a tightly closed container.

In a large pan, place one pound of pork fat cut into tiny pieces. Add two tablespoons of water and four dry bay leaves. Heat over a low flame until fat is melted and tiny crisp pork nuggets appear. Pour in a glass container, let cool, cover, and place in the refrigerator.

Ingredients: for Day of Baking

Have five large round pans which have been greased with the pork fat ready.

5 lb. of all-purpose flour
7 envelopes of dry yeast
1½ lb. of dried salami diced into bite-size portions
1 lb. of Romano cheese diced into bite-size portions
6 tbs. of salt
7 cups of warm water
Black pepper to taste (this bread should be slightly salty and peppery)

Have all ingredients in front of you on a large worktable.
Place about four pounds of the flour on the worktable; make a hole in middle of flour to form a doughnut shape. Place yeast in the center of the flour.
Dissolve salt in warm water. (I have prepared this recipe by dissolving the yeast into the salted water, then slowly adding to the flour to make the dough; you can use whichever method works best for you.)

Slowly pour water into the flour and yeast, working flour and water together with your hands to start forming dough. When a dough ball is formed, knead for a few minutes. You may need to add a bit more flour as you work the dough, especially to your hands.
Now this is the very messy part. By hand, start adding the pork fat in and around the dough. Don't be afraid to work the fat well into the

dough; it will look like a sticky mess, but believe me, the flavor it adds is well worth the mess.

Add the bite-size pieces of salami and cheese, working them uniformly into the dough.

Cut dough into five even portions, and start twisting them into a round braid-like shape. Place each into a pan; put a small glass in the middle of each to maintain the center opening while dough is rising. Cover with a tablecloth.

Let it rise for about two hours or until it doubles in size. Bake in a preheated oven of 425ºF for about thirty minutes or until a golden color and a breadlike crust is formed on the bottom. You can also check with a toothpick, making sure it's completely baked on the inside.

Now I know this is an unusual method of preparing bread, but this is how I watched my grandmother and mother make *casatiello*, and one needs to develop a hand feel for this process. As I watched and wrote this recipe down, my mother laughed at me while suggesting, "Make sure you write down that you need to get your hands messy and that the amounts aren't always the same, you know. Tell them you need to feel when it's right." I guess today, we call it bonding with the ingredients. My mother called it cooking from the heart.

Zeppole di San Giuseppe

Ingredients:

2 large cooked, peeled, and riced potatoes
½ lb. of all-purpose flour
4 whole eggs
1 stick of butter or margarine cut into tiny cubes
1 package of dry yeast
1 tbs. of sugar
2 shot glasses of anisette

On a large work surface or in a bowl, mix flour, potatoes, eggs, butter, yeast, sugar, and anisette; you may use your hand or a spoon to blend all ingredients together until soft dough is formed.

Place the dough in a clean bowl, cover with a cloth or clear wrap, and let rise for two hours or until double in size.

Pinch off small pieces of dough, and shape each portion into a bow shape.

Fry in hot oil until golden. Place fried zeppoles on paper towels to remove excess oil.

While still slightly warm, roll into table sugar.

I have also made these zeppoles with sambuca or Strega and have shaped them into circles, Ss, and candy canes shapes. My mom insists that "since the world was the world," a bow is the shape zeppoles have been made and anisette has always been used, but I have many times changed family recipes with good results and tell her, "Ma, the world is changing." She just waves her hand, shooing me away.

Potato Croquettes (*Panzarott*)

Ingredients

3 lb. of cooked potatoes (I suggest cooking them in their skin and peeling the skin off after they've cooled; the potato does not get soggy and holds its flavor when cooked in its skin.)
4 whole eggs
1 cup of grated Parmigiano-Reggiano cheese
8 oz. of mozzarella diced into tiny portions (mozzarella needs to be dry)
Salt and pepper to taste
1 cup of breadcrumbs

Place cooled potatoes through a ricer or food mill into a large bowl. I have put the cooked potatoes with the skins on through a ricer and have mashed potatoes in the bowl while the skins are left behind in the ricer, which I then discard. Saves a bit of time.

Add eggs, cheese, salt, and pepper. Mix well by hand, incorporating all ingredients uniformly.

By hand—you may dip your hands in some breadcrumbs—take a portion of the potato mixture and shape into an egg-shaped croquette. You can make them into any size you like; after shaping them with your finger, make a hole in the center and place a piece of mozzarella into it, reclosing tightly to cover the cheese.

Gently roll each into the breadcrumbs. You can also mix some grated cheese into the breadcrumbs for extra flavor.

Fry in hot vegetable oil until crispy on all sides, remove, and set on paper towels. It's best when served while still hot and crispy, but served at room temperature for a snack or lunch is also OK.

Now I know the chefs on TV dredge first in flour and then dip into a beaten egg mixture before rolling into the breadcrumbs. I watched my mom cooking for years, and she has never done this. I once tried to imitate the chefs on TV, and the end product was too heavy with coating.

In our family, we enjoy everything from chicken cutlets to croquettes only dipped in beaten eggs which have been spiced with salt, black pepper, and Parmesan cheese then quickly dredged into breadcrumbs and fried, but of course, you can dredge in flour first.

Pasta Frittata

My mom made pasta frittata from leftover pasta in sauce; you can use freshly cooked pasta in sauce or cooked pasta just tossed into butter and grated cheese. Please understand that although a frittata is like an omelet, it is not meant to be creamy or runny but to be set and crispy.

Ingredients:

½ lb. of cooked pasta (you may use spaghetti or ziti)
4 eggs with about 4 tbs. of grated Parmigiano-Reggiano cheese, salted and peppered to taste
1 to 2 tbs. of vegetable oil for cooking the frittata in a round frying pan

Beat eggs well with cheese, salt, and pepper; add the pasta, and toss well until pasta is completely coated with the egg mixture. Heat the pan with oil over a medium flame until hot, then pour egg and pasta mixture into the hot pan. Cook until the bottom is set and has a golden color. While cooking, I lifted the edges of the frittata, allowing more egg mixture to fall into the bottom, cooking it further.

Now my mother has always been strong enough to flip a large skillet with the frittata in it onto a plate and flip it back into the skillet, completely cooking the top side until crispy. I have never been strong or skilled enough to do this and have compensated by sprinkling a mixture of breadcrumbs and grated Parmesan cheese on top, placing the entire skillet under a hot broiler to finish the cooking. The result is very good and crispy.

You will later read how I enticed an Irish American man to flip and love frittatas.

Chapter 2

The Voyage, October 1961

To me, it seemed that in a blink of an eye, we were far away from land and in the middle of a never-ending ocean. The last landmass I recall seeing was as the ship slowed down near the Azores. Small rowboats came close enough to the ship for them to throw thick ropes on deck and send up different goods that they would sell to the passengers. As we all stood near the railing, I begged my mother to buy a colorful wicker basket. My mom was hit in the neck by the knot of the rope that was thrown up to deliver the basket; she winced in pain but still bought the basket.

The first three days were filled with playful excitement. We were given the wrong cabin size, and I had to share the top bunk bed with my brother while my mom shared the bottom bunk with Paola, our baby sister. My mom was very upset about the size of the cabin and was told by the ship's management that money would be refunded to us once we reached New York. I was happy to climb into the top bunk and have my brother read to me until I fell asleep. He read a book of poems written by Signor Sparagna, *Sull Alta Riva*. Signora Sparagna had given us the book for our voyage, telling us to practice our Italian and to not forget our language. The rhythmic sounds of the poems and the rocking and rolling of the ship would lull me to sleep. I still keep that very same book in my nightstand and have thought of donating it to the Italian American Museum but have not yet been able to part with it.

We felt so lucky to have such a large play space. Peppino and I ran around the ship, enjoying looking out at the ocean, amazed as the dolphins followed us with playful jumps. The first English words I recall hearing were on one of those runs around where Peppino was chasing me and pulling my braids. An older American girl yelled at my brother, "Hey, don't pull her hair!" We both look at each other and shrugged in that Neapolitan manner, saying to each other, "What does she want?"

and continued on our way. For the first three days, all was well with calm waters and sunny skies. We ate well, and my brother ate so well, he embarrassed my mother. It seemed that he had a stomach of steel with an attitude to match.

On the fourth day, we were enjoying ourselves in the children's playroom—listening to music, talking to other passengers—when suddenly, it all changed. A massive wave hit the ship, and the chairs we were sitting on went sliding into the wall. My mom held on to my sister, who was only fifteen months old, and stopped her from smashing into the wall. I flew into the wall and off my chair, luckily without a scratch. Other passengers were scattered about, luckily no one was hurt. The rest of the voyage continued in the same manner, with the ship constantly rocking and rolling as the restless ocean tossed us about. I was seasick, not able to eat more than a morsel. In the dining room, plates, glasses, and silverware flew about as wave after wave hit the ship. Only my brother was able to eat double portions of everything as he asked, "Why is everyone sick?"

The most frightening event for me was watching an elderly man's forehead split open. Like most of the passengers, we sought safety in the large common rooms, where the crew tried to keep everyone calm by playing music and having activities. I was sitting with my mother and Paola on a sofa across from an older gentleman who sat on a single chair near the doors. As a wave hit the ship, his chair flipped over, and the doors swung open, hitting his forehead. Blood started to pour out, and everyone began to scream for help. My mom became hysterical as she realized Peppino was not in sight and continued to yell his name until he finally appeared.

He ran to us and, in an adult like manner, told us to calm down as he bent down under the sofa and started to screw the sofa's cable into the bolts on the floor. Apparently, all of the furniture should have been screwed into the floors at the first sign of the storm, but the crew was overwhelmed and forgot. Peppino noticed what the crew was scrambling to do at the last minute and took it upon himself to help. The poor old man was lifted off the floor and rushed to the hospital room, where he received over sixty stitches. We later heard that over two hundred passengers had been hurt on that voyage and found out that we had survived a major unexpected storm.

The day finally arrived that would be etched not only in my memory but my immigrant soul. Peppino had been up early that day, surveying the horizon for what all immigrants look for on their way to America—that great symbol not only of freedom but of hope for a better life. He came running into our cabin breathless, urging us to hurry up, and repeating the words "The Statue of Liberty, the Statue of Liberty." We dressed in a flash and, with hundreds of others, stood on the ship's deck in awe of this most American symbol.

The past days of discomfort seemed to melt away with a renewed energy. As I looked at Lady Liberty and to the Manhattan skyline, I was sure that it all glistened in gold. My mother looked exhausted, and I don't think she even had a glimmer of a smile or hope on her face. I excitedly told her to look up at the American seagulls, but she just mindlessly nodded. What was I feeling in those first few moments of seeing the Manhattan skyline—the only word that describes that feeling is *hope*, the hope for a better life. A childish anticipation of immediate great wealth.

Chapter 3

The Making of an American

We ran down the metal gangplank, me and Peppino, Mom behind us holding Paola. I saw my dad standing at the bottom with the same camel-colored coat that he had worn a year prior on his trip over to America. Within seconds of reaching the bottom, I was suffocated with hugs and kisses. My father noticed how thin I was and commented to my mom that I looked like a slaughtered lamb. As she began to describe the frightful voyage, I started to pull away and was immediately disappointed.

During the sixties, the West Side of Manhattan was a pitiful site; every building looked old and decayed. The streets were dirty and smelly, and this to me could not **possibly be this great country of America.**

I'm not sure what I expected, maybe the wild Wild West or possibly the streets paved with gold and coins scattered about for the easy taking. For certain, I expected beautiful homes with flowery gardens, but none of that was here. I was sure this could not be America. I thought, *Of course not. We were going into a car to reach America.* It was the first car I recall being in. I was dumbstruck by everything I saw—tall buildings, traffic lights, but especially the stairs on the outside of the buildings. This was the first time I had seen fire escapes. I recall excitedly pulling on my mother's coat sleeve and pointing, telling her, "Look, in America, the stairs are on the outside of the building." I thought about what a thrill it would be to climb those American stairs.

After what seemed to me like a very short ride, we finally reached it—this America. We were all getting out in this place called the South Bronx. As I stepped out of the car, the first thing that hit my senses was the smell of burning wood. I lifted my head to look up at the five-story building, which seemed to be staring at me with a menacing grin. The stoop of the building we were entering was dirty, and the door was missing two bottom windowpanes. My young mind struggled to make sense of it all; my emotions went from shock and disbelief to sadness.

Those feelings were intensified upon entering the building. The smell of stale urine overpowered my nostrils, and I began to feel sick and exhausted. The building was very dark and as other family members started to call greetings to us from the top of the stairs, my mom recognized their voices but could not see their faces in the darkness.

We climbed the inside stairs to our fifth-floor walk-up apartment, the last apartment next to the rooftop and as far away from our dreams of America as one could imagine.

What memories do I recall most vividly of the first few months of reaching America? First is the feeling of sadness and disbelief. I asked my mother on many occasions when we could go back to Naples, back home to that sense of familiarity and of safety. My mother seemed constantly exhausted and flustered. I guess trying to adjust to a new country was difficult enough, but add to that the stress of dealing with a hostile environment of burning buildings, drug addicts staggering in the streets, urine-smelling hallways, and a roach-infested apartment was too much for her, and the only comfort she could give me was a straightforward answer. "We're not. This is our home now."

I overheard my parents speaking, my dad telling my mother, "I'd told you in my letters not to come, that I work and send money." I guess he realized the hardships we would need to endure before reaching the land of our dreams, but it was too late to turn back. We could only forge ahead, working our way into America. Even at such a young age, I realized that what we left behind could never be replaced. My parents never laughed as much, never seemed to be as carefree, and never felt as connected to their community again.

Within those few first months, I became a totally different child; that outgoing, feisty, and somewhat belligerent child became introverted, shy, and so quiet that I recall hearing comments from family members that I was in some way intellectually challenged.

The only saving grace was that in the months before we arrived, my dad had worked and saved enough money to buy us not only furniture but our own TV. What else was there to do in America? Our playground in the open field with lizards was gone, Signor Sparagna's home was gone, my cousins were gone, and our walks to the beach were over.

We watched TV shows like *Bonanza, My Three Sons,* and *Leave It to Beaver.* I started to wonder how one reached this America. This America with beautiful landscapes, single homes with white picket fences, and families that had dinner all dressed up with a mom wearing pearls. I watched as these Americans on TV sat around the dinner table, spreading white stuff on fluffy white bread and drinking white liquid in a glass.

A subconscious feeling of being less than others slowly crept inside of me. Nagging questions that I wasn't able to verbalize at such a young age emerged in deepest recesses of my mind. Would I need to do the same to become an American? Could I ever be like those Americans? I began to understand poverty and social class. Most important, I realized that in America, everyone was so different from one another, and I asked myself where I fit in.

The TV America was a totally different place than the one I lived in. My America was a place filled with burning buildings, the constant noise of sirens, with drug addicts and criminals on the streets and in our building. Most confusing of all was that the Americans on TV spoke a different language than the Americans on the streets of my new home. Was I really in America? As a young child, I could not verbalize these feeling or ask these very confusing questions, but as they invaded my being, I became a silent child.

When did I start to speak English? How did I learn to speak English? I guess it was a combination of watching TV and simply mimicking the TV personalities. "Hiya, Mom. Hiya, Pa" from *Bonanza.* Listening to the radio and repeating words to songs like "I like bread and butter, he likes toast and jam." Most frustrating of all was having to repeat rhymes from books like *Cat in the Hat* and *See Jane Run.* My parents didn't waste any time enrolling us into a good Catholic school; their main priority for coming to the United States was to educate us and make sure we had a better future.

By November 1961, Peppino and I were enrolled into Saint Pius V Grammar School, where the mostly Irish Catholic nuns tried to teach the predominately Puerto Rican and black inner-city children, along with a few leftover Italian and Irish, how to be proper American citizens. I started first grade without understanding a single word of English, and the nuns, to ease the transition, placed me in the same class as my cousin who spoke not a word of Neapolitan; she was as foreign to me as the rest of my classmates and even less kind.

The memories of the first three years we lived in that building bring mostly feelings of insecurity, sadness, and a nagging ache in my being that we did not belong. My memory screams with disgust at seeing a drug addict sitting at the top of the stairs near our door inserting a needle into his arm. I along with my brother had been playing outside or, should I say, trying to find something to do on the stoop; we became bored and ran up the stairs.

For some reason, we both turned to look at the stairs that led to the rooftop, and there, we saw a man sitting on the steps with a syringe in one hand and his other arm leaning on his knee. From where I was standing and he was sitting, our eyes briefly met, and all I saw was a deep emptiness; he didn't seem human to me. I felt not so much fear but disgust. That encounter lasted no more than a minute before my brother and I started to yell and pound on the door. He didn't budge but simply looked down and continued to inject himself. My mom quickly opened the door, pulling us inside. I now realize that I need to be thankful for having had that encounter; he was my lifelong motivation, my lifelong phantom with empty eyes that guided me through a drug-free life.

There were also the phantoms with brown paper bags over their mouth and nose that lurked in corner alleyways. They were strange creatures to me as I watched the rhythmic movement of the bag, wondering if that was the way some Americans took their breaths. Most disgusting of all was to pass by the doorway of a neighbor that spewed such a foul urine stench that we would cover our noses and run as fast as we could. We nicknamed them *pisciasott*, meaning "pissing on oneself" or "pants pissers." Later, I was forced to play with a young pants pisser so that I could practice English and start to become an American. I hated every moment with that *pisciasott*.

There was the boring activity of sitting on the stoop and looking across the street to a boarded-up vacant building; on the corner of that building stood a shop which had three gold-colored spheres hanging in front. I always wondered what those spheres were for. I now know that it was a pawnshop.

I got my first taste of young criminals while sitting on that stoop as I munched on a few pieces of candy. Two boys approached me—they were not much older than my brother—pointing a small knife at me, demanding I give them my candy. I just stared with my eyebrows crossed together, not quite understanding what was occurring; they brought the knife close to my hand and removed the candy, laughing and walking away. I did not even cry; I just stared at the boarded-up building, resigning myself that this was life in America.

I had become such a silent invisible child that I never told anyone. I can still hear—or is it feel?—the thought and emotion telling me, "What for?" The only beautiful sight I saw while living in that building was a rose garden that belonged to the only single home left standing in that area. It was wedged between our building, and I often looked down out of our fire escape to watch an old man tending to his garden. I thought the rose garden was like paradise and wanted so much to have one of my own.

It was through that fire escape that someone entered and stole all of our eighteen-karat gold jewelry; the only items not taken were the earrings I had on and a gold pin that was on my mother's coat. I still treasure those items; the earrings were given to me by my paternal grandmother, Filomena, which I was named after and were placed on my ears within the first month of my birth. The pin was given to my mother by my father while they dated as a symbol of his love. When my mother's family in Bagnoli heard of the theft, they started sending replacement jewelry. I treasure all of these items not for their market value but because they remind me of the love they were given with. I realized what an effort it must have been for my family to purchase these items; I know that they denied themselves comforts to show us their love.

What other scattered memories linger in my mind of the three years we lived in that prewar walk-up building? As hard as I try, I can't recall any happy feelings associated with that time or place, having only overwhelming feelings of sadness, fear, and insecurity. I guess the feeling of sadness comes from missing what we left behind in Bagnoli. The feeling of fear was forever present, living near the rooftop where drug addicts hung out and tried to break into our apartment through the front door while we slept. It was by a miracle that on one occasion, my brother, who slept in a room near the door, heard someone trying to break the lock and ran to call my parents. After that, I often wake up in the middle of the night and call out for my mother to show her the witches and demons that flashed on the walls.

I now often wonder how we got through those first three years. I can only guess by the rituals of daily living; my father went to work, my mother cared for the household, and we tried our best to learn our lessons from the Irish Catholic nuns, who at times had little love for the increasing Latin student body. I'm not sure if they were intentionally cruel or just frustrated from being poorly prepared to teach students who spoke English as a second language, but they did not hesitate to smack heads into blackboards, throw erasers across the room to hit a student who did not have the correct answer, or to use a rowboat-size paddle called "Sunny" to establish order.

As harsh as this may sound, I think most of the students were far better off attending Saint Pius than the local public school, where you would have had your ass beaten daily by the criminal-like student body without learning much of anything. If the discipline was a bit harsh, it was offset by the great effort the nuns put forth in trying to instill a sense of morality and achievement through education.

Although I was held back in first grade, with the teachers feeling that I had started school late and with the added disadvantage of not speaking the language, everyone was very proud of me for becoming fluent in English. My father took us to our first American toy store, where I selected a Barbie doll with the classic sparkly black gown. As much as I admired that doll, after a few tries of redressing her, I became extremely bored. I would have preferred to play in an open field, walk to the beach with my cousins, and admire the artwork in Signora Sparagna's home.

Slowly, I resigned myself to the reality that this place was now my new home, and without realizing it, I developed a fierce determination to find America.

After three years of living in that building, my father happily announced that we were moving into these brand-new buildings called the Mott Haven housing projects. The words *housing projects* didn't have a negative meaning to us at all; we simply thought how fortunate for us to have the opportunity to live in an affordable spacious new home. We excitedly packed with great anticipation of finding America.

Loud Silence
Filomena Abys-Smith
April 1, 2004

The silence was always there in the midst of blaring sirens, the fire engines racing to subdue the never-ending blaze of burning buildings.

The ambulances rushing victims to a hospital of despair.

The chasing police after criminals that were themselves victims of ignorance and poverty.

The silence of a child's despair to hear the sounds of a home so far away.

The comforting sounds of a horse-driven cart with calling vendors.

The church bells awaken the heart, mind, and soul to a familiar world.

The soft sounds of breaking waves near the rocky shores.

The calling of well-known neighbors from balcony to balcony.

The music from an open window that lingered in the warm Mediterranean air and forever in my soul.

These sounds were silent in this new home; they were replaced by disappointment and a harsh reality that what we left behind could never be replaced.

Three Little Italian Cartwrights
Filomena Abys-Smith
January 1, 2004

I was always Hoss, Peppino was always Adam. Paola got the best part; she was Little Joe, the one I always wanted to be. It was settled by the Italian Adam that we would be the Cartwrights in order of our ages, and that's how we started our South Bronx Ponderosa in search for the land of beauty and opportunity.

While Ma fried the cutlets before *Bonanza* came on, we started to mimic our way into the Wild Wild West in search of the Americans we hoped one day to be.

We started to talk the talk and walk the walk. "Hiya, Pa! Hiya, Ma!" was called out to the proud parents of the Italian Cartwrights; they would surely one day own a place as big as the Ponderosa away from the noise and poverty.

We rode our horses all in a line around the house. The Italian Adam headed the pack, the disgruntled Hoss in the middle, the curly-headed Little Joe wildly beating her bottom; we were headed to the Ponderosa to find the America we only saw on TV.

Chapter 4

The Mott Haven Projects

The housing authority must have used alphabetic order to start the moving in process for the newly built Mott Haven projects with us being the first family to move in; I guess having a name that starts with *Ab* has its advantages. We were all truly ecstatic to have a spacious apartment on the second floor within walking distance of our school, shops, and transportation. The brand-new housing complex with many buildings reaching over twenty floors had a park with basketball courts and even green space with trees and flowers. The only disadvantage for me was sharing a room with my sister who was five years younger.

By this time, I had started to feel fairly adjusted to my new community and had developed close friendships with many of my classmates. They were all first-generation Puerto Ricans with parents that had immigrated in search of a better future. In that, I found a commonality; our cultures might have been slightly different, but our languages were similar, and there was a Latin rhythm to our lives. A rhythm one needs to feel, a sense of connection I cannot fully explain. I'm not sure if the connection existed because we were all in the same boat rowing toward the shores of a better future or if the Latin-based background helped, but I became very connected to my new friends.

I became the best of friends with Nanette, who entered Saint Pius in the third grade after her family also moved in to the housing projects. I think we became such good friends by fourth grade due to the fact that our personalities were similar; we were quiet, well behaved, and tried our hardest to excel in a classroom where the teacher, Sister Mary John, was either completely crazy or just simply disliked anyone not having an Irish background. She must have felt at a disadvantage due to the fact that she had only two students of Irish descent in our class and showered them with favoritism while unleashing the harshest of punishments on anyone else.

Sister Mary John did not hesitate to grab students by the hair, bashing their heads into the blackboard for not understanding the lessons she herself was incompetent in teaching. I must have frustrated her most due to the fact she did not quite know where to place an Italian; I wasn't Puerto Rican, and yet if I even looked the wrong way, she would remind me of my "Latin temper." It was in trying to cope with this heavenly angle of education that Nanette and I bonded, daily agonizing and sympathizing with each other.

I spent a great deal of time in Nanette's home, and her mom, Liz, was more than happy to teach me to wiggle my hips to the Latino beat. I would hold her hand, allowing the rhythm to guide my feet and sway my body into an enticing dance. I felt sexy and convinced myself that I was as good a dancer as my Puerto Rican family. In reality, I didn't even come close but felt loved and accepted just the same.

I now find it comical that during the month of March, a recital was performed on the school stage with me dancing the Irish jig along with other selected girls. I don't recall with certainty if it was that year or the previous year, but we were removed from class by a nun fully dressed in her down-to-the-ankle outfit who taught us how to skip, hop, and cross our feet one over the other while keeping our arms steady at our side. On the day of the recital, I wore an emerald green outfit with large paper shamrocks around the skirt and danced my way one step closer to becoming "an American."

There was also the very comical reciting of poems such as "The Owl and the Pussycat" with emphasis on the word *pussy*. One would think that anyone teaching in an inner-city school should know enough not to use the word *pussy* to describe such things as a frown on one's face or a dust bunny in a corner, but the nuns used the word often, sending the student body into controlled waves of laughter.

We were often asked to stand and read such lines as "The Owl and the Pussycat went to sea, and the Owl said to the Pussycat, 'O lovely Pussy! O Pussy, my love, / what a beautiful Pussy you are.'" Everyone hid behind textbooks that shook from laughter while the teacher demanded, "What is the meaning of this outrage?" No one was bold enough to explain the inner-city meaning of the word *pussy*, so we all had an hour-long detention.

I still recall with fond amusement trying to figure out the meaning of such songs as "Oh, Susanna / Oh, don't you cry for me / For I come from Alabama / With a banjo on my knee." When Yankee Doodle stuck a feather in his hat and called it macaroni, I was completely lost. The journey to becoming an American was somewhat confusing as I navigated through the different cultures I was exposed to.

Walking home from school, I watched as my young African American neighbors listened to Motown music while moving to the rhythmic beat; I felt the infusion of American soul seep through me. On entering the building, the Latino beat spilling from my neighbors' doors filled my being, and as I walked into my own home, the melody of Neapolitan music reminded me of who I was.

It was in those projects during our dinnertime conversation that I started to understand the gender gap; it became obvious to me as a female that my education was only secondary to learning the fine art of being a "good wife." While we dined on some of my father's favorite soups—like *pasta e fagioli* (pasta and bean soup), pasta and potatoes, or lentil and rice soup—I swallowed not only my soup but my tongue. Housekeeping came naturally to me, and I had always been a clean freak, but the art of being quiet while the men discussed important issues was tortuous.

I would listen as my dad discussed political issues with my brother, wanting so much to ask a question or have a say, but as soon as I formed words, I was told not only by my dad but also my mother to shut up. My mother's reprimand infuriated me even more as she told me, "Be quiet. Why are you getting in the middle of where you don't belong?" My brother snickered as my dad used his favorite line, "Ah a fato o speech," teasingly implying I was making a speech. I don't wish to infer that I was not loved or cared for; they simply believed that the use of my energy should be toward domestic concerns. I silently became very determined to be more than what they expected me to be, a proper obedient daughter and, eventually, a proper obedient housewife. "Not me," I told myself. "Just you wait and see. I will be more than what you ever expected me to be."

It was during those dinnertime conversations that my father started to explain our family history and the reason for not having an Italian surname. As the oral history was told to him, he repeated to us, "You know, the name Abys is Swiss. My great-grandfather came from a wealthy Swiss family, and they were of a noble class." Now you can imagine trying to believe his account while living in a South Bronx housing project with soul music emanating from under our window. My mom laughed with every account of the story, at times asking, "Well, where is the wealth now?" If my father further explained that it was lost through ill fate, she would respond, "Yeah, you're just like Swiss cheese. You have lots of holes in your head." I guess at times my mom had a rough time staying quiet and freely told my dad off.

Many years later, by sheer coincidence, I found his account to be true. As strange as this may sound, it started on a Cape Cod trip where I had driven my new Honda for a weeklong vacation. I sat with my sister in our favorite restaurant, enjoying a well-made pizza, when a waitress announced that someone had hit my car in the parking lot and had quickly sped off.

When I arrived back home, my insurance company had mailed a check for the repairs, and I went to my bank to cash the check, forgetting my bank card at home. The bank officer, knowing who I was, told me not to worry, that she'll quickly bring up my account saying, "With a name like that, you're easy to find." As the Abys names appeared on the screen, I sat in disbelief seeing the name John Abys. We had always assumed that we were the only Abyses in the United States and had no knowledge of this person; before the screen was turned off, I noticed an address in Staten Island. In retelling the story to my sister, she quickly picked up the phone, dialing information, finding his phone number and address.

That evening, I called the number and had a conversation with an unknown family member that was just as shocked to realize that other Abyses existed. In the conversation, I explained who I was, and although he seemed very excited, he was also very afraid, I'm sure, thinking that I was a scam artist. He mentioned that his ancestors were Swiss, and I can still feel the tingling on my arms and the back of my neck as I said, "Wow, that's really unbelievable, so were mine." John continued to be in disbelief, asking me, "Well, if you're really an Abys, then you should know what the family coat of arms looks like." I held back laughter, telling John, "I don't know anything about a coat of arms. My father never mentioned that to us." As John tried to write my phone number, he asked me to please give him time as he was disabled. I had already sensed that by his speech, and when I heard a protective mother in the background telling him to hang up, I was sure of it.

For brevity's sake, I'll conclude this family reunification story by saying that it took over twenty years and the setup of a family website by my cousin Luca Abys of Naples to convince John Abys that we were, in fact, all related. Luca asked me to reach out to John again and forward the family site to him. After many calls without any success, I mailed copies of the family genealogy to him, hoping he would call. I never heard from him until years later, while living in my present home, I received an e-mail from a Denise Dscorce, telling me she had received all of the material I had mailed to John after he had been placed in a nursing home and asked if I would meet with her when she came into Manhattan.

I was as leery as John had been and only accepted the invitation when we decided to meet at Grand Central Station under the famous clock. With my husband, Peter, by my side, I asked half a dozen females, "Are you Denise?" while Peter laughed, saying, "Jesus, Phil, you should have asked what she would be wearing." Finally, a pretty elderly lady accompanied by her husband asked, "Excuse me, are you Filomena?" When I said yes, she reached out, hugging me, and we all went out for coffee, having a great conversation about our family history.

I realized during our conversation that my decision to use Abys as part of my children's surname had been a smart move. Denise was telling me that John, having been the only male carrying the Abys name, had been born with cerebral palsy and never had children, and after his passing, the name would be lost from that part of the family branch that entered the United States in the early nineteen hundreds.

How I wished to be able to sit at a dinner table with my father and tell him that, in fact, he had been correct all along. The reader will find more family history at the end of this journal. For now, let's leave the Swiss Alps and take a South Bronx strut into becoming an American.

The silent introverted child I had become in the first few months of living in the South Bronx had slowly faded away, and that belligerent, feisty person was back to stay. I became determined never to be told by any man when I could speak or have him control my life. I was done with the old-fashioned Neapolitan mentality of family order. I wanted to liberate myself from cultural bonds. I wanted to be a self-sufficient liberated American lady. As strange as this may sound, living in the South Bronx aided in this endeavor.

I spent so much time with Nanette's family, observing her mom work a full day outside the home, and saw great liberation and empowerment. I was starting to think and speak in three languages and, most liberating of all, was watching the civil rights movement. I clearly understood that I was part of the underclass, the poor immigrant American without a voice. It may sound completely laughable, but when I sat in front of the TV hearing Dr. King's speeches, I felt he was also speaking for me. I too was looking for social equality, and when women started burning their bras, I was transformed into a mini feminist.

I now realize how fortunate I was to start my Americanization in a place that most well-established affluent Americans would rather have forgotten. These Americans only saw burning buildings, poverty, and despair, but within all of that was a great education in the struggle to achieve the American Dream. My father constantly reminded us that living in the South Bronx was an education in itself; I never quite understood what he meant until long after he was gone.

As you might suspect, there were also great trials living in a housing project, and after three years, the clean, safe environment slowly disappeared. The phantoms with empty eyes emerged again, and every building had its share of junkies. The fear of entering our building became forever present after being taunted by young addicts with a syringe in the stairwell of our building. That day, I was going home for lunch and decided to use the side stairs to reach the second floor to our apartment. I was halfway up those stairs when three young addicts came running down the stairs, lunging at me with the syringe they had just used. I screamed for my mother, running past them as fast as I could while one grabbed my behind.

Luckily, my mother opened the door to the stairs and pulled me into our apartment. Not much was said between us outside of my mom telling me not to enter the stairs without calling her first from the kitchen window. For the remaining time we lived in that building, it became a daily ritual. I would stand in front of the kitchen window, call for my mom. She would nod from the window and then open the door to the stairs and wait for me to cover my nose to prevent the urine stench from spoiling my appetite while I ran to the safety of our apartment.

You're probably wondering how we managed to live for so long under such fearful conditions. The best explanation I can give is that you adjust to the conditions; you subconsciously prepare yourself for the dangers that exist beyond your door. Once we entered our home, it was like walking into a different world. The house was immaculately clean and organized. The aroma of freshly prepared meals always welcomed us, and the daily rituals of removing our shoes at the door, washing our hands, hanging up our uniforms, doing our homework, and sitting down to dinner at a table set with a linen tablecloth gave structure and quality to our lives.

I can still hear my parents at the dinner table retelling stories of the war, clearly seeing both of them sitting next to each other, sharing a glass of wine as my mother lovingly sliced a piece of fruit for my dad, which he thankfully accepted. I'm certain that the rituals of our culture made living in the South Bronx bearable.

I will only share a few more memories of my time in the projects; it's not my intent to paint a picture of complete mayhem but to emphasize that great adversity with proper guidance builds strong character and a steady resolve to reach the American Dream. Most of our neighbors were all hardworking citizens, and the violence that occurred was caused mostly by the drugs that had invaded the housing projects.

The memory of street violence cannot be denied, and although we never participated in the drug culture that had enveloped our community, it seemed that my brother was forever in street brawls. The first recollection of these straightforward negotiations was being told that my brother had just gotten home from Lincoln Hospital, where his lip had been stitched back together.

The previous day, he had been harassed by a neighbor in the front of our building, where my brother proceeded to use a Bronx term, "kicked the living shit out of." The neighbor's older brother came down to settle the score and split my brother's lip apart. Now as my brother will testify, if he had not panicked during the exchange with the older brother, he could have whooped his ass. For the following months, while the lip healed, Peppino, now called Joe, strengthened his muscles as well as his skills in street fighting. For the remaining time Joe lived in that building until he went away to college, Joe made a point of shoving and harassing the older brother into a form of submission.

The basketball courts of the housing projects were places that not only held vigorous games but also were where disputes were settled. On a sunny Saturday afternoon, I sat on a bench watching my father—all of five feet four, wearing shorts, Converse sneakers, and a headband around his forehead to keep the massive amount of curly hair from falling into his eyes—move like a graceful ballet dancer juggling a soccer ball. First, he lifted the ball onto his toes, foot to foot, then to his knee, knee to knee, from his knee to his chest, side to side, and finally, to his head. He seemed to amaze not only his daughter but also the children playing basketball.

In the sixties, soccer was an alien sport, especially in the inner city, and they watched him as if he was a man from Mars. They stopped pointing at him in appreciative amazement; some started to mimic his moves with their basketballs. I sat so proud watching his graceful moves until I caught sight of a mammoth black man walking slowly toward my father. His fists were clenched, and he had an aggressive strut to his walk. My father must have seen him as quickly as I did and dropped the ball. His relaxed stance changed as he clenched his fists, putting one foot in front of the other, and defiantly looked up at this giant of a man.

For a few seconds, I gasped for air, convinced my dad would be pulverized to the ground. As the black man approached closer, his fist opened into a handshake, and I heard him say, "Can you teach me to do that?" My dad handed him the ball, and he eventually became the first black man to play on the Mount Vesuvius soccer team where my father was the coach.

A strong friendship grew from that encounter, and he proved to be a valuable ally, especially after my brother, while walking with a girl classmate to school, had to again beat the piss out of a young hoodlum for snatching her school hat. It just so happened that the hoodlum was part of a street gang, and the following day, as my brother stepped out of school, a group of boys surrounded him intent on doing serious harm.

I recall a classmate running toward me, yelling about what was happening as a large crowd of people gathered around the circle with my brother in the middle. I could barely see what was occurring except for the occasional sight of a thrusting punch coming out of the circle. Joe threw punch after punch, keeping the jackals at bay, until the nuns called the police. I heard sirens as officers jumped out of their cars to break up the rumble, and then led us inside to the safety of the school.

The police spoke to my father, informing him that they could not ensure Joe's safety, and we should take extra precautions. The soccer team proved to be most helpful with our black friend walking to school with us daily. I'm not sure how long that nightmare lasted, but finally, for whatever reason, a gang member civilly approached my father, telling him that it was over. I was never told why the gang backed off; I was just glad they had.

We were very fortunate to have a stay-at-home mom who prepared delicious lunches for us daily. Unlike most of our classmates, we only ran through the school cafeteria holding a hand over our noses to stop from gagging. My mom was as skilled as a restaurant chef, creating the most tasty lunchtime treats. Even a simple hamburger was made extra special by adding finely diced garlic and parsley. She sliced potatoes so thin by hand that they fried into crispy chips. Thin veal cutlets were quickly dipped into a bit of flour, seared on both sides in butter, spiced with black pepper, and served with crusty bread. Eggs pouched in a zesty red sauce, which my mother called eggs in purgatory, or potatoes with sausages were well worth the walk from school.

It was during one of those lunchtime meals that I looked out of the kitchen window and saw the two Irish sons of the school custodian harassing my brother. Joe was already in the process of holding one down on the ground while the other brother jumped on him. I called my mother who calmly told me to stay where I was as she grabbed the bat we kept inside the closet door. She held one brother at bay while Joe smacked the one on the ground around and then told him to teach the other a lesson as well. When that was over, we washed our hands and sat down at the kitchen table while my mother served us a tasty lunch. She calmly asked my brother, "What was the problem with the two Irish brothers?" My brother responded, "I don't know, Ma. They're Irish. They just like to fight."

My brother graduated from Saint Pius, receiving many awards for academic excellence, and was accepted to Cardinal Hayes High School, where he decided to play football. Now my father was a sports lover and occasionally tried to understand while watching a TV football match the concept of the game. His Neapolitan voice asking my brother, "Joe, why they call this game football when they only use the foot once? I think they should call this game o' munton," meaning "pile up." He laughed as my brother tried to explain the concept of football, saying, "I like all sports, but I don't understand why they knock the crap out of each other, pile on one another, and then call it football."

I don't think he was extremely happy when my brother got on the football team in his first year of high school, but even still, he often went to watch while videoing his Neapolitan son play "pile up." I'm sure he was very proud that his son could compete in an American sport.

It was during those high school years while my brother tried to study for final exams that a group of young men sat under his window with the radio blasting. I prayed my usual silent prayer; I had developed a sharp intuition and felt trouble close at hand. It was the same prayer I repeated when Joe was out late at night, the same simple prayer when Joe was in a street fight. "Please, God, don't let there be trouble. Please keep him safe." I heard the window open in his room as he yelled, "Hey, keep the music down!" He asked not once but three times, and I heard the change in his voice with every request.

The fourth time, he yelled, "If you don't turn down the music, I'm going to shove a stick down your throat and make it come out of your ass!" The group of boys just laughed, not taking him seriously at all; I knew they had made a serious mistake. I heard him go into the hallway closet and grab the bat as I ran into my parents' room to tell them what was happening.

While my dad pulled on his pants, I ran to the window and saw Joe holding the bat a few inches from someone's face, yelling and asking, "Do you want this shoved up your ass or down your throat?" By the time my father joined the mayhem, the laughing had stopped, and I heard someone say, "OK. OK, man, no problem, no problem." The radio was turn off as my father and brother walked away without getting into a physical exchange. With my heart beating out of control and my legs shaking, I finally sat on my bed, wondering when God was going to answer my prayer for a little peace. Education was very important to us, and studying, at times, was a trial in sheer determination. I hope Joe got an A on that exam.

I also graduated from Saint Pius and to everyone's amazement, including my own, received the award for excellence in science, having had the highest grades in seventh and eighth grades. During graduation, I sat in the church with my cap and gown on, hearing my name being called but, in disbelief, not reacting. My friend Nanette, sitting behind me, tapped me on the shoulder, whispering, "Phil, they're calling you." I had always been a good student, trying my best to achieve high grades, but never in a million years did I expect to receive an award. In a daze, I walked up to the altar, where I was congratulated by the monsignor as he handed me a gift box containing rosary beads, which I still have.

Soon after graduation, my friend Nanette moved to Puerto Rico with her family. Our families had been so close; we were the best of friends, sharing all of our girlhood secrets with each other. We said good-bye with heavy hearts, not realizing that this separation was essential to our development. We continued our friendship through letters, often sharing our most intimate feelings.

That summer, I started to work in a five-and-dime store on 149th street, which was a bustling shopping area located under the L train. I was assigned to the material and rug section and, for the first few weeks, cut many fabrics in a zigzag fashion. I hoisted rugs that weighed as much as I did onto the register table and felt like an adult, earning my own money to pay for the extras my parents could not afford. I had desperately for years asked my parents if I could attend ballet classes. They laughed at every request with my father telling me, "You got plenty of room. Go twirl around over there." I was determined to save enough money to take classes and didn't mind walking over a mile to get to work. It now amazes me how my parents, during the many years we lived in the South Bronx, allowed me to walk outside our apartment alone, but I guess you become desensitized and accept your environment as the norm.

I worked full-time that entire summer, saving most of my wages, and when I started my freshman year in high school, I worked part-time. It was from those wages that I was able to purchase my first Christmas gifts for my parents. My dad had always wanted an electric shaver, so I purchased a sturdy black one for him. For my mother, an assortment box of perfumed powder with body lotions. For both of my parents, a music box which I felt so proud to have found. It held a figurine of Tevye from *Fiddler on the Roof* with his arms held high, and when the coil was wound, the tune "If I Were a Rich Man" played as Tevye circled around. I was certain my parents would love this gift since we had all watched the movie together, enjoying the music, but most of all relating to the message of struggle and hope.

I can't say with complete certainty if this happened that summer or the following summer, but it occurred as I walked home with my brother from the train station on 138th Street along Alexander Avenue to reach the Mott Haven projects. We had spent the morning visiting our mother at Lenox Hill Hospital, where she was recuperating from a miscarriage.

The streets were, as usual, crowed with people; it was a hot summer day, and everyone sought relief from the heat by sitting on the brownstone steps, milk crates, or just standing near a wall. We walked quickly and quietly with a South Bronx strut, one that says, "Don't mess with me." It was a walk we developed out of necessity.

Over my right shoulder, I saw a group of older men sitting on the steps of one of the brownstones that lined Alexander Avenue. They were drinking beer, and I said my usual silent prayer, "Please, God, don't let there be trouble." As we passed them, sexual comments were made toward me, comments I had heard so often that their meaning no longer affected me. It was Joe who reacted. He, at sixteen, was strong, determined, and felt indestructible.

As the men laughed after the comment was made, Joe turned and yelled back, "Hey, fucko, how would you like if I said that to your sister!" One of the men stepped off the stairs and started walking toward us, violently cursing and telling Joe, "I'm going to fuck you up." Joe instantly removed his belt, wrapping it around his fist with the buckle right over his knuckles while telling me to run home. I, at thirteen, also felt strong, determined, and indestructible and refused to run, leaving my brother in such danger.

As the man came closer, he too had taken off his belt and swung it over his head. Joe pushed me behind him and took the first blow, with the belt hitting him in the chest as Joe's fist made contact with the man's mouth, splitting it wide open. Blood poured out like an open faucet as he doubled over, gasping for air.

Again, Joe told me to run home, but I refused to leave, seeing the group of men running toward us. While one helped his friend off the floor, the other two jumped on Joe; I automatically, without thinking of the danger, jumped on one, pulling him off by grappling at his hair and face. Joe landed a number of rapid-fire punches at the men, sending them backward as he quickly grabbed me by my arm and started running toward home.

The entire incident lasted only a matter of minutes, and as we ran—with my brother holding on to my arm, lifting me off the ground, urging me to run faster—I saw bottles flying over us and felt the wind of one as it exploded next to my ankle. We ran up the side stairs of our building to our apartment, where my father was getting ready for his night job. He took one look at us and knew we had been in a street brawl. I started to spill out what had occurred as Joe opened his shirt to see what damage the belt buckle had caused. I saw the fury on my father's face as his glare went from me to my brother's chest.

I started to shake, feeling sick to my stomach noticing that my father was grabbing the bat out of the closet while ordering me to stay inside as he went back out with my brother. I sat on the living room sofa crying and having to run to the bathroom to throw up, all the while trying to decide if I should call the police. It seemed like hours to me before my father and brother returned home, but it was probably no more than fifteen minutes. I didn't even ask what happened; I was just glad they were both home safe. Minutes later, a few of my brother's friends called from below our kitchen window. They had heard about the brawl and were asking if he needed help to settle the score. I internally cried, *Oh no, God, please let it end.* I felt a gush of relief as I heard my brother say, "Don't worry about it. We took care of it."

I hope that by now the reader realizes what strong bonds are built between neighbors while they cope with similar struggles. We were all part of the same voiceless family. It didn't matter whether you were black or white, Latin or Latino, Puerto Rican or Italian; we were all held together by the single vision of reaching the American Dream.

We have traveled so far from those housing projects that these stories seem strange to us now, as if they happened to someone else; but no matter how far apart we are, they connect us. On rare occasions when we do talk about our struggles, I still remind my brother that if it wasn't for me, he would have had his ass handed to him on a silver platter, and we both just laugh.

Run-through-the-Cafeteria Lunch

The tin smell of canned products such as Chef Boy-Ar-Dee served alongside a milk carton and fluffy white bread with butter was enough for us to cover our nose and run through the cafeteria feeling sorry for our classmates that had to consume such prefab foods. We ran home to feast on:

Veal in Butter

This recipe can also be prepared with chicken or pork cutlets.

Ingredients:

6 thinly sliced cutlets
1 stick of butter or margarine
Salt and pepper to taste

In a skillet, melt butter while lightly salting and dredging cutlets into the flour. When butter is melted and a bit foamy, place cutlets into the pan and cook until golden. Add a bit more salt and pepper. Serve in a plate with crusty bread. This takes less than ten minutes, and I never quite understood why anyone would waste the time and money on frozen meals that take twice as long to cook. You can also remove the cutlets after they are almost cooked; set them aside on a plate. To the butter, add the juice of a lemon and stir; add a bit of chicken stock, stir for a few seconds. Add the cutlets back in, flip on both sides, simmer for a few minutes, and serve. Easy-breezy lunch.

Sausages with Potatoes and Hot Peppers

Ingredients:

2 lb. of Italian sausages, sweet or hot
5 medium-size potatoes peeled and cut into bite-size portions
4 cloves of garlic cut in half
Sliced hot peppers (these may be fresh peppers or jarred; add as many or as little as you like)

In a skillet, add a bit of oil, maybe two tablespoons. Heat on medium flame. When hot, add sausages; you can leave them in a wheel or cut into links. I find turning individual links easier. Once brown on all sides, remove from skillet and place on a plate.

Add garlic and peppers to the same skillet; cook until garlic has a bit of color, then add potatoes to the skillet. Coat well with oil, and cook covered until potatoes are almost done; you may need to add a bit of water. Place sausages back into the skillet, and cook until potatoes are tender and a bit brown. Make sure that sausages are completely cooked through.

I have also prepared this recipe with Polish kielbasa sausages, and it's a big favorite in my family. Of course, serve with crusty Italian bread—you can also split a hero roll in half and pile the sausages, potatoes, and hot peppers inside—it makes a great sandwich.

Eggs in Purgatory

My mom poached eggs in a leftover ragù sauce which she made extra spicy by adding red pepper flakes. You need to pour the sauce into a skillet, and if the sauce is too thick, add a bit of water. Heat the sauce until bubbly, crack eggs into the sauce, cover, and cook until the eggs are firm.

This is my version of eggs in purgatory.

Ingredients

2 28-oz. cans of San Marzano tomatoes crushed by hand or blender
2 tbs. of "salted" capers
¼ cups of pitted and chopped olives like Gaeta (do not use the green olives with pimentos in the middle)
About 4 gloves of finely chopped garlic
Finely chopped hot peppers like jalapeno or you may use red pepper flakes
4 tbs. of vegetable oil

In a large skillet, add oil over a medium-high flame. When hot, add the garlic, olives, capers, and hot peppers. Cook until the garlic is a slightly golden color. Add the tomatoes, stir, mixing all ingredients together. On a medium flame, cook for about twenty minutes.

You can let this sauce sit until you are ready to crack eggs into it. The sauce will be more flavorful if prepared a few hours ahead. Just before you're ready to serve, heat sauce until bubbly and crack eggs into it. Cover and cook eggs until firm. My mom served these eggs for lunch with bread on the side for dunking, but I have served these eggs on top of cooked rice, or cooked ziti pasta that has been first tossed with a bit of the sauce and then placed the eggs on top, to great reviews from my family. Of course, don't forget to have crusty Italian bread for dunking into the sauce.

"Swallow Your Tongue" Soups
Pasta and Potato Soup (*Pasta e Patate*)

Ingredients:

6 medium potatoes peeled and diced into bite-size pieces
4 cloves of garlic
5 tbs. of vegetable oil
1 lb. of cooked pasta such as cut spaghetti or mixed pasta (my mom purchased this type of pasta in an Italian deli; the bag contained a variety of small pasta in the same package)
Salt and black pepper
Chopped Italian parsley
Optional: about 4 slices of diced pancetta or bacon

Place a large pot of salted water on the stove over a medium flame.

Place another large pot on the stove, add oil. Heat over a medium flame, add the pancetta or bacon, and cook for a few minutes.

Add the garlic, cook until translucent.

Add the potatoes to the pan, coat well with oil, cook for a few minutes until slightly golden, then add enough of the hot salted water to cover potatoes. Cook until tender. At this point, you may add a bit more salt and pepper.

When potatoes are almost tender, cook pasta in the salted boiling water; drain cooked pasta, reserving enough of the pasta water to add to the soup. Add pasta to the potatoes, mix well, and allow the soup to cook on a low flame for about fifteen minutes.

At this point, my mom added bite-size pieces of the ends of the Parmesan cheese. She scraped the back end of the cheese clean, cutting it into bite-size portions, adding them to the soup, cooking until soft. These bits of softened chewy cheese added great flavor to all our soups, and we fought over who didn't get enough.

Pasta and White Kidney Bean Soup (*Pasta e Fagioli*)

Ingredients:

4 15-oz. cans of cannellini beans (or you can cook a bag of dry white kidney beans as my mom always did; I still hide the fact that I use canned beans, knowing that she will scold me by saying, "What does it take to cook a bag of beans?"

½ cup of vegetable oil or olive oil (I know the trend is to use extra virgin olive oil, but I find the taste too overpowering and use canola oil in cooking, only using olive oil on salads and vegetables; of course, you may use what you prefer.)

Optional: a few slices of diced bacon or pancetta

½ cup of crushed tomatoes with the juice

4 cloves of crushed garlic

Salt and pepper

1 lb. of short cut pasta such as shells, ditali, or mixed pasta

Place a large pot of salted water to boil.

In another large pot, add oil (if using the bacon, add and sauté for a few minutes) add the garlic; cook until a slight golden color (do not brown the garlic).

Add the crushed tomatoes; stir and cook until a sauce is made, no more than about five minutes.

Add the beans with all the liquid; stir and let simmer for about fifteen minutes.

You may let this sit on the stove with the flame off until you are ready to cook the pasta; the flavor will improve as it sits.

Cook the pasta. While cooking the pasta start to reheat the beans over a medium low flame. You may drain the cooked pasta over a large bowl or pot to capture the cooking water to be added to the beans or just use a spider to scoop out the pasta, placing it into the beans. Add enough pasta water to make a soup.

Rice and White Kidney Bean Soup (*Riso e Fagioli*)

You may also use this same recipe with cooked rice, but you need to add enough hot water to the beans to make a soup, adding the cooked rice at the very end.

Chopped parsley may be added at the end of cooking. My dad enjoyed eating this type of soup with a raw white onion. He would scoop out the soup with a thick onion piece; I know this sounds strange, but he also dipped raw radishes into a sauce. It's probably an old-fashioned Neapolitan thing.

Lentil Soup (*Riso e Lenticchie*)

Ingredients:

4 tbs. of oil
1 small diced onion
4 cloves of crushed garlic
1 finely diced washed carrot
1 stalk of celery, washed and finely diced
1 large peeled and washed potato diced into small bite-size portions
¼ cup of crushed plum tomatoes (crushed by hand)
Optional: thinly sliced and diced pancetta, prosciutto, or bacon (if you prefer your soup spicy, add a finely diced hot pepper or red pepper flakes)
½ lb. of dried lentils
6 cups of hot water or stock
Salt and pepper to taste
1 cup of cooked rice

Heat oil in a large soup pot; if using pancetta, add to oil and cook for about two minutes. Add the vegetables and lentils; coat well with the oil. Add the hot water or stock, salt and pepper to taste. Cook covered over a medium low flame until vegetables and lentils are tender, about forty-five minutes. Just before serving, mix rice into the soup. You may sprinkle Parmesan cheese over the top of each bowl.

My Maternal -grandparents Nonna
Carmela and Nonno Pasquale. They
taught me the value of hard work

My mom Fortuna holding
me as an infant

Nonna Filomena, holding her name sake {me} with
my brother Peppino and Friend Marica

My dad Ugo holding me, Signora Sparagna,
Peppino, Marica My mom and Zia Tina

On Zia Pinas' sofa with my baby sister Paola and brother Peppino

Nonna Carmela and Nonna Filomena with my cousins,
I'm the tiny one in front

At the Beach in Bagnoli, {Bagno Fortuna} with my dad and brother

At the beach with my cousins—the good old days

Our Playing Field with cousins Ana Maria, Carmela,
Me, Carmela, Rosetta, and Peppino

Carnival 1959 with my cousins and brother.

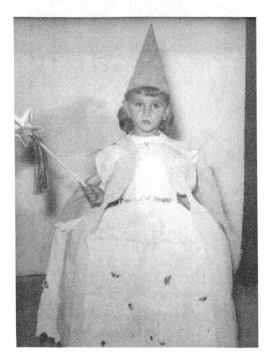

Me dressed up for Carnival 1959

Me ready for the food market

I'm feeling sexy already

My sixth birthday—my last in Bagnoli before leaving for New York

dads' passport—In search of the American Dream

My dad Ugo arriving into New York harbor- never saw his beloved Naples again

This is the original book given to us by Signora
Sparagna for our voyage to the USA

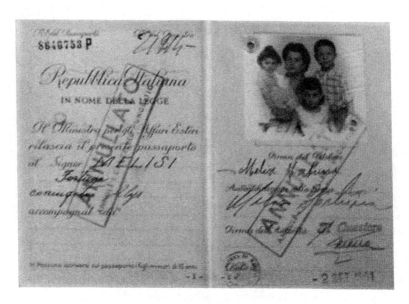

Our Passport photo—Ready to be Americans

This is the steamer-trunk we arrived in the USA with

The Mount Vesuvius Soccer Team—My dad,
{Ugo} is at the bottom third from right

My dads' vision of an Italian-American Soccer Team

PART 2

Chapter 1

First Love

It wasn't until I started freshman year in high school that I bonded with Italian friends; until then, all of my friends had been Puerto Rican, and I was connected to their culture almost as much as my own. I spent so much time at my best friend Nanette's home that we were more like sisters than friends, and our families were surrogates for each other. I was almost completely fluent in Spanish and understood the heart and soul of Puerto Rican life. I was—in every sense, to coin a new term—an Italia-Rican, happy to enjoy both cultures.

After eighth-grade graduation, I was enrolled in Saint Pius High School, a very strict all-girls Catholic school where all the students sat in very straight rows in alphabetical order. I, being first in the row, Susan Adessa second, and Maria Annunziata third, all three of us Italians.

We became good friends, and I was amazed at how alike we were. Our homemade lunches shouted Southern Italian as soon as we opened the bags, relieving slices of pasta frittata, heros made with broccoli raab and sausages, or crusty Italian bread holding a fried chicken cutlet topped with roasted peppers. For the first time since leaving Naples, I was connected to female peers of my own culture.

As teenagers do, we started hanging out at each other's homes and, to use a Bronx term, on the corner. The major problem for me was that I didn't live in a neighborhood where Italian girls were allowed to go, and just the mention of housing projects sent stares of shock in my direction. My friends were kind enough to invite me over to their homes, where for the first time, I was hanging out in an Italian neighborhood.

It was in the early spring of my sophomore year when Susan invited me over for a Saturday lunch. Her mom made a delicious minestrone soup, and we ate hearty portions while dunking slices of bread into the broth. After lunch, her mom asked if we could pick up clothing from the dry cleaners; we talked and giggled all the way there, crashing through the dry cleaners' doors in fits of laughter, and stopped only when we noticed a young man standing near the counter staring at us.

Susan knew him; he was her older brother's friend, and she walked over to say hi, introducing me as Phil. I took one look at him and knew he was not Italian; I was certain that he was Puerto Rican. He spoke with beautiful clear diction that told me he was not from my neighborhood. In a soft voice, he asked me, "Your name is Phil?" I smiled, telling him it was short for Filomena. He nodded in understanding. We chitchatted for a brief few minutes, and as we started to leave, I turned to look back, noticing that he was still smiling and staring. I smiled back and, with too much confidence for a sixteen-year-old, spun my head around, showing off my waist-long hair, walking away with a sexy strut.

I didn't visit Susan until the following Saturday when we got together with a group of friends to hang out on the corner. We were all talking and laughing until the roar of an engine made us suddenly stop. All the girls knew whose car it was; they whispered to me, "That's Mike's car. He built it himself." The Puerto Rican fellow I had met a week earlier stepped out, and although he spoke to everyone, I knew instinctively his sole focus was on me. It was as if everyone else had melted away. We spoke for a long while with all the girls staring at us. They glanced at each other with that "I know they like each other" look.

I started to say good-bye to everyone; it was getting late, and it was time for me to leave. Mike asked me, "Where do you live?" When I told him, the look of shock was comical. His eyes bulged out, and he, with a concerned voice, asked, "How are you getting home?" I had become so accustomed to taking trains and walking around "the hood" that I found the question silly.

Giggling, I answered, "I take the train to 149th Street and then walk to 138th Street to the Mott Haven projects." He stared in disbelief, replying, "By yourself? I don't even walk around that area by myself." I started to laugh, "It's OK. I'm used to it." Mike, pointing to his handmade hot rod, said, "Come on, I'll give you a ride." I hesitated, looking at this strange car with huge wheels and a raised rear. He noticed my concern and softly said, "It's safer than the trains, and I'll drive very slow." The other girls had been listening to our conversation and seemed almost envious. Susan came over, whispering to me, "Don't worry, he's really nice." He opened the door, and that was the first time I sat in a homemade hot rod.

Mike did drive slowly heading toward the South Bronx. We felt completely comfortable with each other and spoke freely. I could smell his cologne and noticed a large silver Indian head ring on his figure. I knew it was a good luck charm, much like the Italians wear the red horn around their neck.

While he drove, he asked me what was an Italian doing living in this neighborhood. I responded, "I always lived there." Mike with a puzzled voice asked, "You were born here?" "No, I was born in Naples. We moved here when I was six." He quickly looked at me in disbelief, and I continued to tell him that until I met Susan, I only had Puerto Rican friends. With that, he started to laugh, saying, "I live in an Italian neighborhood, and most of my friends are Italians." We both started to laugh, I guess, at the irony of our lives.

At a red light, Mike reached into the glove compartment, pulling out a tape while chuckling and saying, "Well, let's get in the right mood for this neighborhood." He blasted Puerto Rican merengue music. I started to laugh out loud, telling him, "I know how to dance the merengue." "Now that I would love to see—an Italian girl dancing the merengue."

He stopped on the Alexander street side of my building and looked at me with concern. "Are you sure you're OK by yourself?" I shrugged, "Yes, I'm fine. I do this all the time. Thanks for the ride." "OK, Phil, see you around." Before I entered the side staircase, I turned looking back; he was still watching me with concern.

How many times did we see each other while I visited with Susan? I'm really not sure. What I am certain of is that we became connected to each other by the mutual understanding of our cultures. Of course, there was playful flirtation, and I, for a young girl, was quite comfortable with my sexuality. The flirtation grew into a relationship on a sunny afternoon when I walked with a group of friends past Mike's home where he was in the driveway, inspecting his car. Everyone stopped to talk to him and check out the hot rod, but as before, everyone melted away, and our focus was solely on each other.

He closed the hood of the car and leaned on it to engage me in conversation. I was more than willing to stand very close, and with very few words spoken, he gently reached for my hand, pulling me into his arms. He held me with one arm around my waist and the other hand wrapped around my hair. I felt completely safe and comfortable; as we smiled at each other, he asked me, "Do you know what you remind me of?"

"No, what?" "You're like those dolls Puerto Rican women place on their beds. Did you ever see one?" "Yes, Italians do the same. My mom has one on her bed." "That's what you look like, a beautiful *muñequita*." He bent down, kissing me. I did not hesitate kissing him back. That first kiss was as natural as taking a breath of fresh air. We continued to kiss for a long while, oblivious to anyone around us, at times Mike holding my head softly on his chest. From that day on, we became inseparable.

We saw each other as often as possible, holding hands, walking to the park, where Mike would take dozens of photos of me. I had my first McDonald's hamburger in his car, surprising him that I had never been to a fast-food restaurant. He watched me open and inspect the hamburger package, laughing when I mentioned, "Wow, this has lots of stuff on it." The hamburger was OK, but I didn't like the catsup. I did enjoy the fries and hot apple pie, but what I loved the most was the kind attention he showered on me.

My parents became aware that I was seeing someone from his phone calls, and I got the usual "Watch your step" warning. I knew that soon, they would ask to meet him. The opportunity came when Mike invited me to accompany him at a nightclub. He asked if my parents would give me permission if he himself met with them. I wasn't really sure how they would react but decided it was time everyone got to know each other. For whatever reason, both my parents liked him immediately. My dad spoke to him in English, giving Mike the once-over, and then shocked me by saying, "OK, you can take my daughter out, but have her home early."

As old-fashioned as my parents were, when it came to Mike, they were quite liberal. It didn't matter that he was Puerto Rican or that he was four years older than me; Mike became part of our home, developing a new language with my mom called Italian-Spani-English, a combination of the three languages, which they understood very well.

Often, on weekends, we would go to clubs, which I was legally too young to attend but never had a problem getting in. Mike had played guitar in a rock band for years and knew everyone. Neither of us drank, and we enjoyed ourselves by talking to friends, listening to music, and being with each other.

On one occasion, when Mike introduced me as Phil Abys to an acquaintance, the fellow, while gawking, asked me if I was Joe Abys's sister. I answered, "Yes, he's my older brother." The fellow responded, "So you're the one he told all the boys to keep away from. He made it clear to all the guys that 'if anyone touches my sister, I'll mess you up.'" Mike laughed, telling the guy, "Yeah, now I'm telling you, keep away from her." He pulled me by the hand, leading me away, muttering, "*Cabron*" I guess he didn't like the way the fellow was gawking.

Mike was a true gentleman and was very sexually reserved with me. As an older male, he could have taken complete advantage of me, but it was I that unusually initiated sexual activity. My parents were correct in trusting Mike; it was their daughter they should not have trusted. When we were alone in his car, I sat so close that, at times laughing, he asked me to move over. "I can't concentrate on driving with you so close." When we parked the car in a quiet area, I didn't hesitate to climb on his lap and, as he put it, "make him lose his self-control." I coquettishly asked, "Then why did you park here?" He smiled, telling me, "Because I'm crazy in love with you." I slowly kissed him behind his ears, whispering, "I love you too."

Before asking me to meet his parents, Mike started to explain the religious practices of Santerismo; as best as I can recall, he told me that it was an extension of the Roman Catholic religion merged with African and Native Indian rituals. He seemed anxious about inviting me into his home, and when I told him I was OK with it, he softly put his hands around my face saying, "I don't want you to be afraid. It's nothing for you to be afraid of. It's not who I am but what my parents are." I was bold enough to tell him, "I'm not afraid of a bunch of BS, and I know that's why you wear that ring." He smirked and said, "Yeah, right, you don't need to believe in it, just respect it." I said, "Yes, OK," all the while thinking, *Boy, what a crock of shit. I don't even believe all the crap the nuns try to teach us in class.*

As we walked into his large brick home, I was immediately aware of a funky smell. I thought, *Wow, the building I live in always smells bad, but as soon as I walk into my home, it smells fresh and clean.* I didn't say a word. We went through his downstairs apartment first, and I didn't find it all that clean and noticed a few religious articles scattered about.

We climbed the stairs to his parents' home, and the sight was a bit shocking. Just about every corner of the very spacious home was littered with statues of saints with bowls of rotting fruit. The home was so cluttered with religious and Indian-like articles that I started to feel claustrophobic. I swallowed the fear, sitting on the living room sofa with his dad across from us.

We chitchatted a bit, and his dad asked me what my horoscope sign was. He continued to tell me that I had a very delicate stomach and that I would eventually have stomach problems. Mike was holding my hand, and he must have felt my increasing nervousness, stopping his dad by saying, "OK, Dad. We're going out. See you later."

As we walked out, I vowed not to let his parents' lifestyle come between our relationship, rationalizing he can't help how they live. Mike put his arm around my waist, asking, "Did my dad scare you?" Even at such a young age, I understood that it was important to be honest in a relationship and told him, "Yes, he's a bit scary, and does he think he can predict the future?"

Mike just laughed, telling me, "Don't pay it any attention. I don't want this to come between us." I replied, "That's what I was thinking." After that, I did occasionally visit his family's home, meeting with his mother, who was scarier than the father. His oldest sister was such a hoarder that you could not open the door to her bedroom without pushing stuff out of the way. Needless to say, we spent more time at my home, even if it was in the hood.

By my junior year of high school, our relationship had become more than the casual dating of a teenager. We had grown so close that it was understood by both of us that we would marry. Although on a very sunny August afternoon, while we walked holding hands, Mike turned to me, saying, "Phil, I can't wait for the day that I can marry you. Will you marry me?" Of course, I said yes. It was only by Mike's self-control that we did not engage in complete sexual intercourse. I was, in every sense, a teenage vixen, willing to entice and arouse whenever possible.

Mike was only human, and the self-control he had practiced for so many months was starting to fade. When we found a place to be alone, I did not hesitate to sit on his lap, facing him, both my legs wrapped around his thighs. I had always been a free spirit and rarely wore a bra; the female liberation movement had inspired me to go without one, and I didn't hesitate pressing my breast that was only covered by a midriff top against his chest while we kissed. He would not have been human if he had not reached for what I made very accessible.

For many months, we engaged in the most sexual forms of foreplay, only hesitating at complete intercourse for fear of pregnancy. Mike kept holding himself back from what I wanted him to do, calling me *muñequita* and softly telling me, "You have no idea how much I want you, but if we get into trouble, your dad will kill us both." I laughed, telling him, "It's not going to happen the first time."

I had just celebrated my seventeenth birthday; Mike's gift was a gold heart locket with matching heart earrings, all of which I still have and treasure. He came over to my home, expecting to pick me up and we just go out. *How lucky*, I thought. My mom had to run to help my dad in his shop, and my pain-in-the-butt little sister was at my aunt's house. Mike walked in, asking, "Where's Mom?" I, smiling, led him by the hand to the living room sofa, responding, "Lucky for us, Mom is working in the shop, and pain-in-the-ass Paola is at Zia Titina's house."

He smiled back, saying, "I guess we need to figure out what to do with all this extra time on our hands." I simply smiled and climbed onto his lap in my usual position, with legs wrapped around his thighs, breast pressed against his chest. His hands pushed my hair back, bringing my face close to his, locking our lips into the most passionate of kisses. It seemed that we kissed for hours, his hands caressing every part of my body. I opened his shirt, kissing his chest and undoing his pants. Our clothes seemed to melt away. I slowly lay back, he bringing himself ever so gently on top of me. That first complete connection was as loving and as natural as the first kiss. My body shook from my inner being outward until we both collapsed from pleasure.

He was the kindest of lovers, and his first question to me was "Are you OK?" I, feeling very sexy and adultlike, pushed my hair from under my back onto the pillows, responding, "Yes, why? Do I look different or something?" He quickly looked up to the ceiling, laughing, then straight at me, softly saying, "I think I'm in love with a witch."

He was not only a friend and lover but also a teacher, always encouraging me to study, kind enough to take time from his own studies to patiently review my homework and explain what I didn't understand. In looking back, he showered me with the attention that my parents did not have time for or see fit to give. He had become my world.

First Love Minestrone Soup

I share this recipe with you with the understanding that I'm using my sensory recall to place the flavors of Susan's mother's minestrone soup into a recipe. I was delighted from the first spoonful not only for the exceptional flavor but also for how similar it was to my own mother's. After high school graduation, I never saw Susan again, mostly due to my own negligence. I have deep regrets for not having stayed in touch with her and still have a gold ring which was part of her own jewelry collection that she gave me as a sign of friendship on the day I met Mike. Years later, by mere coincidence, I met up with Maria Annunziata, and while reminiscing, I asked about Susan. I was heartbroken to hear that she had passed away at a very young age from a blood disorder. Whenever I go through my jewelry box and see the ring, I think of her and regret not having stayed in touch with her.

Ingredients:

¼ cup oil (you may use olive or vegetable oil)
4 slices of diced bacon or pancetta (optional)
1 medium-size onion, finely diced

2 medium-size carrots, washed, scraped, and diced into bite-size portions

2 medium-size potatoes, peeled and diced into bite-size portions

2 small zucchinis, washed and diced into bite-size portions

2 stalks of celery, washed and diced into bite-size portions (try using the inner stalks with the leafy ends)

½ head of cabbage (savoy works well in this recipe, but regular cabbage can also be used; wash and shred cabbage into tiny portions)

1½ cups of white cannellini beans (you may use canned or cook your own beans as my mom always did; I never told her I used canned products as this was taboo in my family)

6 cups of boiling water or stock (in our family, we always used water and the soups were very flavorful)

Salt and black pepper to taste

Optional: the scraped and cleaned back ends of Parmigiano-Reggiano cheese (with a sharp knife, cut into bite-size pieces)

Place oil in a large stockpot that can accommodate all the ingredients over a medium flame; when oil is hot, add the bacon and cook for two minutes. Add the onion, coating well with oil, and cook for about two minutes. Add the carrots, potatoes, and celery; coat well with the oil and onions, adding a bit of salt. Cook for about two to three minutes. Add the zucchini, mix well with all other vegetables, and cook for about two to three minutes. Add the cabbage, toss all the vegetables together, and add a bit of salt. Cook for about five minutes, stirring occasionally. Add the boiling water, giving a good stir, mixing all the vegetables well. Cover pot, and cook over a low flame for about one hour or until all vegetables are soft but not too mushy. Add the cannellini beans and cheese bits, stir well, and simmer for about thirty minutes. This recipe is very versatile, and you may add other vegetables such as steamed and diced green beans, half a cup of crushed plum tomatoes with the juice, or yellow squash. We enjoy this soup over a crusty *frizzele* or toasted Italian bread.

Chapter 2

Refusing to Become a Victim

It occurred only three weeks after my first complete lovemaking with Mike. My brother had left for college only a few days prior; my dad had gone to his night job, and Mike too had gone to his night job, leaving me with good-night hugs no more than two hours earlier. My mom had already gone to bed with my sister, sleeping with her.

I was on the phone with Mike until about ten thirty, and as young lovers do, we sent kisses to each other, saying good night. I fell into a deep sleep, basking in the love that I felt for him. How long did I sleep before I was awakened by the screams of my mother and sister? I'm not sure. The fear in their voices forced me awake, and I jumped out of bed, running into the long hallway, turning on the lights as I ran.

I expected to see my mother sick, but never did I expect to see a tall black man standing in front of our closed door. The same door that I myself had closed with five dead bolts, two chain locks, and a turnkey lock, all of which were still locked.

I can still see myself staring at the man, the locks, and my mother, wondering how he had gotten in. In a hypnotic dream state, I started to scream and push open the locks; the feeling of being violated crushed any sense of fear. As I opened the locks, yelling, "Get the fuck out of my home!" I felt myself being pushed and wedged into a corner between the closet door to my back and the front door to my left shoulder. My sister stood motionless near the archway to the living room in complete shock, while my mother screamed and tried to protect me by hitting the intruder with a broom.

I squirmed, dodged, and pushed against an overpowering forearm, trying to free myself. My only concern was that I needed to continue opening the locks and push the intruder out. I'm still not sure how I managed to free myself and open the door, but as I tried to push the intruder out, I felt myself being lifted off the floor and pulled into the building hallway.

He held me by the collar of my nightclothes and, with one foot, kicked the door to the staircase open. He had pulled me across the threshold of the door and was just about to drag me up the stairs when I heard a neighbor call out, "The police are on the way!" He flung me like a weightless doll against the tile wall, my head and back hitting the upper portion of the wall with enough force for me to hear a vibrating thump. I slid to the floor, landing on my knees and hands. It was only by the strength of youth that I didn't feel any pain and sprang up, running into the house. As I started to lock the door, I noticed blood splattered on the walls; I immediately checked myself, looking down at the palms of my hands and touching my stomach, but I was not injured.

I spun around, looking for my mother and sister, and saw both coming from the kitchen, my mom holding a dish towel on her face that was being soaked with blood. In the struggle, I never noticed that the man had a knife, never realized he was trying to stab me and that, in the struggle to protect me, my mother had her face slashed from her temple to the top of her cheek.

I lost all sense of reason, ran into the kitchen, and pulled out a knife. I started to unbolt the door, ready to strike back. It was only my mother's screams that brought me back to my senses. She had let go of the dish towel, holding me back from opening the door as blood spilled down her face and into her eyes.

In a mental fog, I walked to the phone, calling my father first and then Mike. I'm not certain if I was hysterical or in shock? What I'm completely sure of is that other forces outside myself moved my body to do what had to be done. It wasn't until I placed the receiver of the phone down that I fully realized that this was not a nightmare but a new reality in my life.

The police arrived first and waited for my father to arrive before taking my mother to the hospital. As soon as my father saw my mother's face, he became enraged, yelling at me and my sister for not doing enough to protect my mother. The police tried to calm him down as I tried to explain what had occurred. One officer suggested that he drive my parents to the hospital while one stayed with us. My sister immediately became hysterical, crying to my parents that she was afraid to stay alone with the officer. My father ordered me to call Mike.

I didn't have time to respond; Mike was already knocking on the door. My father didn't take time to explain, telling Mike, "Stay with them while I take Fortuna to the hospital." Mike just nodded and bolted the door behind them. With both hands holding my face, Mike looked to me for an explanation. As I started to explain how I was dragged into the hallway, his face turned ashen white, and with his voice in a panic, he asked me, "Are you hurt? Are you sure you're OK?" His hands moved from my face to my shoulders with his eyes examining me to make sure I was not hurt.

He pulled me into his arms, rocking me back and forth, whispering to me, "Are you sure you're not hurt?" I was barely able to respond, "I'm OK." Sensing that I needed to sit down, he led me to the sofa while reaching for my sister, who was sitting quietly on a chair. He held us in his arms while we both rested our heads on his chest. As I closed my eyes, feeling safe in his presence, he pushed his head back, and I heard him say a short prayer in Spanish. "Thank you, God, for protecting my *muñequita*." I'm not sure how long we sat on the sofa, waiting for my parents to return home. What I am completely sure of is that the stitches my mom received scarred more than her beautiful face and that none of us were the same again.

My dad told us not to bother getting up for school; it was already early morning. Mike had rushed out of his night job and had to get ready for school. I walked him to door, asking him to be careful; his hug told me how much he cared. I've just recently started to wonder why he was the only person to ask me if I was OK, the only one to take the time to examine me to make sure I was not hurt.

I can still see that young girl struggling to free herself from the monster's grip and feel a deep sadness that arms were not holding me back from being dragged into the hallway. After all these years, I still feel a deep internal void that hands were not helping me up from the dirty tile floor. Those thoughts make me feel small and expendable, so I push them back into the recesses of my being, where they have been all these years, not allowing that one incident to derail my dreams of reaching America, not allowing a crazed monster to destroy my right to happiness.

The following day, a detective called us at home. I picked up the receiver, and he asked if I remember what happened the previous night. I can still hear my girlish voice saying, "Yes, a man climbed through the window trying to rob us." He very gently explained that the man was a rapist; he wasn't looking for money. That girlish voice still echoes in my mind, as I responded, "I wondered why he didn't take my mother's gold watch that was sitting right on the kitchen table." The detective must have sensed how young I was, asking to talk to my parents. I handed the phone to my father; after a few brief words, my dad told us the detective was coming over to interview us.

We sat in the living room, the detective informing us that the rapist had attacked two other victims and that undercover officers were searching for him. He turned to me, asking a number of questions. "First, how close were you to him?" I responded, "He picked me up by my nightshirt," and I motioned with my hand to indicate how close he was to my face. "Were the lights on? Did you get a good look at him?" I said, "Yes, I turned the lights on." The last two questions were "Did you notice any identifying marks on the rapist's face? Did he say anything to you?" I didn't know how to describe the crazed look in his eyes or the smell of his breath on me, so I just said no and that the only thing I heard were my own screams.

The detective turned to my dad with a very serious look on his face. "I suggest that until we catch this son of a bitch, you keep a close eye on your wife and daughters. He knows they can identify him, and it's best to be careful." As he started to walk out the door, he noticed the shotgun my father had placed against the closet door. He turned to my dad while pointing to the gun, saying, "I see you thought ahead, can't say I blame you. I do the same," and shook my father's hand.

Mike came over that evening and, as always, showered me with attention, asking if I felt OK, if I was scared, and comforting me with his hugs. I told him I was fine and that tomorrow I was going back to school. That night, as I tried to fall asleep, I finally realized what could have happened to me, and with both hands pressed over my eyes and forehead, I tried to erase the image of that crazed monster raping me. The thought of what I had willingly given only a few weeks earlier to a man I truly loved, and the kindness he had taken it with gave me comfort. I pressed my hands harder over my eyes and forehead, not able to bear the image of being raped. The image of being stabbed or killed was far easier to accept.

The following day, Mike was at my home early in the morning to take me to school. I'm not sure if my dad had spoken to him or if he decided on his own. As he drove, I complained, "This is silly, I can at least walk to the train on my own." He very calmly but sternly spoke to me. "Phil, listen to me, that animal knows you can identify him. If he gets his hands on you this time, he will rape and kill you." That was the first time Mike had spoken to me in a stern voice. He continued, "For now, Phil, this is the way it's going to be." As I turned, looking out of the car window, I felt his hand squeeze my knee, his voice softly asking me, "What is it? Don't you like me driving you?" I almost started to cry, holding back tears only because I didn't want to upset him; he looked so tired. "No, I like you driving me. It's only that you're so tried, and everyone's life has been turned upside down." Only his voice stopped me from crying. "Don't worry, *muñequita*, it's only for a short time. I hope your dad decides to move out of that hellhole soon."

In less than two weeks, the detective called, informing that they had a suspect. The monster was found hiding in the bushes of our housing complex, stalking someone else. We were asked to go over to the police station of the housing complex which was in the building across from ours to identify him from a police lineup. Each of us had to view the lineup separately—first, my mother, I was next, and then my sister, who started to cry and was afraid to look through the window. The police officer in a gentle voice told her, "Don't worry, he can't see you," but she still cried, and we thought it best not to force her. We both identified the same person. The police officer informed us that he had raped two other women in our housing complex.

The word *victim* did not have the depth of meaning until we entered the court system. Once the interrogation by the prosecutor started, I began to understand how a person became a victim twice—first, by the rapist, then by the legal system. We sat in her office, where she had a floor plan of our apartment on her desk, and she began to question me about how many lights were on. I pointed to the spots I had switched the lights on. She continued to ask what seemed to me like ridiculous questions. "Why did you turn them on?" I stared at her almost in disbelief. She stared back, waiting for an answer. I responded, "So that I could see." "What were you expecting to see?" I responded, "I'm not sure I heard my mother yelling."

She again stared hard at me. "When did you last talk to the suspect?" That question made me furious. "I never talked to that man. I didn't know him." "Why was the window opened?" "Because it was hot." "Did you open the window?" "I'm not sure who opened it." She sensed that I was becoming angry and firmly said, "Listen to me when you're on the witness stand. These are the types of questions the defense is going to ask you. You need to repeat the same answer regardless of how many times they ask you." I nodded.

She started prepping me again. "What was the last thing you did before going to bed?" "I spoke to my boyfriend on the phone." "After that, did you invite the suspect in to your home?" With that question, I started to raise my voice. "I told you before—I didn't know that man, and why would I invite a man in to cut my mother's face?" She saw that I was becoming furious and backed off a bit. "I know this is hard for you, but he has already walked twice, and if you can't convince the jury he's the rapist, he'll walk again. The defense attorney may even ask about your sexual activity." I raised my voice. "What business is it of theirs? It has nothing to do with the crime." His attorney may try to convince the jurors that you invited him into your home to have sex. I didn't even bother to respond. I just thought, *This is bullshit.*

My mother came back into the room I was in; she had been with a translator on the witness stand giving her testimony. Her hands were shaking, and she was close to tears. She started recounting what had occurred on the stand, saying, "These people are all crazy. They asked me if you lured that man in and when was the last time I spoke to him." I started to understand why I was being prepped with insane questions.

The next day, before I was about to go on the witness stand, I met with two other victims, the first being a beautiful young girl who was no more than two years older than me with silky long black hair. She told me that it was by her hair that she had been pulled out of the elevator of our building, dragged to the rooftop, and raped from behind. He was acquitted; the jurors did not feel she had gotten a good enough view of him. The next victim was a mother of two young girls whose husband worked at night. The rapist had climbed through the second-floor window of the building next to ours and raped her in her own bed. She looked straight at me, saying, "Don't let that son of a bitch get away with it again. When he was finished with me, he was ready to go into my daughters' room. They're only ten and eight." Now she was close to tears, telling me, "I begged that animal not to and somehow got him out of the house by offering him money that was in my bag near the door. He was acquitted because the jurors did not believe me that he climbed through the open window."

I was starting to feel the weight of responsibility and the importance of my testimony, hoping that I did not buckle under the pressure. We waited outside the courtroom to be called in, and a group of girls stopped in front of us, giving the ghetto stare down. I was so accustomed to those looks, they didn't faze me. They followed us to the bathroom and again tried to intimidate both myself and sister by just standing close and staring. I knew enough not to show fear quickly pulling my sister by the hand, pushing past them. I told my parents and was told not to use the bathroom again. The waiting was causing so much stress that I twisted a tissue into tight long strips. I just wanted to get it over and done with, returning to our normal lives.

Finally, the prosecutor called my parents into an office, and in a short time, they returned with my father in a fury, who started yelling, "OK, it's over. Let's go home." I just stood there in shock, asking, "What about my testimony?" My father responded, "I'm not having you put on the stand with the type of questions they want to ask you. That son of a bitch pleaded guilty to breaking and entering. He's going to get four years." As he spoke, he became more enraged. "I don't understand the laws in this country. That bastard has more rights than the victims. He's innocent until proven guilty. In Italy, he's guilty until proven innocent." He was in a complete frenzy screaming, "Let's get out of here. I can't afford to lose anymore work, and you both need to get back to school."

Mike continued to drive me to school, afraid for my safety, until suddenly, my father ordered us to start packing. I don't think either of my parents realized the emotional toll the incident had taken on all of us and did what Neapolitans have been doing for centuries—forging ahead. I stepped out of line, asking my father, "Why do we have to move? This is our home. We shouldn't have anyone push us around." My father, yelling, told me to shut up and start packing. I guess he didn't realize or maybe didn't care that I was trying to study for exams; after all, I was just a female, and my education was only secondary to being a perfect daughter and, eventually, a perfect wife.

I ran into my bedroom in a rage and started to pull clothing out of my closets. I reached to the top shelves and found the drawing that Francesco Sparagna had sketched of me only a few days prior to our departure for New York. I can still see that beautiful drawing of myself in braids with beads around my neck. I can still recall posing and standing so still for Francesco and his words to me as he handed me the sketch. "Un piccolo regalo per ricordaro (A small gift to help you remember)." I stared at the sketch for a few seconds, and for some strange reason, my rage multiplied tenfold, telling myself, what do I need this for? That person doesn't exist anymore. I wanted to rid myself of that person and ripped the sketch into tiny pieces, throwing it into a waste-paper basket. It was an act of rage, striking out at myself; for what, I am not sure. What I'm very sure of is that I never stopped regretting that act of rage.

We moved into the top floor of a private home in the Morris Park section of the Bronx. The home was owned by an Italian in a very Italian neighborhood. The neighborhood was safe, clean, with many Italian shops; the only problem for me was that the Italian landlady took one look at Mike and knew he wasn't Italian. My father came home very upset one day after having had a discussion with the landlady, who informed him that if she had known I was dating a Puerto Rican, she never would have rented us the apartment. "After all," she continued, "how do I know he's not a rapist?" With that, my father laughed in her face and walked away.

While we were all sitting down to dinner that evening, my father informed us, including Mike, of the great fear our new landlady had of Puerto Ricans, with my mother chiming in Italian-Spani-English, "Yeah, Mike, she thinks she so beautiful you going to go crazy and rape that old hag." We all burst out laughing and moved out of that apartment within eight months.

It would be great if I could remember exactly what we were having for dinner when my dad informed us that our new landlady had an insane fear of Puerto Ricans, but as hard as I try, I cannot recall what we were eating, so I have substituted one of Mike's favorite meals that my mother often prepared for him.

"Welcome to Morris Park" Ragù Sauce

Preparing the meat for Nonna Fortuna's ragù sauce, let's start with the meatballs.

Ingredients

2 to 4 slices of Italian bread, crust removed and soaked in a bit of milk or water
1 lb. of ground beef
5 cloves of finely diced garlic
Finely chopped fresh parsley (you may add as much or as little as you like)
2 well-beaten eggs with about 2 tbs. of Parmesan cheese
4 tbs. of Parmesan cheese to sprinkle on the chopped meat
Salt and black pepper to taste
Vegetable oil for frying

Place chopped meat into a large bowl; add the soaked bread, diced garlic, chopped parsley, eggs, Parmesan cheese, salt and pepper to taste. By hand, roll the meat mixture into a meatball's shape. I suggest making the meatballs into a small or medium size. In a large skillet, fry meatballs on all sides; they need not be cooked completely through as they will finish cooking in the sauce. Set aside on a platter.

Ingredients for Preparing the Braciole

1 lb. of braciole steak (these steaks come from the center cut of the bottom, are round, and are usually less than a ¼-inch thick)
The stuffing for the braciole can be a combination of these ingredients:

4 slices of Genoa salami diced into bite-size portions
4 slices of prosciutto diced into bite-size portions
¼ cup of pine nuts
¼ cup of cheese such as Romano, Parmesan, fontina, or a combination
of all three cheeses diced into tiny bite pieces
¼ cup of finely chopped parsley
Salt and black pepper to taste

Salt and pepper the steaks on both sides; in the middle of each steak, add bits of the salami, prosciutto, cheese, pine nuts, and parsley. Roll into a cylinder shape, tuck the ends in, and tie with a cooking string. Set aside.

Ingredients for the Sauce

¼ cup of olive or vegetable oil
2 35-oz. cans of San Marzano tomatoes (crushed by hand or in a
blender)
1 6-oz. can of tomato paste
4 cloves crushed garlic
1 small onion, finely diced
Salt and fresh basil to taste

Place oil in a large stockpot; when oil is hot, add the braciole and brown on all sides. Add the onion and garlic; sauté until garlic has a bit of color. Add the tomato paste, work well into the oil, add crushed tomatoes with all the juice. Salt and pepper to taste. Cook over a medium-low flame for about forty-five minutes, stirring often, making sure the sauce is not sticking to the bottom. Add the meatballs to the sauce with all the drippings; add shredded basil. Cook for about thirty-five to forty-five minutes over a low flame, adding more fresh shredded basil at the end of cooking. The cooking time for ragù sauce is not so much by the clock but by being able to recognize when it's done; the sauce should have a dense sweet flavor. Serve over your favorite cooked pasta. Often, my mom added short ribs, sausages, or pieces of pork chops to the sauce, browning these meats along with the braciole and then finishing the sauce. If you like, you can also add a small glass of white wine after the meat has browned, and after the foaming has dissipated, you can continue finishing the sauce.

Chapter 3

Young Bride

We moved only a block away from the paranoid landlady into a similar apartment with another Italian landlady who, fortunately, did not have an insane fear of Puerto Ricans. By then, Mike had started working for IBM, and our sole focus was for me to graduate high school and set out on our own.

We really didn't want a big wedding with all the hoopla; we just simply wanted to start living together, having plenty of time and space to fool around. Mike and I discussed a plan and started searching for our own apartment. He was looking forward to moving out of his parents' home since I, as much as I tried, didn't get along with his family. I can only guess that the relationship with Mike's family had gotten off to a bad start by the clashing—not so much of culture, but of lifestyle.

The most devastating incident that occurred between me and his mother was over my accidental disposal of a glass of water. As ridiculous as it sounds, this is what occurred to ruin a family relationship. Mike's mother complained to me that her son was spending too much time with me and not keeping up with his share of the housework. I quietly thought that it would take a bulldozer to clean up the clutter but offered to clean the downstairs apartment for her. Early on a Saturday, I arrived and put my best effort forward, cleaning the only way I knew how, making everything spotless. Mike was upstairs, helping with the major task of machine-washing all of the carpets. As I started to mop under the bed, I noticed an open book with a glass of water next to it. I, in the frenzy of cleaning, assumed that Mike had been reading and drinking water, placing the items under the bed as he started to fall asleep.

I made the fatal mistake of picking up those items, closing the book, placing it on his dresser, and dumping the water in the toilet. I mopped the floors until they shined, hoping to make my future mother-in-law happy. Mike came down first, and I immediately saw the panic on his face as he saw the closed book and the empty washed glass on the dresser. With a voice filled with anxiety, Mike spoke, "Phil, you dumped out the water?" I very proudly responded, "Yeah, of course, the water was all funky. How long did you have that water under your bed?"

I looked into his eyes and saw complete panic. "Oh no, Phil, that wasn't regular water. It's like holy water, and the book was open to a special prayer for my protection." I realized what I had done and immediately apologized, telling Mike, "All right, all right, it's no big deal. Just open the book to the right page, and put some more water in the glass." I didn't see a big problem. As luck would have it, his mom walked in and saw the desecrated items on the dresser. In a rage, she turned to me, and I honestly started to explain what I had done. Mike, in Spanish, quickly started to explain that I didn't know, but she didn't give him a chance to finish as she started to yell, "I don't want her in my house!" Pointing to me, she continued, "She didn't have any business touching what she doesn't understand," along with calling me a few choice Spanish words, all of which I understood very well. I was truly hurt and enraged all at once. I felt she could at least understand that I was trying my best to please her and simply made a mistake.

Even as a teenager, I can't say I had much patience for bullshit, and I lost my temper, calling her a *jíbara* (a Spanish word for mountain person or hillbilly)—regardless of the exact meaning, not a flattering term to call a future mother-in-law. She came toward me, trying to slap me in the face; Mike put up his arm up to block her blow. I yelled back, "Don't you ever put your hand up to me again!" further informing her that all of this, pointing to the religious artifacts, "is a bunch of mumbo jumbo." I saw the stress on poor Mike's face as he stood in the middle, trying to keep us apart.

From that day on, his entire family was very hateful toward me as if I had willingly committed a major crime. If I called Mike on the phone and his mother or sister heard my voice, they would either hang up or place the receiver down on the table, not telling him I was on the phone.

That was the start of a very poor family relationship, making us more determined to set out on our own.

In retrospect, I truly believe that his mother didn't like the idea that her son cared for me so much and would have preferred a Puerto Rican daughter-in-law. On the other hand, I was probably too outspoken and non-compromising when it came to what I called "mumbo jumbo," clashing with my in-laws for the entire marriage, sadly at the emotional expense of my husband.

Mike hesitated in us telling my parents that we didn't want a wedding; we felt it was a waste of money. I clearly recall him telling me, "Phil, this is not going to go over well with your parents. Let's just have a wedding." At the time, I was building what I now call my tower of feminism and wanted to rebel against the established order of society. I closely followed the women's movement, and God, how I loved not wearing a bra. I wanted to free myself from the tightly controlled cultural and social norms. I wanted to live life on my own terms.

Of course, as soon as I mentioned what our intentions were, my parents went plain crazy. My mother, with her hands in her hair, complained, asking me how much shame did I want to bring to the family, yelling the term *brutta figura*, meaning I made the family look bad. My father told me that if I left his house without a formal wedding not to bother coming back. Mike was always more compromising than me and truly loved my parents. Not wanting to upset them any further, he stepped in to quell the fire.

In a bit of a stern voice so unlike him, he said, "Phil, what difference does it make? We'll still be living together. Make your parents happy and keep the peace." I, like a spoiled child, grumpily agreed and started planning a formal wedding. For a very young lady, I must admit I did a good job in not only planning our wedding but in finishing high school and applying to college. When I told my parents that I was planning on attending college, they asked me, "What for? You're getting married." I didn't even bother to respond and just told myself to prove them wrong by being able to do both.

We picked the date of the wedding to fall on August 18, the same day Mike had asked me to marry him a year earlier, and decided to wear the same silver wedding bands we had worn for almost two years. Of course, we were asked by nosy family members what happened to the engagement, why didn't I have a diamond ring, was I expecting. I told whoever asked that a diamond ring didn't make a marriage and, in a very nice manner, told them to mind their own business. I think my mother was actually proud that I put family members in their place and forged ahead.

I was a senior in high school, putting our new apartment together, taking exams, planning a wedding, and applying to colleges without much help from anyone. I just focused and refused to let anyone upset our relationship. My mother insisted on a traditional white wedding dress; I quietly laughed, knowing the meaning behind the color white. In private, Mike and I laughed together as I joked about the church falling in on us when I presented myself as a pure bride. We should have attended Pre-Cana classes for Catholic couples, but I convinced the priest that I was already in a marriage and family prep class in school and would gladly share all the important info with my soon-to-be husband. As we both walked out of the priest's office, I turned to Mike, saying, "Thank God we got out of that. I've had enough Catholic bullshit to last a lifetime." He just held my hand and laughed.

My parents, Mike, and I made arrangements with a well-known Italian catering hall, and as my mom reviewed the menu—instructing the owner-chef how she wanted a delicate soup made not too greasy—I looked at Mike, holding back laughter. She selected a beautiful wedding favor (*bomboniere*), a cut glass plate that sat on a silver carrier holding a small spoon with white almond confetti wrapped in netting. This tradition is very important for Italians to give to their guests as they leave the celebration for not only weddings but for all major events, and I still have two of those favors in my china cabinet.

I with my mother went to Fontana, an Italian seamstress on the Grand Concourse in the Bronx who made for me the most beautiful wedding gown. I had my first visit with her in my school uniform skirt with a Danskin leotard on top that was bunched at the breast. What seemed to me like a very old lady asked one simple question, "How do you want the dress to flow on you?" As I explained that I wanted the dress to flow very similar to what I had on, she started to drape and bunch the fabric over me, forming a gown. I went for eight fittings until the gown was meticulously embroidered with delicate lace and beads. When I couldn't find a headpiece I liked, she had one imported from Italy, a Juliet cap embroidered with the same beads as the gown, the veil flowing from the back. She gave me the headpiece for free as a wedding gift. I've never seen anyone take as much pride in their work as that not-so-old lady.

The most difficult part of the wedding was dealing with family members. On my side, I had relatives that refused to attend because I was marrying a Puerto Rican. On his side, his immediate family refused to attend because they had not participated in the arrangements, which I didn't see how they could since they refused to talk to me. I really didn't care about any of it and just wanted the three-ring circus to end. Our main priority was to get married and start living our own lives.

I refused to recite the traditional wedding vows, which included the word *obey*, thinking, *That's just BS. I'm going to be his wife, not his daughter or pet*, forever more determined to love him but to also be his equal. Mike agreed that I could write the wedding vows any way I liked. The only portion of those vows I can recall is the part where we both pledged to love each other with our whole heart, mind, and soul for the rest of our lives. The church ceremony went very well with a surprise singing of the Ave Maria, which my mother had privately requested without my knowledge. As I heard the operatic voices start to sing, I looked up at Mike, biting my lip, trying not to laugh; he, with a bit of a smile, motioned to me to behave, lowering his head so that we would not look at each other and burst out laughing.

The reception was beautiful with the soup not being greasy at all and Mike singing "Light My Fire" onstage while I was, as always, his admiring groupie standing in front of the stage so proud to finally be his wife. The only downside to the wedding day was that his family refused to attend, claiming never to have received an invitation. I had already anticipated such claims, making sure to have the bridesmaid that was helping me address each invitation write theirs out first, and we both checked it twice.

During the reception, Mike and I noticed that the best man was absent for a good portion of the celebration and, with concern, spoke to each other, wondering where he had gone. Almost at the end of the reception, the best man came walking in with Mike's younger sister, who had decided to attend at the last minute. She called the catering hall, requesting to have the best man leave the reception and pick her up as her escort. At least she walked in with a smile and well-wishes, hugging and kissing us both; I was more than a bit pissed off but, out of love for my husband and family, kept my mouth shut. My mother and father greeted her with warm affection, making sure that the complete meal was served to her in addition to giving her extra favors for the rest of Mike's family. I don't think Mike's sister realized how inappropriate and selfish she had been at all.

The happiest day was not so much the actual wedding day but the day after, when we were finally on our own. Before leaving for our honeymoon, we stopped at my parents' home to say good-bye, and my father shook Mike's hand, which I found quite comical, thinking, *Wow, my father must think that the wedding night was the first time we had sex and feels he, in the old-fashioned Neapolitan style, must shake hands to seal the deal.* I laughed at the irony of it all.

I had graduated high school in June, turned nineteen in July, got married in August, and started college in September. I thought, *Not bad for a little immigrant girl from the South Bronx.* I was confident that I could handle any calamity that came my way.

I would love to give to you the recipe for that non-greasy wedding soup my mom requested for our wedding, but of course, I need to ask that chef, and I'm sure he has long departed his earthly kitchen by now, so I will substitute my mom's own chicken soup, which everyone enjoys.

Nonna Fortuna's Not-Too-Greasy Chicken Soup

Ingredients:

1 whole chicken cut into parts and washed
1 large onion cut into large pieces
3 medium-size carrots washed and cut into large portions
3 stalks of celery with celery leaves on, washed and cut into large portions
2 large Italian canned tomatoes crushed by hand with all the juice

A bunch of fresh Italian parsley
5 quarters of cold water
Salt to taste

In a large stockpot, add chicken parts with all the vegetables, pour water over the top. Over a medium flame, bring to a boil. Skim all the foam off the top as it forms, discard. Lower flame to a simmer, adding salt, and cook for about two hours, being careful to skim off all the foam and fat as it appears on the surface.

Remove cooked chicken parts, set aside on a platter to cool. Remove the cooked vegetables, and place in a sieve over the pot of soup; with the back of a wooden spoon, press the juice from the vegetables into the soup.

Allow the chicken parts to cool so as to be able to remove meat from the bones, cutting them into tiny bite-size portions, adding them back into the soup. If you find that the soup still has too much fat on the surface for your liking, place in the refrigerator to chill, and when the fat hardens, remove it with a spoon.

In this soup, you can cook egg noodles, cut spaghetti, cooked rice, pastina, or alphabet pasta, whatever you prefer. You can also beat about three whole eggs with grated Parmesan cheese and slowly pour the eggs into the hot soup while constantly stirring to form long ribbons. The Italians call this type of soup Stracciatella, meaning "little rags." I guess for the little rags of eggs that form in the soup, and the Chinese call it egg drop.

I hesitate to give this suggestion in fear that my mother will find out, but at times when I don't have enough time to prepare my own chicken soup, I have used low-fat canned chicken stock and slowly poured beaten eggs with Parmesan cheese into the simmering stock; this mock Stracciatella is not bad.

Chapter 4

On Our Own

With the wedding and honeymoon over, our life as a married couple had gotten off to a very busy start. Mike worked; I went to classes and home to housework and homework. Of course, I tried to use all of my family's recipes; I had been writing them down on index cards from a very young age. It was the hands-on experience I needed since my mother very seldom allowed me to cook on my own, and I was only too willing to just write. Was I a horrible cook? No, not really. Was I a good cook? No, not really.

I taught myself the art of cooking mostly through trial and error, reading cookbooks as if they were novels and studying nutrition in college. The most hilarious cooking adventure occurred while I followed a French onion soup recipe from a cookbook that came with a blender that had been given to me at my bridal shower, carefully following the instructions, chopping onions until my nose and eyes started tearing like an open faucet. I stirred the hot liquid on the stovetop and, as instructed, placed the very hot mixture into the blender to puree into a delicious soup, tightly closing the lid and pressing the button, which facilitated a geyser-like explosion to rival Old Faithful.

The hot liquid splattered up against the walls, kitchen cabinets, all the way to the ceiling, decorating the entire kitchen with sparkles of onion bits. For a few seconds, I just stood in shock, trying to understand what had just happened then realizing the kitchen I had just finished cleaning was a complete mess. I held back tears. The only thing I was thankful for was that my face had not been directly over the blender, and as I started to grab towels to soak up the mess, I kept asking myself, "Now what are you going to make for dinner?"

Mike found me on top of the kitchen counter, trying to scrape off onion bits from the cabinets, asking, "Wow, Phil, what happened?" Holding back tears, I started to explain and knew he wanted to laugh but was kind enough not to; instead, he placed both hands around my waist, helping me down from the counter. I complained, "I'll never get this kitchen clean again, and what are we having for dinner?" He helped me clean the kitchen as best as possible, but we did have twinkly onion bits on the ceiling for the rest of our stay in that apartment. As we walked up to the local Italian restaurant holding hands, we looked at each other and busted out laughing.

I managed to keep our tiny walk-in basement apartment clean and very neat. I would come home from school with textbooks in hand, having to do homework, housework, and cook, while most girls my age just flaunted around. I instead had a set plan for not only my days but my life. Finish college, work, and save enough money to buy a home, only placing having children aside until we had the perfect home to raise them in.

I placed great emphasis on being the best wife and, eventually, mother, studying nutrition and family-related subjects so as to improve my skills in those areas. I even enrolled in Puerto Rican studies classes to enhance my understanding of the culture so that I could later teach my children. I sat for weeks, interviewing my Puerto Rican friends and writing a term paper on Puerto Rican cuisine. The teacher gave me an A for the paper, telling me that for the only non-Puerto Rican in the class, I had written the best term paper. Asking me why I took the class, I explained why, and she told me I was a very perceptive young lady. I only wish that I had saved that term paper.

This safe-proof plan for life was our guide, and we both thought nothing could go wrong. We enjoyed our lives, and Mike showered me with attention. He started to teach me to drive, and I can't say that he was the most patient teacher when it came to driving, so I decided to take matters into my own hands, taking the car keys when he was at work and going for quick spins. He was amazed at how quickly I was learning. I simply told him, "You're a great teacher."

I continued with my cooking adventures and, for Christmas, prepared a complicated gingerbread house, which took over two weeks to put together. In such a tiny kitchen, I was placing gingerbread pieces in every section of the house to cool, but with Mike's help, the results were fantastic. Mike took dozens of photos, and I felt like Julia Child carrying my work of art over to my grandmother Filomena's home for Christmas Eve dinner. I had hoped my parents would acknowledge my great accomplishment as a young bride and college student, but when I handed my father my first report card with mostly As and a few Bs, he glanced down, looked back up at me, saying, "Ha, now you a smata housewife." That made me more determined than ever to finish college and prove that I was more than what I had been raised to be, a devoted housewife.

Months before our wedding, I had started taking birth control pills in anticipation of the great sexual lovemaking we would indulge in, but in retrospect, for a young man, Mike's sexual appetite was very poor. It's not that he didn't love me; it's just that he should have had a greater need for sex. I was so young and inexperienced and just assumed that this was simply part of being married. It's not that we never had sex; we did, but I slowly started to notice great changes in his sexual appetite and body structure. At the time, I was so naïve that I put the thought of something being wrong with Mike out of my head, thinking we're probably too busy with other issues, and forged ahead, living life. After the first year of marriage, I stopped taking birth control pills, and we both decided to take whatever came our way.

The walk-in apartment was just too tiny, and we moved into a larger apartment with a very large kitchen. This gave me more space to experiment with food and develop my own style of cooking. For my college experimental cooking classes, I developed a cornmeal-based pancake recipe and banana bread recipe with an assortment of ingredients, ranging from healthy wheat germ to coconut chocolate chip.

I hosted my first Thanksgiving family dinner in that apartment, trying my best to please my family by preparing not only turkey, which my mother insinuated should have a stuffing made from chicken gizzards. I hated pre-boiling the chicken hearts and kidneys before dicing and finally adding them to the stuffing, but I was devoted wife, daughter, and sister, willing to cook my butt off to please my family.

I prepared my own style of deviled eggs, which I stuffed with crispy bacon bits, olives, and capers. Of course, the antipasto was most important, for which I had to slice an assortment of cheese and salamis.

I stuffed red bell peppers with a rice filling and had to prepare roast beef just in case someone didn't want turkey. I prepared a platter of fried vegetables with an assortment of eggplants, zucchini, artichokes, and cauliflower.

A cauliflower salad was necessary to help in digestion, along with a green salad with shredded fennel.

Thankfully, my mother brought the Stracciatella soup. I knew my cooking could never compare to my mother's cooking; she was an exceptional cook coming from a family of phenomenal cooks. The strength of youth helped me complete this most important task in proving my Italian womanhood, and I think my family was truly pleased and proud. I was exhausted but happy that I had finally pleased my family.

We enjoyed our lives, traveling to Cape Cod, Canada, Florida, and Cancún, Mexico, for summer vacations, all the while being not only husband and wife but the best of friends. We were extremely devoted to each other and showered one another with great care and love.

I was in my junior year of college when the unthinkable occurred; the phone call came from my mother as I sat in the comfort of my living room on a May afternoon. We had just gotten back from Mike's parents' home, having had a luncheon to celebrate his birthday. In Neapolitan, she spoke, her voice in a semi-state of panic. "I got a call from the neighboring store. Your father had a heart attack. Pick me up. He's at Lincoln Hospital."

My body and mind rushed to control any emotions so that I could perform whatever tasks lay ahead. I didn't need to speak to my husband; he had already realized something was very wrong and had the car keys in hand. We drove the few blocks to my mother's house in complete silence. As she sat in the backseat, she tried to control her emotions but continued to talk nonstop about the stress that caused this new problem for my father. I thought to myself how unusual this all seemed. My father was always in good health, not overweight, and didn't smoke. I tried to reassure my mother that he would be OK and said a silent prayer. The twenty-minute car ride seemed to take forever, and the panic in my stomach grew with every red light.

We reached the hospital, and I jumped out first, with my mother following and talking, but I was not listening. Mike drove to my father's shop a few blocks away. In the emergency room, I explained who I was and that I was looking for my dad, giving his name and telling the clerks that he had suffered a heart attack. They checked the records for the day and told me the only man that had arrived was a gunshot victim. I repeated that the neighbors had called and told us he had been taken to this hospital and had suffered a heart attack, telling them, "Check your records again." "I'm sorry, miss," they repeated, "but we don't have a heart attack patient. Can you please describe your dad for us?" I described my dad—"five foot four, about 145 pounds, dark wavy hair"—and asked, "Didn't he have any ID on him?" "No, miss, that person had no ID and is in the OR." "The OR? For what?" I repeated. "We're trying to revive him. Please come with me."

My mom stood beside me, completely confused as to what was being said, and as I tried to explain in Neapolitan, other family members arrived. I handed her over to them, as a male attendant approached me, describing the man that was in the OR—a tall man, about six feet, and close to two hundred pounds. I stared at him in disbelief and told him, "That's not my father."

"Miss, can you please come with me? Maybe you can identify his clothing." Through tunnel vision and complete disbelief, I walked along cold bare hallways and felt as if I was gliding more than walking. I was brought to the front doors of the OR. There, my father's clothes lay in a pile on the floor. I recognized them—his maroon sweater on top of his grey pants, the same clothes I so often seen him in. I stood motionless, staring at the pile of clothes that once held so much life. I stared, almost expecting them to come to life, as if they still held his energy. Through a circling dense fog, I heard the attendant ask, "Do they belong to your dad?" I nodded yes.

Other external forces started to take over my body, and I became overly calm, asking, "Can I go in and see my dad?" "No, miss, the doctors are working on him, and that's not allowed. Come along now. I'll take you back to your family." For an instant, I thought of just pushing the doors open and walking in, but those other forces that had taken over told me different, and I quietly walked away with the attendant.

My mother and other family members sat in the waiting room, and everyone looked up at me for an answer. In the midst of this dense fog that had suddenly engulfed me, my lips started to form words, answering the unasked questions. "Yes, it's Dad's clothes. The doctors are working on him. He's been shot." I heard immeasurable cries of pain shrieking in my brain, and all I could do was sit on a chair next to my brother's girlfriend, Lynn.

With the screams from my mother filling my very being, all I could think of is how to call my brother and give him the news. He was about four hours away, completing his final year of graduate work at Brown University. I knew he was busy writing his last research papers, and I mentally searched for the best solution so as not to interrupt his work. For less than thirty minutes, I sat listening to sobbing and prayers from my family. I said my own prayer. "Please, God, this can't be happening to us."

The doors opened, and a doctor walked in, asking to see me, my mother, and Lynn, who was a head nurse at Albert Einstein Hospital. "Please come to the next room." We followed, and he asked us to sit down. He spoke to Lynn first, in medical terms, and explained what the injuries were. "I'm sorry," he said, "the injuries were very extensive. We could not save him. I'm so sorry." My mother, not able to understand what the doctor had said, looked to me for an answer, but all I could do was hold her and cry. Those external forces that had so often guided me took over, and finally, I forced my lips to say the words "Dad is dead."

How long did we sit in that room listening to my mother's unbearable wails? I'm not sure. Everything seemed beyond surreal. My whole being was in a dense fog, a nightmare with no awaking. Those other forces took over, helping me find the strength to pull my mother off the chair as Lynn opened the door to the hallway where family members stood.

Everyone's eyes looked to us and, as I wiped away tears, choked on the words "Dad is dead." The cries of pain and loss filled the hallway. Doctors and nurses came over to help, but what medicine could they offer? Somehow, they escorted us back to the waiting room, and those cries filled the room with such force that I had to leave. I walked out with Lynn following me, asking, "Phil, where are you going?" I spoke through that other being that had taken over guiding me. "I need to find a phone and call Mike to let him know what happened, and somehow, Lynn, we need to call Joe."

I reached my husband at my dad's shop, and he already knew what had occurred. "Phil, the place is a mess, and the police are questioning me. How's Ugo doing?" "He's dead," I responded without crying. My husband's cries filled me with his pain, and I started to sob again. Through the tears, I told Lynn, "You need to call Joe for me. I can't do it. Please call, but don't tell him what happened." "What do you want me to tell him?" "Just tell him Dad had an accident." She looked at me with a questioning stare. "Phil, he's going to ask what kind of an accident. What do you want me to say?" I stood in front of the phone booth with my hands cupped over my face, trying to find the right solution. "Lynn, just tell him that Dad fell off a ladder and is in the hospital. Ask him to come as soon as possible." I stood with her near the phone as she calmly repeated the story I felt would soften the blow until he got home safely.

Mike had been interviewed by the police and a newspaper reporter until they allowed him to lock up the shop that had been taped off as a crime scene. At the hospital, he held me in his arms as we sobbed together, and when there was nothing else to do, he drove us back to my mother's home. I sat on the sofa with her and my sister, holding each other, sobbing uncontrollably. Other family members held and sobbed with us, but all our pain and anger was no match for the subhuman howls of my brother.

A friend had driven Joe to the hospital, where Mike was waiting. The ride had taken over five hours in heavy traffic; they had to pull over a number of times as Joe started to vomit from anxiety. My husband told me very little of what happened when Joe reached the hospital. Who told him what had really occurred? I'm not sure. What I am sure of is that his primordial cries of pain and loss will forever vibrate in my soul, and I have never stopped second-guessing myself if I should have immediately told him the truth.

From that day forward, I started to understand that fate is at times very cruel. My father died only a few months before my brother graduated with his PhD in inorganic chemistry. Only a few months before, he was one of two to be hired in the nation to work at Bell Labs, where he developed a new process that saved Bell Labs millions. Only a few months before my father could have realized his dream for coming to America, the dream of his son achieving what he had never been given the opportunity to do. At my brother's graduation, I made sure to clap and cheer for two, for my dad and myself.

I share these recipes with you in the hope that you will remember how fragile life is and live each day with passion and love.

"It Helps the Digestion" Cauliflower Salad

Ingredients:

1 cauliflower, washed and cut into florets (steam florets until just tender)
1 24-oz. jar of *giardiniera* (this is a variety of pickled vegetables found in any supermarket)
An assortment of olives—as many as you like
Olive oil and white vinegar, prepare enough dressing to coat the vegetable well, about ½ cup of oil with ½ cup of vinegar
Salt to taste

Place steamed cauliflower florets in a large bowl, add a bit of olive oil and vinegar, and toss well. Remove the *giardiniera* vegetables from the jar, and cut them into bite-size pieces, adding them to the cauliflower. Add olives, toss well. Drizzle olive oil and vinegar, toss well, and check for salt. This salad holds up very well when placed in a closed container in the refrigerator and is also great for picnics. When placing in containers make sure the vegetables are completely cover by the dressing, make extra and pour over top if needed.

Fried Vegetable Platter

Neapolitans love fried foods, and whenever we have a family dinner, this is everyone's favorite.

Ingredients

1 cauliflower, washed, cut into florets, steamed until only barely tender
2 to 4 large zucchinis, washed and cut lengthwise
2 to 4 large eggplants, washed and cut lengthwise

Artichokes, as many as you like (you may buy them fresh and remove the outer leaves—using only the center tender heart of the artichoke, being careful to remove the hairy choke on the inside—or just buy the frozen packages of artichoke hearts)

6 whole eggs
6 tbs. of grated Parmesan cheese
2 tbs. of milk
Salt and black pepper to taste
2 cups of unflavored breadcrumbs
Vegetable oil for frying

Have the cauliflower steamed and cooled, eggplants and zucchini sliced, artichokes defrosted. In a large bowl, beat eggs together with cheese, milk, salt, and pepper. Pour breadcrumbs onto a large plate. Heat oil over a medium-high flame in a large skillet; you should have enough oil in the skillet to cover the tops of the vegetables. In an assembly-line fashion, dip vegetables into the beaten eggs then dredge into the breadcrumbs, coating them well. Set coated vegetables aside on a large cookie sheet, or if you have a helper, have that person start frying the vegetables in the hot oil. Vegetables should sizzle as soon as they hit the oil, but the oil should not be so hot that it's smoking. Fry vegetables until they are a golden color, remove with a slotted spoon, and drain on paper towels. It's best to eat these crispy vegetables when hot, and we usually nibble on them before we have dinner.

I have thought of adding the onion soup recipe to this chapter, but almost thirty-eight years after attempting that first culinary magic, I have never had the courage to even look at that recipe again, and needless to say, I have never prepared one. I don't even order onion soup at a restaurant.

Chapter 5

Long Island

After my college graduation, we decided to take our first trip back to Naples. My mom had not seen her family in seventeen years, and with the loss of our father, we all realized how fragile life was. I was not sure how much I remember of Bagnoli but wanted to share the land of my birth with Mike. The five of us, which included my mom, sister, brother, myself and husband, were all extremely excited. We were welcomed with opened arms by my mother's family and spent two glorious weeks in Naples, basking in the sunshine, enjoying the food and landscape. The four of us—myself, Mike, my brother, and my sister—decided to head north, spending three touristy days in Rome, enjoying the culture and antiquity. The tourist nightmare happened as we were leaving Rome, heading for Florence.

As Mike drove past the Tomb of the Unknown Soldier, we parked the car to take a few quick photos of a ceremony that was taking place, the placing of a flower laurel at the base of the tomb. We all stood, watching the ceremony, Mike taking a few snapshots before we headed back to the car. I asked Mike to open the trunk so that I could remove a package of tissues from my luggage. Shock was splashed on my face as I looked inside to find all of our luggage gone. I looked up with my mouth wide open, exclaiming, "Everything is gone!" Everyone ran to look, realizing that we had been robbed and that our long-awaited vacation was over.

I started to work for the New York City Board of Education as a nutritionist that year, and in less than two years of us both working, we had saved enough money for a down payment on a house in Long Island. An extended Cape Cod home not too far from the waterfront, with four bedrooms, two full baths, a finished basement with a built-in bar for entertaining, and most important of all, a backyard where I could release the Italian in me, growing vegetables and herbs. I had waited so long to have an outdoor space to sit in quiet contemplation, enjoying what I had grown. This was my American Dream come true; I had finally reached the land of my dreams.

I resigned from my job, focusing all of my energy on redecorating our home and hoping to become pregnant. While Mike went to work, I painted every room, ripping down old wallpaper, cleaning, polishing and visualizing how I wanted each room to look. I enjoyed the physical labor and relished the feel of grass and soil in my hands as I started a vegetable garden. As I worked in my backyard, I felt a peace which I had never felt before, almost a euphoria from achieving what I had struggled so long for. I would feel the sunshine on my shoulders and smell the sea air, smiling to myself that I was no longer looking out of the housing project window, hoping to fly away to a beautiful landscape, but was actually there.

A poem ("Summer." by John Clare) that I had read years earlier constantly echoed in my mind; its verses of separating from a beloved place frightened me, and I dispelled the feeling of loss that it evoked. I was certain I would never leave my sanctuary. The ending verse—"Summer sometime shall bless this spot, when I, / Hapt in the cold dark grave, can heed it not"—made me fear for my beloved outdoor space where I found so much peace. I asked myself what would happen if I was not here to care for this space. I had given so much of myself to my first love, to my first home, to my cherished space in the sun that I could not bear the thought of being separated from them.

Mike, extremely skillful with his hands, changed every door in the home to six-panel colonial doors that shined like glass. Each door handle, each hinge, and each light plate was replaced by solid brass, and we purchased furniture for every room with extreme care; after all, this was to be our home of a lifetime, where we would raise healthy, educated American citizens. We became active members of the community; Mike becoming a member and secretary of the Kiwanis Club.

I, as a devoted wife, hosted parties for our friends and neighbors, at times cooking for as many as forty guests. I spared no expense preparing veal marsala made from the center cut, requesting from my mother's butcher that they all be uniform in size. I stuffed mushrooms with a mixture of Genoa salami, breadcrumbs, and cheese. Each deviled egg had a creamy filling of whipped egg yolk and mayo speckled with tiny bits of crispy bacon, chopped capers, and olives and a minute crisscross of red pimentos on top for visual appeal.

I conducted house tours of the historic homes in our village, and during the Christmas holiday season, I prepare an elaborate gingerbread house to be raffled off by the Kiwanis club, the profits going to charity. I now think of what a novelty we must have been to the all-white members of our circle of friends. A Puerto Rican, or to use an inner city term a New York Rican man, with an Italian immigrant wife. We never gave it a second thought, continuing to live our lives within the comfort of a supportive community.

We were living the picture-perfect American Dream. All of the basic human needs were filled, except for the most valued of all, sexuality and procreation. From the first years of our marriage, I had sensed that something was very wrong but also understood that in dealing with the male ego, a wife must be very careful not to upset the image of manhood. I gingerly hinted at seeing a fertility specialist. We had not used birth control from the first year of marriage, and I thought it very peculiar that I never became pregnant.

I knew how much my husband wanted to have children; he had made that so clear on the first Christmas in our forever home. Teasingly, I had asked him to write a Santa note telling me what he wanted. He laughingly replied, "Phil, all our money is in this house. There's not much left for fancy gifts this year." "I know, but you still must want something."

To please me, as he sat in his gold-colored armchair near the fireplace, he grabbed a scrap piece of Santa wrapping paper I had on the living room floor, and while I continued to wrap gifts for our family, he wrote on the back: "Dear Santa, what I would truly love to have this Christmas is good health and happiness for myself and wife but most of all to fill our home with a few healthy and happy children. Children would make my life complete and a very happy man." He gently tossed the paper to me, and as I read, I felt such a deep void quietly saying a prayer that his wish would be granted. I placed that note inside a carved wooden box where I kept coins from different places we had traveled to. Occasionally, I would open the box, read the note, and say a silent prayer to conceive a much-wanted child.

Finally, after more than five years of living in our forever home, we decided to see a fertility specialist. The blood results revealed a heart-wrenching diagnosis. Mike's hormonal levels were completely out of balance, suggesting a possible pituitary gland tumor. We held hands as the doctor explained that Mike would need to have a CAT scan to verify the diagnosis. I can still feel his grip tightening around my hand as the doctor continued to explain that this type of tumor is usually not life-threatening but causes infertility.

We walked out of his office in a daze, not being able to understand how this could have happened to us. I internally asked myself, *God, why us? We worked so hard to have a comfortable home to raise children in, we live such a healthy lifestyle, we've loved each other for so long. Why us?*

The scan confirmed the diagnosis of a pituitary tumor. We both sat across from the doctor as he explained that he would prescribe medication to shrink the tumor and hormonal injections to increase testosterone levels. As he spoke, I started to sink into a dense fog, understanding the lack of sexual desire and the constant mood swings Mike was prone to. The doctor turned, looking straight at me, and spoke about the remedy I did not want to hear. "At this point, the best chance for conceiving is to consider artificial insemination." I immediately started to feel like a science project, hearing the doctor's voice in the midst of the dense fog that was slowly engulfing both our lives.

He turned to Mike to explain that artificial insemination is not that uncommon and that the donor would be matched to his own skin, hair, and eye color. Through the fog, I heard my voice asking, "Donor? Who is this donor going to be?" The doctor turned to me, smiling, and very matter-of-factly explained that most of the donors were college students looking to make extra money. He continued to explain that we need not worry, that the donor will never know the identity of the recipient. "The recipient," I repeated the words silently to myself, knowing that it would be me.

We never looked at each other during that visit, Mike not asking any questions. The doctor's last recommendation was to give it some serious thought, that we had a good chance of having a child by this method. We walked out of his office not in our usual fashion of holding hands, but apart. It was the first time since we met that I felt Mike distant from me.

We sat in the car, Mike turning the ignition key, looking straight ahead, not speaking.

I quietly sat, trying to digest how our lives were changed in a few moments by a random occurrence we had no control over. I finally spoke. "I don't know about that artificial insemination method. It seems such a cold and medical way of having a child, like going to bed with a stranger." Mike's head snapped, turning to me; the glare in his eyes told me I had stepped on a very sensitive area.

The mere mention of going to bed with another man had inflamed his male ego; his machismo was in question. He responded, "Well, I guess it's the only way to have a child." He turned, driving toward home. We never spoke about artificial insemination again and instead focused on getting him better and trying to have our own child.

The medication to shrink the tumor was in pill form, easy enough to take, but the testosterone injections had to be given in the buttocks. On the first attempt with the nurse instructing me how to inject my husband in the butt, I passed out. I awoke on a gurney with the nurse next to me, checking my pulse, telling me to lay still. I looked up at Mike, who seemed totally frustrated, feeling so inadequate and stupid.

Our lives were becoming unraveled—a vicious cycle of going to doctors, checking sperm counts, checking my body temperature, and keeping a chart to estimate the best time for conception. With the biggest problem being that Mike very rarely came near me. On a number of occasions, I spoke to the doctor, explaining my concern. He very firmly stated that Mike's test results were not encouraging and that we would most likely never conceive our own child. I clearly recall his words as they reached through the phone, ripping at my heart. "Please consider other avenues, maybe adoption."

When did his behavior become so different than the man I married? At first, it was so subtle; I recall the first evening of him not coming home as usual, and I, in a panic, called the state police to see if they had any news of a car accident. For hours, I paced the kitchen and living room, looking out of the window, hoping to see his car pull into the driveway. By the time he came home, it was late in the night, and I frantically asked, "What happened? Where were you?"

His response felt cold; without emotion, he replied, "I felt tired and sick. I pulled over and fell asleep." At first, I immediately believed him, caressing his face and forehead, asking him if he wanted a cup of chamomile tea. As he slowly started to sip the tea, the cold hard look on his face told me that something other than falling asleep had occurred. I asked him if he wanted to talk about anything else; with a monotone voice, he said, "No, I'm fine. Go to bed." A great divide was being gouged between us. From whom or what, I was not sure.

Nothing was the same after that episode; he found fault with everything I did. Whereas in the past, he adored everything I did, he now complained that I did nothing right. He told me that he found me unattractive and that my breasts were way too small for his liking. I didn't even bother to respond, telling myself, "OK, stay calm. You know he's not well. Seek counseling."

I found a family counselor, asking Mike to attend the first session with me. The counselor was a down-to-earth black man more accustomed to dealing with drug—and criminal-related issues than infertility. That first meeting will forever reverberate in my memory, still being able to tear at my heart.

The counselor asked both of us to state what issues we would like to resolve; I'm not sure exactly what I said, something to the effect that Mike was not happy with anything I did and was being very cold toward me. Mike's statement is still imbedded in my being like an unwanted tattoo. "I don't have any issues to resolve. I'm not in love with her anymore, I don't find her attractive, I just want a divorce."

The counselor stared at him for a few seconds, not saying anything, then turned to me, asking, "What do you have to say to that?" I wasn't sure how to explain the great amount of stress Mike's medical condition was causing without hurting Mike's ego, so I just shrugged, not saying anything.

I now laugh thinking of how protective I was of a man who didn't want to be around me, who had just stated that he wanted to be rid of me. At the end of the session, I do remember the counselor asking both of us to have a written list of issues we wanted to iron out in the next session. I tried to make light of the situation by saying Mike may have a book written. The counselor laughed; I smiled at the silly joke, and Mike was straight-faced, not saying anything else.

As soon as we sat in the car, Mike turned to me, asking, "Are we going to the Kiwanis dinner tonight?" I told myself, *Hold on to your temper, be kind, your husband is not well.* Like a good devoted wife, I accompanied my husband to dinner.

I was so completely devoted to my husband that I treated him like a fragile piece of china, and every word I uttered was carefully thought over so as not to upset him. For months, I worked up the courage to ask him to go for a second medical opinion at Memorial Sloan-Kettering, hoping to find a solution and happiness again. His response was spoken in that now familiar monotone voice. "I'm not going to any other doctors. My mother sent Sissy," his younger sister, to Puerto Rico, where she was meeting with a very skilled Santeria, a type of mystical healer, and Sissy would bring back potions to help him feel better.

I had made it clear from the beginning of our relationship that this type of nonsense was not to be part of our lives, but my heart was breaking for him, and I gave in. "OK, if it helps you feel better." Sissy brought back an assortment of male colognes, and I realized that I should not have given in; he was now depending on cologne to make him better. I quietly thought to myself, *Maybe that's where he is when he's not home. He's having rituals performed.* How crazy was his family? Their son had a brain tumor, and they were encouraging him to use cologne as a treatment. I said nothing to anyone and suffered in silence.

For over two years, my life became a torment of dealing with a husband that was not in any way the man I married. A *Dr. Jekyll and Mr. Hyde* type of behavior that affected my own health so severely that I developed fits of vomiting. I became so ill one day after having an episode the previous evening—him demanding that I leave the house, that he couldn't stand being in the same room with me—that on the route home from work on the Throgs Neck Bridge, I started to uncontrollably vomit.

I was stuck in heavy traffic, not being able to move left or right, with vomit gushing out of me as if a pump had been turned on at full force. By the time I reached home, I and the car were a mess of splattered vomit. Mike saw the condition I was in, and when I asked for his help, he coldly looked at me, telling me, "Help yourself. It's not my fucking problem." I had never heard my husband curse at me before, and with every distant cruel word, my very sense of self-worth was being shattered.

I became so ill, barely able to keep a spoonful of food down that I had to seek medical attention. My doctor ran a battery of tests with the only conclusion being that I had a nervous stomach due to excessive stress. He prescribed Librium, and as I read the warning label, the drug-addict phantom with empty eyes stared back at me. It was an automatic reaction. I flipped the bottle upside down, spilling the contents into the toilet. I would rather have died from malnutrition than become a slave with empty eyes.

I alone attended counseling, Mike refusing to attend after the second session. The counselor was my only salvation, the only person that gave me validation to live my own life. I can still hear his encouraging words. "Filomena, listen to me. You've been coming to see me for almost two years, and your marriage has not gotten any better but from what I hear, much worse. You're still a very young woman. Do yourself a favor. Go on vacation by yourself. I don't think you're going to have a hard time meeting other people." I sat, trying to absorb the meaning of his words. I think if we had not been in a professional setting, his words would have been very different, maybe recommending, "Tell this guy to go fuck himself." I knew what he meant by meeting other people. He was, in a very careful manner, referring to other men.

At the time, I could not fathom the idea; I had been with my husband from the age of sixteen, and the thought of even holding hands with someone else seemed impossible. I responded, "I'm not sure about that. I'm too old to start over again. I just want my marriage to be the same. I want my husband to love me again." The counselor leaned forward in his chair, looking straight at me with great sadness on his face. He spoke kindly but firmly. "Filomena, this has been going on too long. I don't think that's going to happen. It's time for you to move on." He continued to speak, filling me with the notion that I had the God-given right to live my own life. His final words will forever resonate in me. "When the union cannot stand, you must stand alone. When the union cannot be saved, you must save the self." I left that session, promising the counselor that I take a Club Med vacation and start to live my own life.

The Long Island Housewife's Veal Marsala

Ingredients

1½ lb. of veal scaloppine cut from the top, round and flattened (I always had the butcher do this and asked to have each cutlet about the same size.)
1½ stick of butter
Flour, spread on a plate for dredging
Salt and black pepper to taste
½ cup dry marsala wine

Melt butter in a large skillet over a medium-low flame. While butter is melting, salt and pepper each cutlet. Dredge each cutlet into the flour, shaking off the excess, and place them into hot melted butter, browning both sides. Make sure each cutlet has enough room in the pan to brown; do not overlap cutlets. Remove all the cutlets, and place them on a warm platter. Add the marsala, and while it foams, scrape lose all brown bits with a wooden spoon. At this point, you may add two more tablespoons of butter and any juices the cutlets have released onto the platter. Cook until a dense sauce is made, no longer than five minutes. Add the cutlets to the sauce, flipping each over once to coat well. Lower flame to a simmer, and cook for about another five minutes, adding salt and black pepper to taste. This makes a great meal served with mashed potatoes.

"Let's Party" Stuffed Mushrooms

Ingredients

1½ lb. of mushrooms (whatever type you prefer, such as cremini or portabella)
4 cloves of very finely chopped garlic
6 slices of finely diced Genoa salami
4 tbs. of grated Parmesan cheese, fontina cheese, or any good melting cheese (you may even use crumbled goat cheese or Swiss)
6 tbs. of finely chopped fresh parsley
½ cup of unflavored breadcrumbs
¼ cup of olive oil

Remove stems from mushrooms and discard; with a wet Scott towel or cloth, wipe mushrooms clean and set aside. In a bowl, add the chopped garlic, salami, Parmesan cheese, melting cheese, parsley, and breadcrumbs. Mix well. Slowly add oil and toss all ingredients together. Fill each mushroom with stuffing, and place in a buttered baking dish; drizzle tops with olive oil, and bake at 375°F for about twenty minutes or until cheese is melted and tops are crispy. You may add chopped prosciutto or finely diced ham to the filling. For extra crunch, you may add a topping of breadcrumbs and Parmesan cheese to the tops of the stuffed mushrooms before baking.

True Lovers' Deviled Eggs

Ingredients

1 dozen hard-cooked eggs cut in half (remove yolks, place in a bowl)
½ lb. cooked bacon, must be crispy and broken into tiny pieces
¼ cup of chopped olives (whatever type you prefer)
Optional: 2 tbs. of salted capers, finely chopped or finely diced prosciutto, finely diced ham
½ cup of mayo
Salt and black pepper to taste

Remove yolks from eggs, place in a bowl; with a fork, break up the yolk, adding a bit of mayo, and whip together. Add the remaining ingredients and additional mayo; whip until fluffy. Add salt and pepper, whip again, and by teaspoon—or if you really wish to be fancy, use a pastry bag with a swirly tip—fill the egg whites with yolk filling. You may decorate the tops with tiny pieces of pimentos, celery, or olives. If you have leftover yolk filling, you can use it to fill celery stalks or fennel wedges, serving them next to the deviled eggs.

Chapter 6

To Save the Self

I planned my vacation at work, arranging all the details with a travel agency located in that area. In the brochure, Paradise Island seemed so peaceful, a place for me to find what I had not felt in over two years—peace and harmony. Mike's behavior had become so verbally abusive that at night, I rarely slept, and whatever I ate, I threw up. I knew I was reaching the breaking point and had started to feel that maybe, for all those years, he never really loved me at all.

He started his usual rant as soon as we were in the same room. "I don't want you here. I want a divorce. You've been nothing but a burden to me, and I know you want to go to bed with other men."

I watched his insensitive behavior, listened to his cruel words, and started to feel that I had never really been a wife or friend to him at all but only a *muñequita*, a doll to merely dress up and parade around as a display for his own ego. With deep sadness, I realized that now he no longer had any use for me and was willing to discard me like an unwanted toy. More than my heart was being ripped apart, my soul and sense of what I had been to the man I loved was in shattered bits. I questioned my own stupidity for having been so faithful to a man that had not loved me for so many years. I felt like a complete fool without much value.

I went on my first Club Med vacation expecting to find a bit of peace and not much else. Instead, I found that without trying, I had the surprising ability to attract men. I'd sit on a lounge chair, reading a book, and in a short amount of time, a male would engage me in conversation. Of course, they asked what I was reading and where I was from, but the direction of their eyes told a different story. I was both amused and shocked.

Most entertaining of all was my ability to control the situation with cool composure; I can only guess that I had acquired this innate ability to stay on my guard from living in the hood and started to understand how hard times can serve as an emotional bank where one can make withdrawals when necessary.

There was one persistent French Canadian who was very free with his hands. As he sat next to me, chitchatting with a sexy French accent, he slowly rubbed my thigh with his hand, telling me how soft my skin felt. I very calmly smiled and leaned toward him, removing his hand, telling him, "Keep your hands to yourself." He responded, "You are very tempting." I thanked him, telling him again, "Keep your hands to yourself." I enjoyed the much-needed male attention and was able to eat, hardy without vomiting.

It amused me to watch other females make complete fools of themselves by overdrinking and allowing men to have the advantage; I told myself, "Nope, that will never be me." The vacation proved to be not only relaxing—I no longer had tightness in my stomach—but also educational. While I participated in all the activities outside of drunkenness and casual sex, I realized that I attracted men very easily.

I was sure that was what my counselor was suggesting, and I was very happy to have taken his advice. At the end of the vacation, as I was leaving, my Canadian friend ran up to me to say good-bye, handing me his business card, and with a peck on the cheek asked me to visit him in Montréal. Smiling, I thanked him and placed the card in my bag, later disposing it in the trash.

The nervousness began as soon as I reached the airport; my sister's boyfriend, Jim, picked me up, and as we drove home, the tension in me soared. I prayed that Mike would not be home, but instead, as I opened the front door, entering the living room with Jim behind me, Mike was sitting in his chair, eyes glaring at me. Jim spoke, telling Mike, "Don't give her any trouble." Mike, unlike his usual behavior, leaped from the chair ready to . . . I'm not sure what he was ready to do. I grabbed Jim by the arm, pushing him out the door, thanking him, and quickly locked the door behind me.

Mike imminently started with the belittling comments. "Where where you? You were gone for a week?" Without taking a breath, he continued, "You see my hand? I almost cut two fingers off, remodeling the bathroom cabinet the way you wanted it. I had to ask our neighbor to drive me to the hospital. You weren't around."

I stared at his bandaged hand quickly, deciding not to have him make me feel guilty and start pampering him like I had done for years.

I grabbed my bag and started to climb the stairs to the bedroom that we had not made love in for years. Mike continued to yell. "Where were you?" I quietly said, "On vacation." "With who?" Mike demanded. My voice barely audible, I replied, "By myself."

I felt the tide of change in me; I was tired of his temper tantrums and his controlling me through guilt as if I had caused his illness, but most eye-opening of all, I realized I was tired of not having a real marriage. I started to feel rage at the thought that maybe he felt I should be contented with a sexless marriage void of passion. I was feeling like a display doll to be propped on the bed just for show. Mike's tantrum continued as I closed the door to the bedroom. "I don't believe you. Who were you with? Answer me, I'm still your husband." I stepped out of the bedroom, seeing him looking up. I almost answered, "You could have fooled me!" but thought, *Why bother?* Our eyes met for a brief second as I closed the door to the top of the stairs and then the door to the bedroom.

I met with my counselor a few days after that, and his first question to me was "How did your vacation go?" He had a new sly look in his eyes and a bit of a smirk on his face. With my very simple response of "It went great. I enjoyed myself and ate like a piglet without throwing up," his smirk got a little wider as he asked, "I bet you met lots of new friends?" The smirk made the question clearer than words; I knew exactly what he meant. I smiled back, reporting to my most valuable confidant, "Yes, I met a lot of new friends." We stared at each other, understanding the meaning of our conversation. "Good, Filomena, I knew that you would." We ended that portion of the counseling session with those positive words of encouragement.

For the rest of that session, as I explained Mike's increasingly aggressive behavior, he coached me on how to handle the situation. He leaned forward in his chair, intently listening to my silly high school—girl emotions. I mentioned, "Oh, I don't think he would ever physically hurt me. I think he still loves me but doesn't know how to show it anymore." "Filomena, carefully listen to me. You are not dealing with the same person you married. I'm not sure what's caused the change in his behavior. It may be his medical condition, the medicine he's taking, or drugs." I stopped him from continuing. "Drugs? He doesn't even drink. We've never had that type of problem."

My counselor took a deep breath, sitting back in his chair. "I'm not sure what his problem is, but I'm sure that if he becomes physically aggressive, you need to get out. Don't hesitate to pick up the phone to call the police or just walk out of the house. Please don't take any chances, and don't make a threat unless you're going to follow through." I pushed my head back onto the wall, thinking out loud, "I can't believe this is happing to me. We've loved each other so much." At the end of the session, my counselor made me promise that I would protect myself. I knew that he was right. I had not felt comfortable and safe in my own home for months.

It was almost as if my counselor had had a premonition about what was to follow, and he was correct in telling me to protect myself. Soon after that session, I came home to find the phone wires cut, and as I sat in the kitchen trying to calm myself with a cup of chamomile tea, Mike walked in, picking up the receiver, slamming it into the wall, demanding that I pay more of the house bills. I sat staring at him for a few seconds, hearing my counselor's voice echoing in my ears. "Don't make a threat unless you're going to follow through." I didn't become very upset. I just sat in my chair, telling him, "Mike, if you don't stop, I'm going to call the police." He yelled back, "Yeah, how? You don't have a phone." I got up and pushed past him, walking out of the house in my nightclothes with his eyes following me in complete shock. I continued to walk across the lawn to my neighbor's house, asking them if I could use their phone to call the police.

I had been very friendly with them, and they pulled me right into their home, realizing that something was seriously wrong. I first called the police and then, as we waited, I started to explain what was occurring. Mrs. Flores put her arm around me, sitting me down at her kitchen table; Mr. Flores looked out the window, waiting for the police to arrive as he told me, "I knew something was very wrong these past months. Mike's behavior has been just too different." When the police arrived, we stood in the doorway as I explained what had occurred; Mike, seeing the police, jumped into his car, speeding away. The police asked if I want him arrested. I quickly responded, "Please, no, don't arrest him. He's very sick. I just don't know what else to do." "OK," one police officer said, suggesting that when he came back to the house, they would speak to him.

I agreed, and they helped me climb through a window to unlock the door to my own home. Mike spent a good half hour driving recklessly around the block, and one officer told me that if he didn't stop soon, they were going to arrest him anyway. My neighbors stood next to me in the night air, waiting for his tantrum to cease, and as he pulled into the driveway, the police walked over to speak to him. I watched from my neighbor's lawn in complete disbelief that my life had turned to this nightmare.

I saw Mike nod his head as the police spoke to him, and then he walked into the house. An officer walked over to inform me that Mike had been warned not to harass me in any way when I went home, asking me to call again if he did. Mr. Flores spoke, telling us that he didn't think it was safe for me to go back to my own home and that I should spend the night with them; his wife agreed. I was becoming numb. I didn't cry, I didn't vomit. I was simply dazed, walking away with the Floreses, realizing that my counselor was right; this was not the same man I married.

I spent a sleepless night mostly sitting on the bed in the Flores guest room. I tried to lie down and close my eyes only to see the images of my husband slamming the phone receiver into the wall and had to sit upright, trying to erase the thought from my mind. I asked myself over and over again, What does he want? and came up with more unanswerable questions. For months, he said he wanted a divorce, but didn't follow through with it. He said he wanted me out of the home, but when I would leave, he would become upset. He had even tried to block me in the garage one day when I was trying to leave with my bike on the carrack.

He had placed his car in front so that I couldn't back out, demanding to know where I was going. I angrily told him, "You know where I bike-ride. Move your car." "Yeah, right, you're going by yourself." I yelled back, "Yeah, by myself! Do you want to come? If not, move your fucking car." He defiantly refused to move. I started my car, backing so close to his that I almost hit the car until he realized I wasn't fooling around and moved his car. Was he trying to test my will? Was he trying to break my spirit? Was his manhood so in question that he now needed to control me? If that was the case, he should have known better.

Mike had understood my emotional makeup more than anyone else and should have realized that I could never be a submissive, controlled wife. If that was what he now needed to feel like a man, he had to find it with someone else.

I sat up all night in a strange room, admitting to myself that we had grown so far apart in the past two years that we were no longer married, no longer friends, and I could no longer live this way.

In the morning, Mr. Flores called my home to tell Mike I was going over to get ready for work. I sat at the kitchen table with a cup of tea in front of me in the same emotional state; I was dazed and confused from lack of sleep and nourishment. I heard Mr. Flores say, "Mike, I hope you've calmed down. Your wife is coming over to get dressed for work. Please don't give her any trouble." When he hung up, I simply got up, thanking them. Mrs. Flores put her arm around my shoulder, telling me not to hesitate to walk over if I needed help. I simply nodded, and as my insides started to shake, I walked across the lawn to the house that was no longer my home.

I don't have any recipes to end this chapter with, only a sense of deep sadness at having lost my best friend, my devoted husband, and my first love.

Chapter 7

I Stand Alone

From that day on, I, who had once relished the comfort of my home, felt nothing but fear. I could never have imagined that a man who had been for so many years my protector, my teacher, my sole source of security, and my admiring lover was now attempting to push me out of my home without any regard for my well-being.

I often wondered who was giving him such misguided advice. Was it his family who may have felt animosity toward me or friends who may have been jealous of the strong love we once had? I was certain that he was being coached by others as to how he should dispel of this unwanted toy. I felt not so much anger but deep sadness and a loss of respect more than love for him. Mike, in his confused mind, did not realize that I still loved him so much I would have given him anything he asked for. A divorce, as painful as it felt, was fine; I never wanted to be with a man that didn't want to be with me. Our home with whatever possessions he wanted—I would gladly give him anything if they made him feel better. I didn't need them; all I needed was to find a sense of peace and harmony again.

I entered my home every day feeling so tired from work, seeking solace, finding only the cold material possessions staring at me, and became so agitated that I would run toward the waterfront, hoping to find a peaceful solution to my sad existence. One day, I found myself on an empty lot looking toward the open bay; we had walked to that same lot holding hands so many times, just daydreaming of buying the property and building a home with windows facing the waterfront.

Now as I tried to catch my breath, I did not even dare to dream of happiness. I felt so unwanted, so tired and old, struggling to just make it through another day. I asked myself, *What for? Why struggle? For what purpose?* On an impulse, I stepped onto the bulkhead with my toes hanging over the edge, looking down into the deep water. I pictured myself drowning, my lungs filling with water, not being able to breathe, my lifeless body floating away. How long did I stare down at the water wanting to jump in? Was it minutes or hours? I'm not sure. I stood there until I felt those external forces place their arms around my shoulders, holding me back, and I heard the echoes of my mother's cries after my father's murder.

Those cries frightened me more than my own death, coaxing me off the bulkhead with my inner voice speaking to me. The voice whispered to me, "You have become a flashing neon sign to your husband, a constant display of what he cannot have. The sign reads loud and clear every time you're in the same room: 'Here is the wife you loved for so long. This is the wife you will never have children with.'" At that very moment, I understood that I could do nothing else for him but leave; in my leaving, I hoped he would find peace.

I ran home hearing my own breathing pounding in my ears, realizing that I really didn't want to die but wanted the freedom to live, to live without the burden of being a wife. To just be without being part of someone else. I walked into my home, a home we both had put together with so much care; it no longer gave me happiness. I felt anxious and queasy every time I entered the front door.

I walked through the living room, running my hand across the fabric of the sofa, glancing around at all the beautiful possessions. In the dining room stood a china cabinet filled with silver and crystal, the walls decorated with an array of scenic plates. I realized I didn't care. I walked into the kitchen and looked up at the shelves that held my cookbooks and told myself, "What does it matter? You have not cooked a meal in months." Turning, I stared at the back door that led to the porch and into the backyard; I took a few steps forward, stopping. I could not bear the thought of leaving my outer sanctuary; my heart was crumbling into tiny pieces knowing that I would never sit in my quiet place again.

I pushed back tears, turning away. "What did it matter?" I told myself. "You didn't even plant a vegetable garden this year." I walked into the study; the furniture was beautiful, the bookshelves holding a complete edition of *The Hobbit* with Royal Doulton figurines of each of the characters next to it. The Lladró, the Lenox, the handmade stained glass hanging in the window were so perfect, but I did not care. My marriage was anything but perfect, and those objects did not make me feel beautiful. I walked out not caring about them at all.

I walked into the gym and stood there for no more than a minute, walking back out into the hallway toward the basement door. With my hand on the doorknob, I hesitated, becoming frightened, telling myself, "There's nothing down there you need." I walked away, hearing the distant echoes of friends laughing and music playing, wishing once again to have happiness in my life.

I climbed the stairs to the bedroom, not caring how large and beautifully decorated it was. I once had cherished waking up in the morning, seeing the sunshine stream though the window hitting the flowery stained glass that had been made just for me; now I hardly ever slept.

Looking at the bed, I could not remember the last time we had made love. I packed a few pieces of clothing into a bag, knowing that this was best for both of us. In the deepest recesses of my being, I was certain I was taking with me the most precious possessions of all, my dignity and self-respect.

Before walking down the stairs, I stood in the bedroom doorway, looking across the hall into the bedroom that should have been a nursery; it now held a new gadget called the IBM Personal Computer. With a gouging ache in my heart, I admitted to myself that it would never be a room for our child.

As I started to walk down the stairs, the methodical control I had felt going through my home gave into sadness, turning into tears. I placed one hand over my eyes, trying to stop the flood of tears, realizing I was crying not so much because I was leaving my forever home but because my fairy-tale romance didn't have a happy ending, and I knew I had to stand alone. With streams of tears soaking my cheeks, I walked down the remaining stairs, telling myself, "Be ready. Be very ready to lose your innocence." I walked out the front door slowly, closing it behind me, and never lived in that home again.

I cannot think of a single meal that I enjoyed during this heart-shattering period of my life, but I can still feel the distant residual pain of betrayal and know that it will never completely heal.

Chapter 8

Loss of Innocence

Before driving away from my home, I wiped my tears, telling myself that the hardest part was yet to come. I needed to explain to my mother why I was leaving, and worse yet, I needed to stay with her and my sister for a few months until I got settled in my own apartment. I drove, dreading the thought of not so much explaining what my life had been like for the past two years but of not having my own space; I had not lived with either of them since the age of nineteen, and I knew the transitions would be very difficult for me.

My mom was standing on the front porch when I pulled the car into a spot, and I immediately saw the perplexed look on her face. I climbed the front steps feeling beyond exhausted, hoping to find a quiet refuge, remembering my father's warning from years earlier—"Once you're married, don't expect to come back when things get tough." I understood that divorce would make the whole family look bad (*brutta figura*), and I had been raised from birth to be the perfect wife, forsaking any of my needs for the well-being of my family. My parents never foresaw how intently I had followed the women's movement and could never have imagined that two years of discussions with a street-smart black counselor would give me not only courage but society's blessing to live my own life.

I started to explain to my mother before I stepped off the last step. In Neapolitan, I tried to explain, and at that every moment, I realized I was not proficient enough in the language to explain complicated matters. My mind was thinking in two languages, struggling between two cultures to explain a great deal of emotional turmoil. I tried my best to explain that Mike was not happy with the marriage and had asked for a divorce and that I had tried for two years to seek help but to no avail. She already knew to a very limited extent that we were going through difficulties, but like a good Neapolitan mother-in-law, she said little and expected her daughter to stick it out. I explained as much as I could without compromising Mike's medical situation, still being very protective of his privacy.

My mother, with a stern look on her face, spoke, "Of course your husband is not happy with you. After all these years, you've never given him children." I can't say I was surprised by her summation that I was somehow at fault; I had expected as much. The remark left me with no other alternative but to further explain. She stared at me in disbelief, asking, "Are you sure? All these years I thought it was you who couldn't have children?" I knew she wouldn't refuse my request to move in with her for a few months, and as we started to climb the stairs to her apartment, she rambled on about the kitchen renovations she was having done.

I walked into anything but a quiet refuge as workmen tore down the kitchen, and my mother pointed to a pile of mail that needed to be sorted. I simply nodded while I opened the mail, and she informed the workmen that I would be painting the kitchen, proudly stating that I had painted most of my home in Long Island. I had to explain, telling her I was not well enough to paint, and hid my feelings of disappointment at her insensitivity, telling myself if you can get through these next few months, everything else will be a piece of cake.

That Monday, I went through my usual work routine of picking up all the paperwork from my four schools, bringing them to the office. For the first time since working with the same supervisor, I was pulled over to the side and asked, "Ms. Abys, since when do you come to work dressed in jeans? You've always dressed in a professional manner. What is the problem?" With extreme embarrassment, I stood there, looking at my supervisor of many years, knowing the shock my explanation would bring. She knew Mike, and when I started to explain why I had left my home, she stared in complete disbelief, saying, "I can't believe it. You always seemed like such a happy, loving couple." I, through my embarrassment, told her, "If I hadn't been living this nightmare myself, I wouldn't believe it either."

That weekend, along with my mother, I drove to my home, hoping to simply pack more of my clothes. As I pulled in front of the house, a car that had been parked there quickly sped away. We both saw that it was Mike's older sister. I walked into the living room to find my in-laws and my husband in a complete frenzy. With one glance, I didn't need to ask why; I knew they had ransacked my home.

I had been absent for such a short time, and most of my good china was gone; all the decorative wall plates were gone, the Llardó, the Lenox, the Royal Doulton, the Dresden tea set, the Japanese geisha girl tea set, the silver and crystal champagne glasses, all the stained glasses. Even a sewing kit my aunt Vincenza had given me at my bridal shower was gone. She had saved a collection of antique buttons for me, placing them in the basket; they too were gone. In brief, all items of either emotional or market value were gone, which led me to believe that this had been a well-thought-out plan.

Mike was completely disheveled and seemed emotionally torn, almost on the verge of a complete nervous breakdown. I surprised myself by being very calm, avoiding my in-laws, looking straight into Mike's eyes, asking, "What happened? Where's everything?" He started with one of his tantrums, yelling, "I broke everything! I smashed everything to bits and put it in the garbage." I could see that his parents were very anxious that he might not repeat the well-rehearsed story, with his mother rubbing his back and his father telling him in Spanish to be quiet like I didn't understand the language. I merely responded, "Oh," and walked outside to see what was in the garbage, finding not a bit of shattered glass or anything else.

My mother, following closely behind, told me, "His sister drove off with everything. Who do they think they're kidding?" I simply nodded, saying, "I know." I walked back into the living room, looked straight into my husband's eyes, and—with a soft smile, in a very calm voice—spoke, "I didn't see anything in the garbage, not even a bit of glass." With that, he crawled up into a fetus-like position in front of the fireplace, yelling, "I burned everything first and then put it in the garbage!" If my heart was not breaking for him and if I didn't feel so much love and compassion for him, I would have started laughing at the absurdity of his situation.

I'm not sure what they expected from me, maybe that I would call the police or make a big fuss. Little did they know that two years of dealing with constant emotional turmoil and through deep soul-searching, I had come to care nothing about material possessions and was simply there to remove my clothes so that I could go to work.

I no longer reacted to Mike's temper tantrum; I had spent too much of my youth dealing with that. I simply walked upstairs to pack the rest of my clothing. For the first time, I could sense anger in my mother against Mike as she complained, "What nerve they have. They took all the best stuff we gave you. His family never gave you a thing, and now they have." I stopped her in midsentence, telling her, "Ma, I don't give a damn about all the stuff. They need to live with themselves." With increasing bitterness, my mother continued, "The nerve of them to just walk in here and take." I heard her voice in the distance and continued to pack, refusing to listen.

I'm not sure if it was that day or on one of the many occasions I had to enter the Long Island house to remove whatever belongings were left for me that the final dagger was thrust into my heart. I walked into the basement to remove family memorabilia; I opened the grey metal closets, pulling out the light wooden wine box that I kept not only photos but a treasured memento of my father. It was the broken music box and electric razor I had given my father as a Christmas gift.

Mike knew that as a young girl, I had purchased those items with one of my first paychecks, and both my parents treasured the music box until it was knocked over and broken. My father, not being able to part with it, had taken the top portion of Tevye with his arms held high and taped it on the cash register in his shop. I can still hear my father's voice telling me, "My life is just like that fiddler, always on a shaky roof."

After my father's murder, as we cleaned up the shop, Mike himself removed the figurine from the register, handing it to me with tears filling his eyes. I had found the razor in the back of the shop on a shelf, still plugged into the socket. I kept those items with a newspaper article of Mike's interview by a *Daily News* reporter on the day of the murder. In addition to those articles, there were—and I hesitate to mention this, fearing that the reader may think I'm a bit touched in the head—dry rose petals which I found the day after my father's funeral at the foot of my bed.

That night, before going to bed, I mentioned to Mike how I had forgotten to take a few rose petals; he, while hugging and kissing me, told me not to worry and helped me into bed. The next morning, as I stepped out of bed, I felt those dry rose petals under my foot. We both stared down in disbelief, I asking Mike if he had placed them there. He seemed just as shocked as I was, said, "Where would I get dry petals from?" We both stared at each other in complete disbelief. After a few brief seconds without saying another word, I picked them up, placing them in an envelope with the newspaper article, and placed all those items into the wooden wine box along with the broken music box and razor.

That day, Mike followed me into the basement, already knowing what I was looking for, and closely watched as I opened the box to find everything missing. I didn't need to ask. I just looked up into his face, and he spoke with a very deliberate frozen voice, "I smashed it with everything else and put it in the garbage." At that very moment, I understood his illness was no longer just physical but had become a chronic malady of the heart and soul. If there had been a slight chance for reconciliation, it was forever lost on that day. He had already displayed a great lack of respect for me, but to disrespect the memory of my murdered father was the point of no return. The emotional divorce for me was complete; I said nothing, closing the box and walking away.

The last memory I have of seeing Mike—and I cannot say with certainty if it occurred on that same day or on one of the many other occasions I was given permission to enter my own home—was in the company of a young attorney from the law firm I had hired to assist me in entering the home to remove whatever articles I needed.

Mike was in the living room as we entered and said nothing, allowing me to go through the house, removing what I needed. After many trips to my car, packing as much as I could, the attorney started to walk toward his car, leaving me to push the trunk closed. Mike came running out of the house, grabbing me from behind, spinning me around to face him. The attorney came running over in fear that Mike might hurt me; he quickly stopped when I put my hand up, and he saw that Mike was in tears, begging for forgiveness, telling me how much he loved me, and asking me, "Please don't leave."

I felt so much sadness, so much sorrow, but no longer felt the love and respect I once had for him. I almost started to cry myself, but with every bit of strength, I held back the tears, telling him, "I know, but it's too late for us now. It's really over. I can't be with you anymore. I don't want to be your wife." I pushed myself out of his arms and sat in my car with the attorney walking over to ask if I was OK to drive.

On that day, refusing to shed any more tears, I drove away, never looking back, realizing that if I had stayed, it would have been solely for material comforts, nothing more than legal prostitution. "That" I was not willing to bear; we both deserved better. I didn't care what the legality was, I didn't care what the Catholic Church's views were, I didn't even care what my family thought; I was no longer his wife.

That day, while driving, I subconsciously reached inside myself, grabbing the shattered bits of my broken heart, vowing never to be anyone's perfect little housewife again. In the deepest recesses of my being, I watched not only the bits and pieces of my heart roll off my hand as I dropped them one by one into my internal frozen pond. I also ripped my sense of who I was into a thousand tiny parts, scattering them into the icy water.

The actual divorce took four years as Mike, with the help of both our attorneys, tried to delay the inevitable. During those four years, I became a completely different person, immovable in my resolve to live my own life. I purchased my own apartment, worked two jobs, went out with friends, vacationed, and did not hold back from male attention as I had done before. As much as I enjoyed my single life, there was always a nagging feeling of something absent—a void I could not fill regardless of how hard I worked, how much I traveled, and how much male attention I received.

At this point, it does not serve any purpose to mention other male acquaintances outside of the two you will meet in the next chapters. This book is meant, first and foremost, to reveal the deep passion I have for living life well. I share these next chapters with you, hoping that it will inspire you to live with great passion and that you will not misjudge the men or the relationships I had with them.

I definitely don't have any recipes to share in this chapter.

I had watched my mother all my life prepare meals for family and friends with so much love and care that it had become an intricate part of who I was. The preparation of meals was an extension of my heart; it was how I displayed my deepest love. I refused to prepare a meal for any man after leaving Mike, but what I was truly refusing to do was *love*.

A Friend's Friend

I had known Annie from my college days; now we were colleagues working together, and as we both walked from the train station to the Department of Health building to take the required class for food safety, the one clear recollection I had of her was how she had come running to me in class after my father's murder to express her condolences. She agonized with me over how unfair it all was to have to take final exams only a few days after my father's funeral. Not really wanting to talk to any of my teachers about what had occurred, I was willing to take the exams and take whatever grades came my way. Annie kindly went to our biology instructor, explaining what I had been through, and the following day, that instructor along with all of my other instructors outside of one informed me that I need not take the finals.

I was truly happy for her help, and now years later, as we walked chitchatting about what had occurred in my marriage to Mike, she expressed her shock, asking if I was dating yet. I simply replied, "I've dated a few guys, nothing serious," honestly stating, "I really don't want to be serious with anyone." She asked if I like to meet a close friend that was her daughter's godfather, saying, "He's not bad-looking, works for the transits" and then stopped with hesitation. I could sense her concern as she continued, "He's really very kind, but you know, a bit aggressive. Sometimes he just needs to be told to shut up. He's looking for someone nice. I can give him your number. You can talk and take it from there."

While she spoke, I thought to myself, *He can't be a bad egg. He's her daughter's godfather. Just talking on the phone is harmless.* But her hesitation made me hold back, and I said, "*Oh*, I don't know. I'll give it some thought and let you know later." During the class, I told myself to just say no. I had always been a very private person and didn't want coworkers knowing too much of my personal business. At the end of the class, as we walked back to the train station, I decided not to mention the issue, hoping she had forgotten our discussion.

Annie spoke up, asking, "Well, can I give William your number?" Shrugging my shoulders, not sure what to do, I simply said, "I guess just talking on the phone is OK. I don't think you would set me up with a nut. After all, he's your daughter's godfather." I continued, asking, "His name is William?" Annie smiled, saying, "Yeah, he's Irish. William really needs to meet someone educated and nice like you." My last thought was *I'm flattered, but what type of woman has he been dating?*

Two days later, as I lay in bed watching TV, the phone rang. I picked up the receiver, hearing, "Hi, Filomena, it's William O'Conner, Annie's friend." By this time, I had reached an emotional state where I didn't give a damn about impressing any man and was fairly content with single life, simply said with little excitement, "Oh yes, hi," and waited for William to continue. He didn't need encouragement to continue talking, and the conversation followed in this similar fashion:

"Annie told me you went to college with her and now work together."

"Yes, we've know each other since college. She told me you're her daughter's godfather."

"Yeah, I've been good friends with her husband for years. Ah, Annie told me to watch what I say, that you're one of those very educated refined bro—" And then he stopped himself from saying "broads" and said "gals."

I smiled, not knowing what to think, placing my hand over my forehead, thinking to myself, I *hope you didn't make a big mistake.* I sensed from his tone of voice that the phrase Annie had used, "a bit aggressive," had been as serious understatement. I didn't respond, allowing him to continue.

"Yeah, she also told me you're into bodybuilding and work at a gym." At that point, I had to stop him to explain, "I'm not into bodybuilding, but I work out almost daily and teach classes." With that said, I heard a quick laugh, and William honestly stated, "Lately, I've been more into body softening. I haven't done any serious working out since my boxing days in the army. So listen, let me take you out to dinner." I pushed my head back onto the pillow, telling myself, *It's only dinner. How bad can that be? An old friend wouldn't set you up with a madman.* But the vibrations that reached through the phone told me different.

I must have been subconsciously looking for a madman because I said, "OK, dinner sounds fine," and processed to give him my address, setting up a dinner date within two days of that first phone call.

The mismatch was obvious from the moment I opened the door, and there, William stood nicely dressed in a suit and tie. Over the phone, I had explained where we were going for dinner and dressed in jeans with a causal top. Of course, it was only that he was Annie's friend that I had agreed to meet him at my apartment, and as we both cordially greeted each other, I asked him to come in.

William's eyes moved from my face to my tight jeans and quickly glanced around my apartment. From the beginning, I found him unappealing and thought, *Why is he dressed in a suit? I told him the restaurant was casual.* He sat on the love seat in the living room, and I sat on the sofa facing him. I can only guess that his next statement came from nervousness or just not knowing what to say, but now, so many years later, I laugh thinking of him blurting out, "So what did you do, clean up because you knew I was coming over?"

I never imagined that anyone could be so rude and sat for a few seconds in disbelief, digesting what he had just said, simply responding, "Ah no, my home is always this way." William, with a bit of a laugh, said, "Yeah, right, you just stuffed everything into the closets."

I had a momentary urge to throw him out but held back, telling myself, *Stay calm. He's Annie's friend. Just have dinner, and leave it at that.* I gave a slight laugh, saying, "No, I didn't stuff my closet."

I rose from the sofa, asking, "Are you ready for dinner?" His eyes canvassed my body as if he was looking at a painting, responding, "Yeah, sure, let's go." As we were walking out the door, he quickly mentioned something unflattering about my husband. I knew instantly that he had had a long conversation with Annie, thinking to myself, *OK, you just made a big mistake. Next time, keep your personal business to yourself.* Refusing to dignify his comment, I said nothing.

He drove to the restaurant, and I can't recall the exact details of the conversation, only that his insinuations toward my divorce and aggressive manner of speaking made me thankful I was only a few minutes from home. During dinner, he again directed the conversation to my marriage and subsequent divorce. I was shocked at his lack of etiquette, finding him too presumptuous. I said very little, trying to avoid the conversation. I now know that a good portion of his aggressive behavior was to cover up for nervousness and insecurity, but at the time, I couldn't wait for dinner to end.

After dinner, he drove me back to my apartment, and I quickly said, "It was very nice to meet you. Thank you so much for dinner," and started to walk away. He didn't ask but told me he would walk back to my building with me. I very quickly said, "Oh, that's not necessary," angrily thinking Annie had some nerve setting me up with this madman.

William simply started to walk and informed me, "It's too dark. I don't want you to walk by yourself." I smiled, not saying anything but thinking, "If this nut thinks he's coming into my apartment, he's completely out of his mind." At the foot of the stairs, I said good night, and he simply watched me climb the stairs with a smile on his face. As soon as I locked the door behind me, I told myself, "Call Annie first thing in the morning, and tell her that you didn't like him at all and to please not have him call again."

Early in the morning, I called Annie and explained that I didn't think we were a good match, asking her to please not have him call anymore. Annie's voice seemed very disappointed, telling me, "Are you sure? He really liked you." I knew by that comment that they had already spoken, and it was before nine in the morning. She continued by saying, "I know William is a bit rough around the edges, but he's really very kind and nice when you get to know him." I truly felt sorry and disappointed that

I didn't like him but honestly told Annie, "Ah, I don't think we're a good match. It's better that he doesn't call. Thanks, Annie. I'm sorry."

I can't say exactly how many days it took for Annie to call me and ask if William could call me again, probably no more than two weeks. She plainly told me that he was driving her crazy about wanting to see me again and that he promised to keep his mouth shut. Although hesitant, I found it flattering, recalling with great relish how he had reviewed my feminine assets. I thought to myself, *Give it another try. A bit of a madman might do you some good.* I agreed that William could call me again, and a day later, I sat on my bed, trying to have a conversation with a madman.

He apologized for talking too much and actually made me laugh by saying, "Ah, you know, sometimes my big mouth gets in the way." We chitchatted for a while, William asking if he could take me out again. I agreed, and a few days later, he picked me up at my apartment. This time, we were both dressed in jeans, and as he walked in, I, laughing and motioning to my surroundings, said, "See, my apartment is always this way." William, laughing along with me, responded, "Sorry for saying that, but I've never seen such a clean apartment." I just smiled, thinking, *Only God knows what type of woman he's being seeing.*

We went out to dinner again, and this time, the conversation went along not perfect but better than the first as we talked about arriving in New York around the same time. If nothing else, we had immigration as a common factor, but William made it very clear that this polite chitchat was not on top of his priority list by plainly asking, "Why did you get divorce?"

I looked down, taking a few deep breaths, thinking, *Who does he think he is asking me such personal questions?* I held tightly onto the edge of the table, my temper almost on the verge of exploding, when a flash of realization occurred. That internal voice that had so often cleared my cluttered mind spoke, "He's here with you because he's looking for something different than what he can find in a barroom." As I looked up, he was staring at me, waiting for an explanation. With a smirk on my face, I began by saying, "I usually don't discuss this with someone I hardly know," and then proceeded to explain a very complicated situation.

I can't say he was very sympathetic or that he gave me a feeling of comfort; it just seemed to me he was trying to make sure I was not the type of female that easily walked out on a relationship. I saw the potential for possessiveness, telling myself, *Be careful. You're just looking for a friendly, fun relationship.* He again took it upon himself to walk me to my apartment, and as I thanked him for dinner, he didn't ask but told me, "I'll call you tomorrow." I didn't give it a second thought, knowing that the following day, I was working at the gym until 9:00 p.m.

Before our first sexual encounter, William had many times pulled me into his arms, kissing me with almost a crazed passion, but it wasn't until after I had finished Easter dinner with my family while driving home to meet William that the uncontrollable vixen in me took hold, and I decided to let nature take its course.

William walked in with a large fluffy Easter rabbit, shaking it in my face and pulling me into his arms. With a sexy smile, I thanked him with a prolonged kiss, not on the lips but on his cheek. I can only guess that William's other female friends had never kissed his cheek in such a fashion, seeing the intense pleasure it aroused in him.

A great sexual passion developed from that kiss, with William surprising me by being the most careful and considerate lover. I gave him sexually what I could not give him from my heart, keeping steady in my resolve never to love or be another man's wife. Although not willing to verbalize my lack of heart in the relationship, he became increasingly possessive and demanded what I was not yet able to give, further pushing me away.

I must admit that I thoroughly enjoyed his attention and greatly anticipated our time together. William's emotional makeup fascinated me, and I found his willingness to please very endearing. He showered me with attention and was so willing to make me happy that one afternoon, after I had been out the previous evening with a group of friends to a male strip club, he, with a bit of a smirk and raising his hands in a questioning manner, asked, "What do you need to go to those places for? You have me," and proceeded to run his hands down his body.

Sitting at the foot of my bed feeling ever so ready for entertainment, I softly said, "Yes, but those fellows dance and strip." He looked up at the ceiling and laughingly said, "Yeah, watch this."

I pushed myself back onto the bed, resting on the pillows, and with a wave of one hand, told him, "The floor is all yours." William was completely delightful, slowly removing each article of clothing down to his underwear; before removing that last item, he grabbed a small straw hat that sat on my doll's head, carefully placing it in front of his very substantial male anatomy. As he removed that last piece of clothing, I, with both hands over my eyes, peeked through my fingers while convulsing with laughter, noticing that the hat was way too small. Dropping the hat, he crawled onto the bed like a stalking lion; I wrapped my arms around him, giving him a prolonged kiss near his ear, whispering, "You're so right. Those male strippers can't compete with you."

I fondly recall William putting his clothes on after that passionate afternoon, informing me, "You know, Phil, this is not a genetic disorder. It's from an accident." Looking at him with crinkled eyebrows and a perplexed look, I asked, "What genetic disorder? Everything seems to be just in the right place."

William, with a look of disbelief, asked, "Didn't you noticed my toe?" "Your toe?" I responded. "No, I was concentrating on other parts. I didn't look at your toe." He laughingly pointed to his foot, and as I took a closer look, I noticed that the top portions of his big toe and pointer toe were missing. I softly grabbed his toes, teasingly shaking them, and asked, "Wow, what happened to these pigs?"

He fell back onto the bed, laughing, and as I climbed on top of him, he began to explain, "Ah, I was about twelve, working with my dad, unloading a soda truck when my foot got stuck under the lift and was crushed." "*Oh* God, that was horrible. Couldn't they put it back together?" "Nah, it was too badly mangled." William, while laughing, continued, "The doctor told me not to worry, that it would grow back. It didn't affect me too much, except I had to readjust going up the stairs. For a while, I kept slipping."

I spontaneously hugged and kissed him to show that I felt sorry, noticing that he enjoyed that as much as the sex. Those emotions frightened me, and without my knowledge, my own hand reached inside myself, removing my melting heart, tossing it back into my internal frozen pond, refusing to let me love.

We dated in much the same fashion for no more than three months. Enjoying his attention and sexual appetite, I was becoming frightened whenever I sensed he wanted more than this friendly causal affair. I didn't realize how serious he considered our relationship until we were having dinner at my mother's home and he ever so gently slipped a small box containing an Irish claddagh ring into the palm of my hand. I opened the box, staring at this strange ring, not knowing what to make of it, not understanding the significance of it at all.

I merely thought that it was a friendly gift, thanking him, and placed it on my finger. William didn't hesitate to quickly remove the ring from my finger, explaining that I had it on the wrong way, and proceeded to adjust the ring with the heart pointing toward me. He continued to explain the sentiment attached to the ring, saying, "Phil, you wear the ring this way. It means your heart is taken." I sat speechless, thinking, *Oh my god, I didn't want this. I'm not ready for this. I just want to fool around and have fun.* Not knowing what to say, I avoided eye contact with William and decided that it was best not to discuss the matter any further.

In June, William told me that he was going to Ireland for a few weeks for his sister's wedding and that he had given serious thought to taking me to meet his family. As was William's custom, he never asked but told me what he planned on doing with my life, and as was my custom, I gave it little thought, secure in my resolve to live life by my own rules. We briefly discussed the matter with William telling me, "I really want to take you to the wedding, but so many people are staying in my mother's home. I don't think you'll be comfortable."

Not ready to meet his family, I quickly responded, "Oh, no, don't worry about me. Just go and enjoy your family." I felt relieved and didn't give the matter a second thought. As heartless as this may sound, I didn't care about William being away, wanting only to live life without the burden of a serious relationship. I was unaware that the winds of destiny were blowing me into a new encounter that would change my life forever.

Grammar School Graduation
St. Pius V Grammar School
Bronx, New York

My High School Photo
Aquinas High School
Bronx, New York

Two Bronx Sisters

Birthday cake from my first love

19 and ready to be a bride

A Young bride with her dad

A Young Bride with her family

Just married and ready for my honeymoon

Honeymoon Fun

Young Bride busy with homework

A young wife feeling like Julia Childs

Happy young wife

Joe's wedding day

PART 3

PART 2

Chapter 1

How I Met Your Father

It must have been destiny that I decided to work instead of taking my usual July vacation that year. I had taken a July vacation since 1980, when I started to work for the New York City Board of Education as a nutritionist. That year, a colleague asked if I would take care of her favorite school while she was on vacation. I agreed and, a few weeks later, at 7:00 a.m., rang the doorbell to that school.

I rang the bell, expecting the custodian to open the door; I rang a second time without any success. I waited on the front steps for my colleague to arrive and start the process of handing over all the information for summer work. She arrived, and I informed her that the school was locked. With a puzzled look on her face, she rang the bell, but no one answered.

She quickly assured me that this was very unusual and that something serious must have happened to Pete; he was always on time and such a great person to work with. Together, we both waited on the steps. The kitchen staff arrived along with the principal, and we all waited on the steps. The children arrived, expecting a warm breakfast before classes, but stood in line, waiting to enter the locked school.

After an hour of waiting, I became very irritated, telling my colleague that this was not what I expected and if it happened again, I would not hesitate to inform the superintendent of schools. She again explained that this was extremely unusual and was now concerned that something very serious must have happened to Pete, the custodian.

Finally, he arrived from the back alley of the school, and with one look at him, I realized that the only serious thing that had occurred was a night-long party. His eyes were bloodshot, and he looked exhausted. I couldn't believe it; he very calmly stated, "Why didn't someone ring the doorbell? I was inside waiting." I caught him glancing at me from the corners of his eyes, and even though they were bloodshot, I noticed how beautifully blue they were.

I thought, *Great, just my luck, I'm stuck with this wiseass savage to work with. That's what I get for being nice.* For the next few days, I worked at other schools, dreading the thought of having to go back and deal with the wiseass. Finally, I had to go back. On my next visit, the doors were open; I walked in with a briefcase in hand, vowing to myself to make the best of it.

As usual, I said good morning to the staff and jumped right in to work, checking inventory, payroll, and orders. I was asking the cook questions about staff hours when who came strolling in but the wiseass custodian.

Not only did he walk into the kitchen with coal-dusted clothes, hands, and face but he had the nerve to pour himself a cup of coffee. For a few seconds, I just stood there in shock. I finally gathered my thoughts, asking the cook, "What is going on? You know only kitchen staff in proper clean uniforms are allowed in kitchen."

Giggling, she made light of the situation, saying, "Oh, we only allow this for the summer, and everyone from the principal down *loves* Pete." As I stood there listening to her excuses, he casually walked over, asking me my name. Of course, I responded with "Ms. Abys." I saw a devilish spark in his eyes and a smirk under his mustache. "*No*, what's your first name?"

I took deep breath, thinking, *The balls on this guy . . . who does he think he is?* I suggested he call me Ms. Abys but, without taking another breath, gave him my first name. I was shocked at myself, and he, with a wide smile, said, "Great, I'm Peter Smith. If you need anything, let me know." As he started to walk away, I had to admit he was a good-looking wiseass.

I spent the rest of that day making sure every last detail of my work was taken care of. I had always taken great pride in my profession, and my reputation followed me. Everyone knew I was strict on sanitation, organization, and honesty. I refused to let this summer put a dent in my reputation.

For the following three days, I worked at other schools and cursed myself for changing my vacation. I didn't need any more complications in my life, and my gut feeling told me different. On the next visit to the wiseass's school, the door was open and the kitchen was unlocked, with Mr. Smith sitting on the stainless steel kitchen counter, having his cup of coffee.

I was furious; he was blackened by coal dust from head to toe. There he sat, sipping his coffee and swinging his legs. On top of that, I felt his eyes glaring at me, almost beckoning me to say something. I refused to play his game, not paying him any attention. I told myself, *This is only a summer assignment. Let someone else deal with this savage.* He may have everyone in the school wrapped around his pinky, but not me.

That same day, as I sat having my lunch, I felt him slip onto the bench next to me. His face and hands were semi-clean, and a smell of cologne mixed with his sweat filled my nostrils. Those blue eyes pierced me as he nonchalantly said, "I hear you're Italian. I bet you like growing tomatoes."

In any other situation, I probably would have been highly insulted, thinking, *What an ass! Just because I'm Italian, he thinks I like growing tomatoes.* His matter-of-fact manner made me laugh instead, and I admitted to enjoying gardening.

He smiled back, asking, "Would you like to see great-looking tomatoes? I'm growing some on the rooftop of this school." I laughed out loud, asking him, "Is this a joke? Don't you have a better pickup line?"

Peter, with a devilish smile, ever so softly responded, "I'm not kidding. Come and take a look." For a few brief minutes, while smiling at him, I contemplated the invitation. I always considered myself a professional at work. Was I willing to give that up? What would the staff think?

I'm not sure why I agreed, but there I was, climbing the six flights of stairs to view this guy's tomatoes. As he climbed ahead, his male scent filled my female senses. He reached back, offering his hand in help, and immediately as I held his hand, I felt the sexual energy pass through us. I knew exactly why I was climbing those stairs, tomatoes or no tomatoes.

I was pleasantly surprised when he pushed open the door to the roof. There, in the bright sunshine, stood several compound buckets growing great-looking tomatoes. I placed a hand over my mouth, laughing and blurting out, "I can't believe it! I've never seen tomatoes grown in buckets before." Again, with that devilish smile, he softly said, "See? I wasn't lying."

It was beautiful on top of that roof; the view was clear, and the sky blue. As we both took a few deep breaths of air and chatted for a while, I felt completely comfortable and safe. I casually mentioned that it was getting breezy, and he offhandedly stated, with a smile on his lips and that devilish look in his eyes, "Yeah, when the wind blows, my dick gets hard." With any other man, I would have felt threatened and insulted, but not with this guy. I sensed a kind soul behind the tough-guy facade. I gave the proper response, "We should be getting back to work. We're on Board of Ed time." I bit my tongue, telling myself, *Don't you dare say what you're truly thinking—"Well then, let's have a look."*

As I turned toward the stairs, our eyes met; at that very instance, I was certain that it was going to be a very hot complicated summer. My next thought was what to do with William, my possessive Irish boyfriend, who was visiting his family in Ireland.

Chapter 2

Sex in Southold

After our rooftop rendezvous, I found myself scheduling more time at Peter's school. Whenever I was there, we had coffee, had lunch, and laughed so often together that the staff teased me with comments like "Old Pete, he sure sweet on you. He's like bees to honey when you're around." I smiled back and admitted that we were very fond of each other. They always answered with "*Uh-huh.*" I told myself to stop acting like a silly high school girl and worked out harder than ever, I guess to bring my female senses into order.

He again slipped onto the bench next to me, and immediately, I felt our sexual energies flow together. His devilish smile and the sparkle in his eyes drew me to him.

"Hi there, Ms. Abys, how's it going?"

"OK."

"Can I ask you a personal question?"

"Sure."

"Are you married? I didn't notice a ring on your finger."

"No, I'm not anymore. I'm divorced."

"Are you in a serious relationship with anyone?"

"No, not really. I do date someone."

"Great, that's what I wanted to hear. So then, why don't you come out to Southold, Long Island, with me? My family has a summer home there, and I think you'll like it."

"Sounds nice. What day are you going?"

"No, not for the day, for the weekend. It's too far for just one day."

"Oh! I don't know. I hardly know you well enough."

"I'm not going to rape you. You can have your own room. You don't have to sleep with me, if that's what you're thinking."

The simple thought made my heart beat out of control. I gave it a thought for no more than a minute, saying, "OK, sounds like fun, if I have my own room."

"No problem, don't worry."

We decided to meet on Friday after work at the back of the school, away from peering eyes. I wanted to maintain some level of the professionalism, which I was quickly losing.

Every day, I anticipated our weekend together, imagining what it would feel like to be wrapped in his arms. That Friday, precisely at three, we met. "Great, Phil, let's get the hell out of the city. Would you mind if I drive? I know the road, and it would be quicker." I scooted over, and he took over; I was happy not to drive. I listened to Phil Collins, while he talked nonstop; I sensed he was nervous.

In about two hours, we arrived at a quaint home within walking distance of the beach and marina. True to his word, he picked up my bags and set them in a separate bedroom. "OK, this is your room. I'll stay in this room. Is that OK with you?" "This is great, Pete. This is really nice." Not sure if I was glad or disappointed at the separation.

We changed and went for a walk on the beach, and as we talked, I was very disappointed that he didn't even try to hold my hand. I thought, *This is OK. It's nice. We'll just be friends.* We went out for dinner; spent some time in the backyard, watching the stars; and finally, I just said, "I'm tired. I'm going to bed." "Yeah, let's get some shut-eye. Tomorrow, I'll take you for a ride on the boat." I tossed and turned in that bed all night, cursing myself for not being able to sleep. I knew why and hoped he was tossing and turning as well.

We woke up early and walked to the marina; this time, he was holding my hand, and I sensed he had spent a night of feeling very uncomfortable.

Once I saw him hop on to this tugboat, I hesitated, saying, "Pete, is that thing safe?"

He started to laugh. "Yeah, it's safe. I know it's not what you expected, but I've caught a lot of fish on this tug, and it's safe. I wouldn't put you on it if I thought different."

I stepped on board and asked, "Where are the seats?"

He smiled with that devilish smile. "Phil, you don't sit. You stand, you drink, and you fish. By the way, that's where I was the day I was late in opening the school. Technically, I wasn't late. I had been out all weekend—you know, fishing, drinking, and driving back to the school—that when I got there, I fell asleep."

I didn't say anything. I was having a good time and didn't want to spoil it with heavy conversation.

"Pete, it's really beautiful out here."

"Yeah, I've been coming out here for years."

As I watched the shoreline, he seemed to be watching the bathing suit I was wearing or, should I say, the lack of bathing suit. A yellow and black tiger-striped one-piece with a back so low it went down to my behind, zippers on both sides that went all the way up to the underarms. I was so very much enjoying his stares.

"Where are we going?"

"To Goose Creek. It's not too far. Have you ever steered a boat before?"

"No."

"Come over. I'll show you how."

I stood in front of him, and his arms wrapped around me with his hands steadily holding my hands over the wheel. "See? It's not difficult."

"Phil, do those zippers really work?"

"Yes, they do." I simultaneously opened up the sides, revealing most of my behind. "I hope you like the view."

He took a few steps back, staring for a few seconds, responding, "Looks great from back here."

"I'm glad you like it." He held me even closer, and with every thump and bump of the waves, I was enjoying the ride more and more. He occasionally let go of one hand from the wheel, caressing my waist, hips, and behind. I felt as if I was about to explode.

If the weather had not changed so quickly, I'm not sure what would have taken place. The water suddenly became so choppy that waves started to come over the sides.

"Phil, move over. Let me take the wheel." I saw the concern on his face as he steered the boat around, heading for the marina.

"Pete, can you get this thing back to the marina?"

As the cold waves hit my body, he noticed how scared I was and reassured me with a smile and by saying, "Phil, don't worry. I've done this a hundred times. We're only a few minutes from shore."

I became so frightened that I started to explain how on my voyage to the United States, a number of serious storms battered the ship and how I was afraid of deep water. With him still focused on steering the boat, he continued to comfort me with his words. "Umm, that must have been terrible. Don't worry, we're almost there."

By the time we reached the marina, we were completely soaked, and I was shaking. Was I shaking from fear, the cold water hitting my body, or the sexual desire he had aroused in me? I'm not sure. As soon as we stepped off the boat, he wrapped a towel around me, gave me a bear hug with both hands on my bottom, asking,

"Were you scared?"

"Yes. I was very scared."

He felt me shaking. "Come on, let's get out of these wet clothes and have lunch."

He held my hand as we walked home, while asking, "Now tell me again what happened on your trip to the US." I didn't know it then, but I was starting to fall in love.

We had lunch in Greenport, and I shopped at one of the many antique shops. I noticed how he watched me analyze every piece I picked up and asked,

"Phil, are you always so fussy?"

"Yeah kind of, I never buy anything unless I can visualize it in a space in my home. It doesn't make sense to just buy."

"You're sure different than any other chick I've been with, and as for me, I throw any old crap around." He made me laugh out loud, and his matter-of-fact, this-is-how-I-am attitude made me like him more.

As we started to drive back to the house, he said, "Phil, tonight, I'll cook for you. You know, I can cook. Can you?" Since I didn't know what level of culinary expertise he was referring to, I just said, "Oh, I can put a meal together." We stopped at a supermarket that I was not impressed with, where he purchased chicken and tomatoes.

While I sat in the kitchen, ready to watch his culinary magic, he suggested that I sit outside in the backyard and just relax; proudly telling me he had it all under control in there. I didn't understand what was there to control; there really wasn't much to do. As I started to walk out, he asked me, "Wait a minute. I have a shirt I'd like to give you. It doesn't fit me. Maybe you can use it." He handed me a very flowery Hawaiian shirt that I really liked. "Thanks, Pete, this is really nice to hang out in." I went into the bedroom and removed all of my clothes, putting on only a knitted bikini bottom with the shirt over it.

I sat on a lounge chair in the sunshine with sunglasses on, legs slightly apart, hoping he would forget about the damn chicken and take care of me. After what seemed to me like hours, I felt so restless and irritable that I sprang up and walked into the kitchen.

"Phil, go relax. I'm fine in here." I watched as he pulled chicken parts out of the package and just had to ask,

"You're planning on washing and spicing that chicken?"

He seemed a little annoyed, replying, "Phil, I know how to cook."

I thought, *Fine, let him play at being chef. I'll just go outside and stretch my muscles out.*

I went into the bedroom, removed the shirt, and pulled on terry cloth shorts. The shorts were so short that they came up to only my crotch. On my upper body, just a sports bar. In the sunshine, on the garden deck, with Kenny G music playing, I started the stretch routine that I had being doing for years.

The stretch routine had so many forward straddles and legs-spread-wide-over-the-head positions that a blind man could have seen my most intimate assets. I was ending with deep breathing when from behind, I heard

"Jesus, Phil, I haven't seen a girl do that since high school."

I turned around, and there he stood in the doorway with a plate full of raw chicken ready to grill. "Oh, I didn't know you were watching." I was so very happy he had.

"Where did you learn to do that?"

"Some in dancing school, most on my own with the help of yoga book."

"You must be in really good shape."

"I guess so. I work out and teach at a gym at least five days a week."

His smile told me he had enjoyed the stretch more than I had. While the chicken sizzled on the grill, he started to make a tomato salad with oil and sugar. I was shocked, and although I thought better not to ask, my curiosity got the best of me.

"Why are you putting sugar in the salad?"

"To make it a little sweeter. Why, don't you do that?"

"No, not at all. I just add olive oil, fresh basil, a little salt, maybe oregano and ice cubes."

"Ice cubes, what for?"

"It chills the tomatoes and makes a dressing to pour over *frezzile*."

"Over what?"

"*Frezzile*, it's this hard Italian round cracker."

"Oh yeah, I've seen them in the Italian delis. I always wondered what they were for."

I was truly touched that he was trying to please me, telling myself that, somehow, I needed to get that chicken down. I ate and told him how good it was, wondering if I would ever cook for him. We stayed in that night just watching TV—with him sitting on the couch, me laying down with my head on his chest, his arm around me. I felt so comfortable with him, as if I had known him for years. My thoughts as I snuggled were *Wow! This is nice. Just being friends is really nice.* After a long while, I started to fall asleep, deciding that it was best to go to my room. Peter simply said, "OK, good night, see you in the morning."

I tossed and turned in bed again, cursing myself for not being able to sleep. How long did I toss? I'm not sure.

I tossed until the door opened, and he stood in the doorway. I heard his voice softly saying, "I'm going to bed with you tonight."

I reached out for him. As he slipped into bed with me, I wrapped my arms around him, "Peter I was wondering what was taking you so long."

"I didn't want you to think that this was just about sex. It's not like that with you."

My palm caressed his cheek as I whispered, "I know."

The morning came much too soon, with Peter deciding that we should go for a swim before heading back to the city.

We walked hand in hand to the marina with Peter suggesting, "Come on, let's jump off the pier."

I instantly replied, "No, Pete, I'm not a good swimmer, and I'm afraid of deep water."

He pulled me closer, "Don't worry Phil, I'll be with you. I won't let anything happen to you."

I pulled my hand out of his, backing away from the pier. "No, I'm happy sitting here. You go ahead."

"OK, see you in a bit." And he dove in.

I only saw him for a few brief seconds, and then he vanished. After a few minutes and in a bit of a panic, I started to call his name until he came quietly from behind, grabbing me in his arms. I yelled, "You crazy SOB! First, you almost drown me, and now you're trying to scare me to death."

Laughing, he spun me around. "Come on, admit it. You like me just a bit." I had to honestly admit, "*No*, much more than a bit." His kisses sent flames of passion through me.

We quietly drove home, and the nervousness he had on the drive there was gone. We reached his apartment, and after sweet good-night kisses, I drove home. As I drove, I prayed that no one would call me that night. I just wanted to enjoy the memories of the weekend.

I hadn't even turned the key in the lock when the phone began to ring. At first, I refused to pick up, and then I thought, *Maybe it's my mother*, and I don't want her to worry. In frustration, I lifted the receiver.

"I've been calling you all weekend. Where have you been?"
"*Oh*! Hi, how's it going?"
"Where were you?"
"I went away for the weekend."
"With who?"
"A friend."
"A male friend?"

I guess I could have lied but felt William didn't have any right to even ask. Slightly annoyed, I said, "Yes, a male friend."

"What! I leave for my sister's wedding, and you're out with another man."

"Look, William, we've only been dating for a few months, and we don't have a commitment to each other." He was trying to keep his voice low so that other family members could not hear, but his voice was very loud with assumptions.

"That's not the way I see it."

My voice was getting louder; I didn't need to worry about anyone hearing me. "Well, that's the way it is."

"Thanks, Phil. Thanks for ruining my sister's wedding for me."

He continued, "As soon as I get back, we're going to talk about this."

I thought, *Who the fuck does he think he is?* and slammed down the receiver.

Chapter 3

Irish Diplomacy

I slept very fretfully that night. William's phone call had ruined the end of a wonderful weekend. Only thinking of seeing Peter again made me happy. On Monday morning, I stopped at his school first; it was the closest to my home, and I needed to pick up all the paperwork for the office. I entered the kitchen, seeing Peter; he was having coffee with Jeanie, the cook.

With a wide smile, he said, "Good morning, Ms. Abys. Did you have a good weekend?" "Good morning, Peter. I had a very good weekend. How was yours?"

With even a bigger smile, he replied, "Great. Just great."

I turned away from him, trying not to blush, and spoke to the cook. "Jeanie, I need the weekly paperwork for the office."

Her smile told me she knew something. "You wait right there. I'll get it for you."

After she walked away, I asked Peter, "Did you tell her I spent the weekend with you?" "No, Phil, but she's sharp, and she knows we're good friends. It's not a big deal. We didn't commit a crime."

"I know, but I just don't like my personal business interfering with my work."

"You're too uptight about work. Relax. I'll see you later."

"I'm working late tonight at the gym."

"OK, I'll call you later." He brushed his hand against my arm, sending heat waves through my spine, and went to work.

Jeanie returned with the paperwork, "Here you go everything is in order." Her smile told me she knew that Peter and I were more than just friends.

"Thanks, Jeanie. If you need me, just call."

"OK, no problem."

I went to the gym after work, teaching classes until nine. I should have been exhausted but was only looking forward to Peter's call. As soon as I got through the door, the phone rang. I hesitated, not knowing for sure who it was. I mentally spoke to myself, *Please don't let it be William.*

"Hi, you're finally home."
"Hi, William. How's it going?"
"You worked late at the gym?"
"Yes, I'm really tired. I need to take a shower."
"All right, I'll be home soon, and we can get together and talk."

I hung up, thinking of how I could tell William that I really wasn't ready for a serious relationship and wanted to also date someone else.

After my shower, as I lay in bed, feeling clean and comfortable, Peter called, his voice putting a smile on my tired face.

"Hey, workout queen, did you knock them dead?"
"Yeah."
"You sound tired, Phil."
"Yes, I am." And then I fumbled for words.
"What's wrong? Are you OK?"
"I'm fine. It's just that the other fellow I was seeing is kind of possessive, and I don't know—"
Peter stopped me in midsentence. "Is he hassling you?"
"No, not really. He's very good to me. He just thinks the relationship is more than it is."
"Oh, I see. You know what? Get some rest, and when you come in to work tomorrow, we'll talk about it."
"Thanks, Pete. Good night."

I placed my head on the pillow, drifting into sleep, thinking of how pleasant Peter's personality was compared to William's.

We were both busy with work that morning, and I didn't see Peter until he slipped onto the bench next to me at lunchtime.

"Come on, let's go out for a walk."
"Pete. We're working. We just can't leave and go walking."

"You're entitled to lunch, aren't you?"

"Yes, but I never leave the school."

"This is a good time to start." He took me by the hand and gently pulled me off the bench.

"Jeanie, if anyone calls for Ms. Abys, tell them she having lunch and to call back later."

"Pete, I never do that."

"There's a first time for everything. Come on, let's get out of here."

We walked up the hill to White Plains Road, and as usual, the streets were busy with shoppers. I had completely forgotten about our conversation from the previous night, but he had not.

"So, Phil, tell me what's the problem with this other guy you're seeing. He's not pushing you around or anything like that?"

"No, no. He's very kind, but I think he wants a more serious relationship and didn't like the idea of me spending the weekend with you."

"Well, it's just too fucking bad about him."

I immediately saw a change in his usual mellow behavior; it made me nervous.

"Where did you meet this guy?"

"Through a college friend that I now work with. He's her daughter's godfather. He's in Ireland for a few weeks for his sister's wedding."

"Jesus, Phil, a fucking donkey from the other side. God, they're the worst kind."

"Pete, you're Irish."

"I'm an American."

"If he gives you any trouble, just let me know." We left the conversation at that.

The avenue was bustling; the once mostly Italian neighborhood—now mostly Jamaican—reminded me of my days in the South Bronx. I enjoyed the vibration of life, the hustle and bustle of the markets. We browsed, and he noticed that I had picked up a coconut.

"You like fresh coconut?"

"I love fresh coconut. They remind me of my childhood days in Naples."

He took it and bought it for me. "You ate a lot of coconut in Italy?"

"Mostly on the beach after we had lunch. My dad bought fresh coconut slices from the vendors for us to snack on."

"Your parents are still here in the US, or did they go back to Italy?"

"My mom lives here in the Bronx. My dad passed away many years ago."

"Sorry, Phil, was he very sick?"

He sensed my hesitation and stood still.

"No, he wasn't sick. He was shot in a holdup in his shop."

"Oh God, I'm so sorry," and he reached for my hand.

"We're all OK now. It happened a long time ago." The look on his face told me that he felt truly sorry for me.

He started to talk about his parents, and the bitterness in his voice filled his being like thick overflowing bile. "My parents are in the middle of a messy divorce. My father fucked around on my mother for years, and she drank, I guess to ease the pain. They should have gotten divorced when I was very young."

He sighed, continuing, "Instead, they did the good Irish Catholic bullshit, sticking it out while having two more kids and making everyone miserable."

I saw the intense tension in his jaw, and my heart started to ache for him. I didn't say much, not knowing what to say to comfort him.

"How many children did your parents have?"

"Six."

"Wow, that's a lot to handle," and left it at that.

We started to walk back to the school, passing a seedy, dirty-looking bar. Peter shocked me by stopping right in front, turning to me, placing both hands on my arms, and telling me, "Wait right here. No one is going to bother you here," and went inside. I guess he thought I would be afraid of standing outside by myself in a less-than-upscale neighborhood. He didn't know that I had spent so much time in the South Bronx maneuvering out of danger that this was like a walk in Disney World. I was touched by his display of protectiveness.

I waited for a few minutes and then started to get annoyed, deciding to walk back alone. I was just about to start walking when he came out and noticed how annoyed I was.

"Phil, I didn't go in there to have a drink or anything like that."

"What the hell were you doing in that place?"

"Oh! Putting in the numbers."

"Are you crazy! The illegal numbers? For who?"

"The school."

"The whole school plays the numbers?"

"Yeah, just about."

"My staff is playing the numbers while working?"

"Well, technically, I am . . . come on, Phil, don't be so annoyed. It's not a big deal."

We walked in silence for a while, and then he grabbed for my hand, asking, "Have you always been so straight?"

"What do you mean straight?"

"Well, let's see—you don't smoke, don't drink, don't do drugs, or gamble. That's called being very straight."

"So now you're making fun of me for living, as you call it, 'straight'?"

Peter wrapped his arm around my waist pulling me closer. "No, Phil, not at all. That's why I like you so much. You're the only straight, well-balanced chick I've ever met. You definitely have your shit together."

We continued to walk in silence.

We entered the kitchen, and without me asking, Jeanie said, "Nope, no one called." "Jeanie, can you crack open this coconut for Ms. Abys. She loves coconut. It reminds her of her childhood in Italy." Jeanie, with a broad smile, responded, "Sure enough."

Great, I thought, *now he's running my kitchen*. I had never seen anyone open a coconut as quickly as she did.

"Jeanie, that's the fastest I ever seen anyone do that."

"Done a lot of this in South Carolina. We eat lots of fruits and vegetables, just like Italians."

I had to smile telling her, "I know. We both like fresh home-cooked food."

"Ms. Abys, there's nothing better."

I asked her to put the slices into a bowl of ice water along with the coconut milk so that it stayed fresh for everyone to snack on.

"Just like we do in South Carolina."

I rubbed her back to show gratitude and connection. Her smile warmed my heart.

The coconut was really delicious, and as I stood looking out over the counters, munching on a piece, Peter came so close behind me that I felt his breath on my neck.

"Ms. Abys, is the coconut to your liking?"
"It's really good."

Without thinking, I spun around and put the piece in his mouth. My fingers lingered in his mouth too long, and his stare gave us away. With a devilish look in his eyes, he whispered,

"It really is good, especially from you."

How long did we stare at each other? I'm not sure, probably too long. The staff pretended to be busy at work, but who was I fooling? They all knew.

How to Crack Open a Tasty Coconut

I still cannot believe that was Peter's first taste of a fresh coconut. No wonder he enjoyed it so much, and he has been cracking and eating fresh coconut since that day.

Tools you will need to crack open a fresh coconut: a hammer, a screwdriver or corkscrew, a sharp paring knife, and a vegetable peeler. Wash the outside of the coconut, place a thick dish towel on your kitchen counter, and place the coconut on top of the towel. Be careful, and insert the screwdriver or corkscrew in the eyes of the coconut, hitting the object hard enough to make a hole in each eye. Pour coconut water through a sieve into a bowl, set aside. Carefully hit the middle of the coconut hard enough to break it in half, hit each half with the hammer into smaller pieces. Insert the paring knife in between the white pulp and the hard shell, maneuvering the knife to loosen coconut meat. Rinse the pieces under cold water, removing any fibers. Place them in the bowl with the coconut milk, and add more cold water to cover the tops of coconut pieces. You may use a vegetable peeler to remove the dark skin from the coconut meat, just like peeling a potato.

The easiest and tastiest recipe to enjoy fresh coconut is by melting semisweet chocolate into a bowl and dipping by hand bite-size pieces of coconut into the melted chocolate. Slowly place these chocolate-dripping coconut pieces into your husband's mouth, allowing the fingers to linger for no more than two to three minutes. When other senses are aroused, push the coconut aside and carefully take care of the hard issues at hand. Works like a charm.

Chapter 4

Mistaken Commitment

While William was away, I didn't see any reason not to enjoy Peter's company. We didn't have a commitment to each other, and I refused to be forced into a serious relationship. I had spent too much of my life in one and, for the present, only wanted to savor the pleasures of single life.

While with Peter, we continued our playful sexual charade at work. The conversation usually started early in the morning when we had coffee. "Good morning, Ms. Abys." "Good morning, Mr. Smith," and we smile and stare at each other with sexual anticipation.

In the evening, we go out to the movies and for dinner, ending the night at my apartment. There was no hesitation, and he approached me with such sexual hunger that at times I was worried the neighbors would hear and call the police. I would always ask him to leave after the lovemaking, and I saw that he was becoming annoyed.

"Jesus, Phil, talk about making a guy feel bad. First, you screw my brains out and then ask me to leave. It's usually the other way around." I felt that we were getting too emotionally involved, and that feeling made me very uncomfortable. I would give him the excuse that we both had to work early and that it was better this way. In reality, I was afraid of the commitment that I knew he too wanted. I hadn't received my final divorce papers yet and knew I needed time to myself, without the responsibilities a serious relationship required (in plain old Bronx English, "just to fuck around"). The problem for me was that both lovers wanted it to be serious.

William didn't even ask if he could come over. He just came over, and I thanked God Peter was not around.

"Hey, I didn't know you were coming. You didn't call." I think he wanted to see if anyone else was there and take care of the matter in his own way.

174

"Hi, you look good, Phil", placing a bag full of gifts in the living room and holding my face in his hands, while softly kissed me.

My body didn't react as before, and I wondered if he noticed. He sat on the love seat as if he owned the place; I hadn't even asked him to come in. I sat across from him on the sofa.

"How was your trip? Was the wedding nice?"

"Phil, who's this fuck you're seeing?"

I just defiantly looked at him and didn't answer.

"I asked you a question."

Now he was getting me annoyed. "And I'm not answering. It's none of your business."

"What!"

"This is not the type of relationship I want. This is not what I expected from you."

I clearly saw the hurt in his eyes, and the anger in his voice frightened me.

"Look, William, I think you misunderstood the relationship. I'm not ready for such a serious commitment."

"Did you go to bed with that fuck?"

Now I was starting to get furious. I got up, stood right in his face, and yelled, "It's none of your business!"

He didn't move, just sat there and stared at me. I sat down, trying to calm myself. We sat quietly for a few minutes, and then I tried to reason with him.

"Look, William, it's not that I don't care for you, but I'm not ready for this. I need some space. You can't demand a commitment from a person. It just happens. We're not there yet." I was hoping that maybe he would get up and tell me to fuck off. Instead, he put both elbows on his lap and placed his hands on his forehead, trying to calm himself.

"Phil, do you know what it's like for me to think of you being with another man? When you told me that you had spent the weekend with him, I sat out in the night air, drinking and getting fucked up. I had to get the thought of another man touching you out of my head. It was making me crazy. My whole family knew something was wrong. They want to meet you. I told them I'll bring you to Ireland soon. I just don't do that with anyone."

I saw the hurt in him, and my heart started to melt. "I'm sorry, William, truly sorry. I didn't mean to hurt you in any way. I'm just not ready for this. I need to live my own life for a while."

We both just sat there for a few minutes, not knowing what else to say, and then he just agreed. "OK, Phil, I understand. You're right, but don't play this man's game for too long. You're too much of a lady for that. Open up your gifts. I bought them for you."

The bag was filled with Irish crystal, teas, jellies, cookies, and cakes. I opened them and told him how beautiful it all was, thanking him. He came over and put his hands around my face and started to softly kiss me; again, my body didn't respond as it had before. I guess he had the answer to his question. We said our good-byes, and he left. I put on my Kenny G music and started to stretch.

Both lovers showered me with so much attention, friendship, and sexual desire that I could not give up one for the other. As wrong as it might have been, I felt entitled to such luxury. I had spent years caring for a sick husband, and now it was time to care for myself.

Dating both lovers would have been easier if they too only wanted to "fuck around," but both had spent their adult lives in shallow sexual affairs and were now ready for commitments. I had to navigate the affairs very carefully as I knew both were very possessive, and having to share was inflaming their male egos.

I'd go out with Peter, enjoying his easy outgoing personality, his humor, and his hunger for true friendship. When he simply touched my face and kissed my cheek, I would melt in his arms, helpless to refuse him anything.

When William came over to pick me up for dinner after I had explained that I was not ready for a serious relationship, he simply walked into my apartment, put both hands on my hips, pulling me to him, and told me, "You're going to make me lose my mind." His forceful kisses and raw male sexuality made me want him. As he started to unbutton my shirt, I realized that I could not stop him nor did I want to. He picked me up, placing me on the bed; I took one look in his eyes and knew he was in love. The combination of love, sexual desire, and possessiveness scared me.

He was always a kind, considerate lover and showered me with compliments—"Jesus, Phil, what did you do to me? I can't think of anything else but you" or "Please don't see anyone else. I can't stand the thought of another man putting his hands on you. I'm going to kill that fuck if I find out who he is." I simply ran my fingers through his auburn beard, caressed his cheeks, and whispered to him, "William, let's go for dinner. I'm starved." "OK, I'll take you anywhere you want to go."

Somewhere in the back of my being, I knew that I was wrong but felt entitled to live my life by my own terms. I guarded my emotions like prized jewels, vowing not to love either of them.

Both lovers splurged gifts and entertainment on me but knew that I did not need or require them for a relationship. Unlike most women they had dated, I had always worked and had more assets than both of them. That was one reason they probably found me so appealing in addition to having a clean, well-organized, nicely decorated home. They didn't know what I had left behind for a husband that I had to leave because my mere presence caused him physical distress. Out of love for my husband, I took the blow of leaving our beautiful home; his medical condition was enough for him to bear.

William's demanding "I'll kick anyone's ass that gets in my way" attitude worried me. This was clear one evening when we were having dinner in a place that he frequented, and everyone knew his behavior.

I sat at a table while he went to the men's room, and a fellow stared once too often. I didn't think anything of it, but when William came out of the men's room, this fellow asked him a question. With an instant reaction, William grabbed the guy by the shirt, pushing him up against the wall. I sat there motionless, wondering what the guy might have said to him to make him so upset. William said a few words to the fellow, and then he must have noticed how still I was holding on to the table and thought better of doing what he had started to do. He released his grip and pushed the fellow in the back. The fellow quickly walked away.

"William, for God's sake, what happened?"

"Ah, don't worry about that guy. He's an asshole. I didn't like the way he asked who you were. Next time I see him and you're not around, I'll remember to give him a beating."

"William, just let it go. It's not worth it. What's with the Irish anyway? I know they like to drink, fight, and fuck, but let it go."

With that, he started to howl with laughter that made me laugh. "Yeah, Phil, that's true. Not always in that order, but yeah, we do. Come on, let's eat."

Peter had a completely different personality; his charm made me melt. On his first visit to my home, his words made me feel like a queen in a palace. "Wow, Phil, now I understand why you're so fussy about what you buy." He noticed the bowl and plate I had purchased in Greenport. "Phil, that looks great there. You have really great taste. As I said before, you're a different type of chick." His personality always made me feel so comfortable, and I felt my emotions getting the best of me when I was with him. I checked them into place.

I assumed that he had developed this very diplomatic manner from working for a film production company for many years. When he first told me that he had worked on filming ads for I Love NY, Breakstone's, and Miller beer, which he himself had been in, I didn't believe him. "Pete, I don't believe you. You're full of it." "Phil, you never believe anything I say. Tomorrow, I'll show you photos." True to his word again, he handed me a photo album filled with pictures of him with top models like Christie Brinkley, Cheryl Tiegs, Jerry Hall, as well as other TV personalities.

"*Wow*! Pete, I can't believe it. Why did you leave?"

"I usually worked twelve-hour days and then partied all night. That life was going to kill me. I got fed up and left."

As I thumbed through the photo album, I saw a photo of him on a NASCAR car with a big smile, holding a Miller beer. "Pete, that's you! You look great."

"Yeah, the producer-director asked me if I could catch a beer while sitting on the car. I told him, 'No problem, I been catching beers most of my life' and made the commercial. It aired for a while, and I made money from it, but as usual, I pissed it away. If I had a penny for every dollar I wasted on drinking and useless women, I'd be a millionaire."

"Well, you seem to very friendly with . . ." and I pointed to different women he was with. His smile gave him away as to what went on. "Yeah, she was nice. That one, not bad." I got a bit jealous and gave him a shove.

He started to laugh, pulling me close, softly telling me, "All these women had nothing over on you and not half as much between the ears."

He continued, "You're just as beautiful and smarter than all of them." I never felt so special.

Although Peter pretended to have a mellow, nonaggressive attitude, I felt for sure that that was not so. I noticed how quickly his personality changed when we had gone to the Halloween parade in New York City, and if any unsavory person approached us, his attitude quickly changed. When I wasn't able to see the parade over other people's heads, he simply picked me up with one hand bringing me over his head and onto his shoulder.

"Pete, you're crazy. I'm too heavy."

"Jesus, Phil! I picked up bags of flour heavier then you. Don't worry." He held me on his shoulder for a good portion of the parade until I insisted he put me down.

We had dinner at Pete's Tavern before the parade, and while I ate a hearty steak dinner, he was having trouble finishing his veal.

"What's wrong, Pete? Don't you like your meal?"

"Ah, no, it's OK, but, ah, I was out the night before, and well, it was a rough night." I didn't think he had been playing bingo and left it at that.

When I mentioned that I was in the mood for something sweet, he drove to City Island to my favorite dessert cafe for a late-night treat. I watched him staring at me, and his beautiful deep blue eyes made me ask,

"Pete, does everyone in your family have such beautiful eyes?"

"Yeah, would you like to have a baby with blue eyes?"

The remark took me completely off guard, and I had to look down. I didn't know what to say or think, but I knew his intentions were serious. We went to my apartment that night and did some serious practicing on having that blue-eyed baby.

William's intentions for me were also very obvious when he asked me to have dinner with his brother and family. I hesitated. I wasn't sure if I wanted to meet with family members and give the wrong impression as to my intentions with William. He was always persistent with whatever he wanted, and I finally agreed. We drove to his brother's home, and as soon as I saw them together, the deep affection they had for each other was clear. Unlike Italians, they didn't kiss or hug, but the simple handshake and thump of the shoulders was as loving as a kiss.

William was so unlike his brother Gavin, a soft-spoken gentleman with a very nice wife and two little boys that seemed to adore their uncle. I connected instantly with them and enjoyed watching William so playful with his nephews. On the drive back home, I asked William if he was like his dad. He replied, "Oh God, no. Gavin is just like my dad, quiet and . . ." He couldn't finish the sentence as he was searching for words. I finished it for him. "Soft-spoken and non demanding?"

He replied, "Yeah, kind of. He looks like my dad too, but don't let his easy personality fool you. I wouldn't want to piss him off. He's a tough son of bitch when he is mad and not bad with his fists. I remember when we were young teenagers, helping my mom move into another apartment, and we were fighting over who was carrying what boxes. We beat the shit out of each other all the way up the stairs until my mother came out and told us if we didn't stop fighting and start working, she was going to beat us both." I had to laugh and placed my emotions in my well-guarded vault.

We went home that night, and he made the most passionate love to me. I was starting to fall asleep in his arms as he gently stroked my hair away from my face. The phone rang, and I didn't want to pick it up but thought better of it in case my mother was calling. I always worried about her living alone.

"Hello?"

"Hey, Phil. It's Pete."

William was so close to me that he heard his voice.

"I can't talk now."

William's rage was instantaneous. "Give me that phone. Let me talk to that fuck!"

He grabbed over me to reach the phone, but I had already put down the receiver.

"Why is that fuck calling you?"

"William, we're friends. What's the big deal?"

"Friends, my ass."

"Don't make a big deal of it!"

"What!" Another man is calling you, and you think I'm not going to make a big deal of it?"

His voice now filled with such rage I started to shake. He had got out of bed and pounded on the bedroom door.

"I want you to be my wife, not my bitch. I don't want another man calling you, touching you, and if you don't stop seeing him, I swear I'll find out who he is and fucking kill him!"

His rage filled me with fear, and for a moment, I thought he was going to shake me to find out who I was seeing. He started to get dressed and pounded another fist into the bedroom door that made the house shake. "I want you to be my wife, do you understand? If I wanted just a bitch, I know where to go." I whispered so low that I don't think he even heard me in his rage. "I don't want to be a wife."

I watched him leave and walk down the path to his car from my living room window, praying that he would go home and not to a bar in such a rage. As his car drove away, I sat on the floor in my living room with my head in my hands, telling myself that I needed to explain to him that it's easier to be someone's bitch than a wife. That I had been a wife from a very young age, had spent most of my life under that burden—a burden that I was no longer willing to bear.

That in the end, I had to leave not only the comfort of my home, the comfort of a circle of dear friends, but the comfort of the only man I had been with from the age of sixteen. The comfort of a man that could no longer be my husband and that I no longer wanted to be anyone's wife.

I thought I could tell him all these things, but I knew he would not understand. I wanted to cry, but the tears did not come. I guess I had used up all my tears years ago, and my heart had been frozen from deep sorrow. I forced myself up and into the shower. I needed to wash off his scent and his sweat from me. I wanted to wash away the love I knew he had for me and the guilt that I could not return his love.

The next day, Peter called me at work, not in his usual pleasant, easygoing manner.

"Hi. Who was there, that donkey fuck?"

"Pete, I don't want to talk about it."

"Yeah, right, me neither." He slammed down the phone without saying good-bye.

Chapter 5

Male Pride

After that episode, I told myself not to see either of them. It wasn't worth the stress, and I was afraid someone would get hurt. For weeks, I went to work, exercised to the point of exhaustion, and occasionally went out only with my female friends. My female friends encouraged me to date other men. I listen to their advice, dating an attorney twice. His conversations were so boring that I nearly fell asleep at dinner. I had the attention of my mother's doctor, and he even asked me to work for him, which I tried for a few months. His secretary, in confidence, told me that he was a very wealthy man and that the reason he asked me to work for him was that he really liked me.

I thought of this not bad-looking man, who was well over six foot tall, using such an unmanly excuse to be with me instead of just asking for a date. I pictured him trying to make love to me with his medical journals in hand for instructions. I didn't care about his money or status; I never worked for him again. I dated the director of the hiking group I belonged to, and his calculating personality made me cringe when he even touched my hand.

I also realized that each lover had found out who the other was. That thought scared me more than anything as I had affection for both. When I explained to Peter that William knew who he was and that I was nervous, he responded in a sarcastic way. "Yeah, I'm really worried. I'll fuck him up, and by the way, I know who he is. If that donkey pushes you around, let me know. I'll take care of it." "Pete, he's not like that."

The difference between Peter and William was that Peter never demanded I stop seeing William. He would just say, "I understand you're not ready for a commitment" and suffered in silence. William, on the other hand, was very clear about what he wanted. "Phil, if you don't stop seeing that fuck—I know who he is—I'm going to give him the beating of his life." I yelled back, "Don't tell me how to live my life!"

All the while, I still spoke to both lovers often but refused to see either of them. I needed to get away, far away from everyone. I decided to take a trip to Yellowstone Park with my family. I was sure that the distance, physical activity, and beautiful landscapes would cure me of my unbalanced emotions.

I was packing for the trip when Peter called, his voice filled with physical pain and emotional stress. "Hi, Phil, can you come over for a while? I fell down the stairs at work and hurt my back. I need your help." I stood with the receiver in my hand, not knowing what to say, not wanting to give of myself to anyone. I didn't want to start melting for him as I always had. I didn't want to be in a relationship that required so much effort.

"I can't. I'm leaving for Yellowstone Park. I'm sorry, Peter. I just can't come over." I put down the receiver, wanting to put my head through the wall; maybe that would erase him from my mind. I didn't realize that he had already entered my frozen heart.

While I hiked, toured, and absorbed the beauty of Yellowstone, I made the decision to only see one lover. I was so concerned that one would hurt the other and knew I was being completely selfish. Why did I decide to continue to see William and not Peter? I enjoyed Peter's company so much more than William's; we got along so well, and when we made love, it was like hot flames swirling in unison.

It was only the bitterness that Peter felt for his family that pushed me into a commitment with William. I knew that if I made a commitment to Peter, I would one day have to deal with his family. He had never even asked me to meet with any of them. I sensed that there was a great deal of family turmoil.

William, on the other hand, was always asking me to attend family affairs, and I saw the deep affection he had for them. Although we argued often, I felt the deep affection and passion he had for me. When we made love, both our passions burned to the boiling point. I also found William's "I want you to be only mine" attitude very appealing.

A few days after my return from Yellowstone. William asked me to have dinner with him. His demands were very clear. "I don't want you to see anyone else, do you understand? I can't stand the thought of you with someone else." "William, I know you're right. I've been a bit selfish. I just wasn't ready for a serious relationship. This time, I'm going to try. I won't see him anymore." I could see the relief on his face, and if his male pride had been a boxer, he would have raised his arms in victory. Deep in the depths of my frozen heart, a small spark had started to burn. I didn't know for whom; I only knew that I needed to try at being committed again.

Over the phone, I spoke to Peter and told him I didn't want to see him anymore. I had made my commitment to William. While I spoke, I felt my heart being ripped apart. I truly didn't want to stop seeing him. I enjoyed his company so much, but I also understood that I could no longer have them both. I felt like a little girl in her favorite candy shop being asked to only pick one piece of candy when she much preferred to have two. I wanted to reach through the phone, grab and shake Peter, while yelling at him, "For God's sake, stop being so understanding! Be more demanding. Ask me to be only yours." Peter was just too understanding; I thought, *Maybe I'm not that important to him.*

"Fine, Phil, I understand. Call me whenever you want. If anything goes wrong, I'm always here for you." Peter didn't seem that upset, just very understanding, and I felt very rejected by him but said nothing. I told myself, *Be strong. It's time to move on.*

What I didn't know was that the next phone call he had made after I refused to go over and nurse him was to a whore, who had gone over with substances for instant relief. What she offered didn't exactly have the *Good Housekeeping* seal of approval and started him on a frenzy of drinking, drugs, and whoring. He too had felt rejected by me. To this day, I still blame myself and often ask for his forgiveness. He kindly tells me, "There's no need for forgiveness. It wasn't your fault," but my heart breaks whenever I think of what he went through.

Chapter 6

Undivided Attention

William was happy for the undivided attention, and we settled into a routine of going out to movies, dinners, and shows. I even started to cook for him, which I had not done for any man since I separated from my husband. For me, this was a pivotal point in the defrosting of my heart. At first, I had to almost force myself to cook for William. As an Italian, food had been so central to my emotional makeup that in order for me to truly give myself to a man, I had to cook for him. For other women, the bedroom might have been a problem after a divorce, but not for me; I didn't have a problem there. I had to start heating up the pots in the kitchen again.

When we were home, we enjoyed our sexuality to the fullest. We both loved to listen to black soul music, and I allowed the rhythm to move my body into an enticing dance. I slowly dance for him, removing my clothing one garment at a time, while my hips swirled him into arousal. I would finally straddle him with only my panties on. William's hands slowly caressed my face down to my neck and linger over my breast until he took me with such passion that at times he frightened me.

We made love to the point of exhaustion, and as William held me in his arms, he breathlessly asked, "Where did a nice little Italian girl learn to dance like that?" I answered, "In the hood, my blue-eyed soul brother." "In the hood?" We both howled with laughter. I guess coming from the ghetto has some benefits.

I can't say the relationship was a smooth compromising one. The divide between us when it came to issues such as politics, gender, race, and religion was as wide and as deep as the Atlantic Ocean. We both had arrived in New York the same year (1961) and, as immigrants, had been toughened by hard work. I could deal somewhat with his arrogant, bigoted old-fashioned attitude but constantly mentally spared with him. The debates were never-ending, and at times I felt that the mental sparring was an arousal factor for him.

When he complained about the illegal Hispanic population, I just mentioned all the illegal Irish on McLean Avenue, further sending the point across by using an Irish saying, "What's good for the goose is good for the gander." He complained about the Jews controlling the media. I just reminded him his oldest brother was married to a Jewish girl. He quickly responded, "Yeah, well, she converted." I smirked at him, taunting him with, "You can't convert genetics or culture." It would make him crazed and aroused all at once.

He became so agitated with my skills that one evening, during dinner, he playfully slammed his hand on the table demanding to know where I had learned to debate so well. "Jesus, Phil, where did you learn to debate like that? In college?" "Nope, William, at the dinner table." "You debated with your brother?" "Not exactly. I was told to be quiet while my father and brother discussed issues. I swore that I'd never be told to be quiet in my own home." William, while laughing stated, "God, I wish your father was still alive maybe he shut you up again." I gave him a shove, putting my face right in front of his. "Well, if you're looking for a stupid piece of ass, you're in the wrong place." He pulled me closer. "Nope, just your beautiful ass." The debate sessions served other purposes outside of intellectual stimulation, and I quietly wondered if William realized that the quiet thoughts of a spouse make you more of a fool without even the pleasure of a debate. Regardless, I enjoyed his attention and knew I could never compromise enough to meet his old-fashioned expectation of a silent submissive wife.

The most infuriating remark from William came after I had prepared a cauliflower and pasta meal for him that he enjoyed. "Damn, Phil, you really know how to cook." Out of the goodness of my heart, I asked if he wanted to take some to work. "Yeah, sure, Phil. One thing I gotta say about your husband is that he trained you good."

I was in the kitchen, scooping the pasta into a Tupperware, and without thinking, I flung the bowl across the kitchen into the living room, hitting William in the back. "What the fuck is wrong with you? Are you crazy?" "You make a comment like that, and you're asking what's wrong with me? You ignorant son of a bitch!" Now I was yelling at the top of my voice and was sure the neighbors would call the police. "I was his wife, not his dog! You don't train a wife! I did everything for him out of love, and he demanded nothing!"

"Jesus, Phil, it's just an expression." I was in a complete rage, yelling, "It's an expression that shows me how you truly feel! Get the fuck out of my house!" I grabbed him by the shirt, trying to push him out the door. His laughing infuriated me even more, and as he walked out the door, he casually said, "I'll call you in a few days when you've cooled off." I yelled back, "Fuck off! Stay away from me." He laughed all the way down the stairs. I slammed the door, knowing I was stuck with cleaning up the mess.

Of course, he called in a few days, and I had cooled off. At first, I was very standoffish with him, not wanting to give in. Then he started to apologize, "Come on, Phil, let's go to dinner. I miss you." "What you miss your trained dog." "It was just an expression. I didn't mean anything by it. I miss the way you cook, in and out of the kitchen." My frozen heart was ever so slowly starting to thaw, and I gave in.

He tried so hard to please me with gifts and entertainment; I guess it was his way of securing my love and faithfulness. I don't think he understood that they were not for sale. I hoped that, eventually, he would understand that those emotions came from years of friendship, but I did enjoy the attention.

William always pretended to be a hard-ass in front of family and friends, but I saw a softer loving side of him. One day, he came home, and while pulling me into his arms softly whispered, "I have a special gift for you, soul sister," giving me tickets to a Smokey Robinson concert at Radio City. He saw the happiness on my face, and as I hugged and kissed him with a thank-you, he held me tighter, saying, "I do anything to make you happy." He also tried to keep his emotions in check and, I think, was trained from birth not to show too much outward feelings. For the Irish, this is very unmanly.

During our relationship, William became as possessive as he was passionate and felt that it was his male obligation to protect me. I found this very flattering and truly appreciated his manly display of love. On one of the many occasions I had to enter my house in Long Island that had been placed on the market for sale, William refused to let me go alone. It was unlike him to take a day off from work, but when he realized I was going alone, he didn't ask but told me, "I'm going with you. It's not safe for you to go alone." I hesitated, knowing how explosive his temper could be, and made it clear to him that if Mike was in the house, he was to stay outside.

As William drove out to Long Island, he asked, "Is your ex going to be there?" I really was not certain, telling him that Mike was not letting realtors in to view the home, and that I had to do it. William's face displayed his anger, and I started to regret having him come along. I again reminded him that if Mike was in the house, he was to stay outside and, most of all, to keep his hands to himself.

William's words didn't put me at ease but only made me more nervous. "You know, Phil, I can't believe that your brother didn't put his head through the wall. If you had been my sister, I would have given him the beating of his life for robbing you blind." I tried to explain that Mike was sick and that it didn't matter what he had taken. I further tried to explain that I had no ill feelings toward Mike, hoping that he find his own happiness. I could sense the jealousy in William when he said, "What? You're still in love with that faggot?" I just turned my head, looking out of the window, not responding, realizing that William was not comfortable being in love with a divorcée who may still have feelings for her first lover.

We entered the home, and I was relieved that Mike was not there. As we waited for the realtors to arrive, I toured the house that once had been my home with an array of emotions. I realized that regardless of how skilled Mike was with his hands, it was I that had added the touches that made a house a home. The house barely resembled the home I had left behind.

The cleanness was gone, and a strange smell gave me a queasy feeling in my stomach. I mentally spoke to myself, I *thought you had gotten over that sick feeling. I guess not.* William was unusually quiet as he followed me around the house and only surveyed the property without extending a word of comfort. I spoke to myself again, I *wonder if he realizes that you were once very happy and loved here. I wonder if he really cares.*

We climbed the stairs to the bedrooms, and as I entered the bedroom that I had slept in for years, my heart broke all over again. The brass hooks that once held matching cascading plants now held a grotesque Halloween mask, and the plants hung dry and lifeless. The sight of those dry lifeless plants that once had been so green and healthy almost made me cry. I saw shadows of myself dusting the leaves off with a wet paper towel. I had given so much of myself; now it was all as dry and lifeless as those plants. I turned to William, telling him, "You know, we didn't live this way. When I lived here, it didn't look like this." He just smirked, responding, "I didn't think you did."

We walked across the hall into the smaller bedroom, and feeling safe with William's presence, I opened the closet door that lead to the storage area. I cannot describe the shock when I saw my wedding dress that I had years earlier scrunched into the garbage can along with the lace bridal shower umbrella my aunt Vincenza had hand-made for me back in the closet.

The dress hung there like a shrine with the umbrella propped up against the wall next to the dress. My hand reached out to touch the dress I had so carefully designed, but my new self would not allow that weakness. I backed away, thinking that I should at least take the umbrella my aunt had made for me; she had put so much love and time sewing the white lace and beads. Again, I would not allow myself even that small weakness. Those were the treasures of a young naïve girl; I was anything but that now. I quickly backed out of the closet, not sure if I wanted to laugh or cry, thinking that maybe Mike loved the dress or the vision of his doll all dressed up more so than the real person; he had discarded me but kept the dress.

I stepped out of the closet, telling William what I had seen; his very cold, callous remark put it all in order for me—"He's fucking nuts."

If I had expected sympathy from William, I received none. Not a word of understanding for what I had gone through for so many years. William simply wanted to make sure that what he now wanted was safe, and later, as we drove away, he very honestly said, "I still think your brother should have given him a beating. That fuck of your ex was crazy like a fox." I turned, looking out of the window, and didn't answer.

William's final display of intention came with a very strong request that we go to Ireland for Easter. "Phil, I want you to meet my family in Ireland. They want to meet you. Let's go for two weeks during the time you have off from work." I hesitated, not sure what my feelings were for him and if we were compatible for a lifelong relationship. He sensed my hesitation but continued, "I'll pay and plan for everything. You don't need to worry about anything. I'll take you from the north to south of Ireland. We'll have fun."

He continued with a bit of a smirk on his face, "Oh, three important things you need to know: You'll be cold. Bring heavy clothes. You wouldn't like the food. It's not like yours; and we can't sleep together in my mother's home until we're legally married."

With that, I said, "Thank God. Give Patty Boy a rest." We both started to laugh.

Flying Cauliflower and Pasta

Ingredients

1 cauliflower cut into small florets
½ cup of vegetable oil or olive oil (if using olive oil, lower the heat as it burns easier)
6 cloves of garlic, crushed
Salt and red pepper flakes to taste
1 lb. of short cut pasta (you may use ziti, bow ties, small rigatoni, or shells)

Place a pot of salted water on the stove to boil. In a large skillet, heat oil with garlic and red pepper flakes until garlic is slightly golden. Add cauliflower tossed well into the oil, add a few tablespoons of hot water, cover, and let cook on a medium flame until tender but not mushy. While cauliflower is cooking, add pasta to boiling water, cooking according to package directions. When pasta is done, drain and save about a quarter cup of the pasta water, or you may just scoop out the pasta with a slotted spider and add to the cauliflower, tossing well. If you like a soupier product, add more pasta water. I have always had a debate with my mom about this. She claims I don't add enough pasta water; I telling her we don't like it soupy. You can also make this recipe with broccoli florets. If you're cooking for an Irishman, add a few slices of diced bacon into the oil, allow it to become a bit crispy, then add the garlic, red pepper flakes, and cauliflower or broccoli. I have prepared this recipe and placed it into a buttered baking pan, adding shredded cheese on top, and baked it until the cheese melted. Everyone seemed to enjoy it.

Chapter 7

An Irish Easter

We left for Ireland a week before Easter. William's youngest brother, Seamus, picked us up and drove to the farm that has been in the O'Conner family for generations. Seamus, a very soft-spoken handsome gentleman, was a complete contrast to William. I saw the affection between them as they shook hands.

The farmhouse was a quaint Irish home that stood on acres of land. William's mother came out to greet us, and immediately, I saw who William looked like. As his mother greeted us in the driveway, she beamed to see her son but didn't hug or kiss him. She warmly greeted me with a smile and said, "Come in, come in, I have the fireplace going." As they walked ahead, I whispered to William, "Don't you kiss your family after not seeing them for so long?" With an amused look, he whispered, "No, Phil, not in Ireland."

We walked into a family room with the fireplace roaring, and his mom quickly told me to sit by the fire, placing a shawl around my shoulders. "Here, Filomena, you'll be cold for a while. You need to adjust to our climate. William smirked and winked at me. His youngest sister came to greet me, and she too was a soft-spoken beautiful blonde lady. I wondered how William had developed such an aggressive personality.

His mom had prepared a very tasty stuffed chicken breast, which she served with potatoes, vegetables, and her own homemade bread. I commented on how delicious it all was. William quietly whispered to me, "You really like it?" "Yes, it's great. I especially love the bread."

I was given his sister's room in the front of the home, while William was staying in a very large room at the back of the house. He rolled his eyes at me, indicating he was not happy with the separation. We took our first walk on the farm that day, and as we started to walk out the kitchen door, William stopped me. Laughing, he said, "Phil, you need to take those fancy leather boots off and put these Wellies on. It's mucky out there." "Oh! OK, it's always muddy outside?" As he smiled, answering, "Pretty much," I saw a softer, mellower person.

As we started to walk and talk, I was actually shocked at the change in his personality. "William, this is really beautiful." "Yeah, it's been in my family for generations. When my father immigrated to the US, my mother was pregnant with me and had my three brothers. He worked in the US, and we stayed here until I was six. We finally all moved to New York in 1961, just like you. In New York, they had my two sisters and youngest brother. Now the ones born in New York live here, and the four boys born here live in the US." We both started to laugh.

I was surprised at how muddy it was and was thankful that William had told me to change my boots. William continued, "When my father retired, my parents took the three youngest back here, and they finished their schooling here." All I saw ahead of me were miles of green pasture and at times an old half-collapsed brick home and a very large old barn. The family dog had been following us, and when we passed a group of grazing cows, the dog immediately started to chase them. William called the dog back with a whistle. "Are those your family cows?" "*No.* After my dad passed away, my mom started to lease the land to other farmers."

He then asked, "Phil, why don't you have an Italian last name?" I started to snicker. "I was wondering when that question would pop up. Most people ask it right away. My ancestors were Swiss. They immigrated to Italy in the eighteenth century. Most people don't see you as an Italian unless you have a name like macaroni or something." He started to laugh, pulling me close to him, and gave me a soft kiss. He felt my hands. "Let's get back. You feel cold." We spent the rest of that evening sitting in front of the fireplace in the family room, and I noticed a beautiful drawing of a man I knew immediately was his father. I asked William, "Is that your dad? Your brother Gavin looks just like him." "Yeah, I know, and they have the same mellow personality too, but don't push them too far, you know what I mean?" I nodded, asking, "Who drew it?" "My sister Mora. She's very artistic."

That night, I slept in his sister's room with flannel sheets, two regular blankets, and an electric blanket. I had my flannel pj's, a sweater, and a robe on and still felt cold. He came to the bedroom door, put both hands around my face, and kissed me passionately. "I hate this not being able to sleep with you. Two adults and we can't sleep together. Catholic bullshit." "William, this is your mother's house. We follow her rules. Go to bed."

His mom had a very hearty Irish breakfast prepared for us the next morning, and I especially enjoyed her homemade bread and jams, the same type of jam that William had brought back for me when he had attended his older sister's wedding and I had gone to Southold with Peter; for an instant, the taste of the jam made me think of Peter. I shook the thought from my head, telling myself, *Be happy. You're with a man that loves you, and most important, you get along with his family.* When I couldn't finish the breakfast, William's mother asked if everything was OK. "Oh, yes, it's great, but it's way too much. I never eat this much." "Ah yes," she responded, "you're so thin, not much to you at all." William, with a smile, responded, "She has it where it counts." I kicked him under the table. His mom made like she didn't hear.

He made travel plans for us and decided to rent a car. We spent the next few days visiting with his family. I met his older sister Margret, who was married to a dairy farmer; that's the wedding he had been attending when I went to Southold with Peter. She seemed to be more like William, looked like him, and was not as soft-spoken as the others. Margret was extremely friendly and had tea and sandwiches ready for us. I admired her home, an update farmhouse with imported Italian marble in the bathroom. I commentated on how beautiful it all was, and William teased her, "Yeah Margret, it pays off to be the young wife of an Irish farmer." She took us to see the newly born calves and the dairy production. I was amazed at how clean it all was; the smell was of fresh hay.

Later, as we walked on his family farm, I asked about the collapsed brick home. "Who did it belong to?" "I'm not sure, Phil, but when we get married, we can build a home here and even come back to live here." I was shocked at the idea. First, he hadn't formally asked me to marry him; he just assumed I would. Second, I had spent most of my life trying to become an American and had no intention of trying to become Irish; the weather alone might kill me. "Oh, I don't know about that, William. My Mediterranean blood would freeze in this climate."

"Yeah, I know it takes a bit of adjusting. I'm freezing in that back bedroom."

We passed a big open barn, and he pulled me into it. Teasing me while trying to undo my sweater, he whispered, "It's an O'Conner tradition that you take care of me in this barn." "You're nuts. Leave me alone," I responded, pushing him away. I started to walk away, and laughing, he followed grabbing my hand, and we went back to sit by the fire.

I had always heard of the political trouble between Irish Catholics and Anglo Protestants, but all seemed very peaceful here. It wasn't until I shopped with his sisters in the village that I sensed the great divide. As I approached a shop and tried to step in, they would very kindly tell me, "Oh no, you don't want to shop there" and diverted me to another shop. When I approached outdoor vendors that seemed to be from India, they very gently said, "Phil, come this way. It's best not to encourage them." This happened a number of times, and I became so curious that I just had to ask, "Why not those shops?"

They both looked at me in unison, saying, "You can't shop in a Protestant store. We're Catholic." I was truly shocked. "How do you know who is who? Everyone looks the same to me." They both started to giggle. "Phil, the last name gives them away, and they're not really Irish. They're British." They giggled again and took me to lunch, I guess in an Irish Catholic cafe. I didn't say much more. I really liked them both and respected their feelings.

We walked again that evening, and I told William about the shopping incident. His voice was very clear as to how he felt. "I should have mentioned it to you before, but you're going to be the wife of an Irish Catholic. You don't shop at a British fuck's store." "William, I don't get it. They've been here for generations, and what difference does religion make as to where one shops?" "It makes plenty of difference. They don't belong here. The Irish would be better off if they all leave Northern Ireland." "William, that's like the American Indians asking all of us to leave. It's never going to happen. It's better if everyone just get along." "Oh, for God's sake, I'm looking for a wife, and I got a politician." I didn't say any more on the matter. I could see he had been branded with this hatred, and

I wasn't going to change it. I knew the issues were far more complicated than both of our understandings and felt it was better left alone.

"Phil, why is it that you never used your first husband's name?" "I didn't want to change it. I like my name. My father gave us great pride as to who we are, and there are very few Abyses around. I don't want to lose my name." "Well, when you marry me, you'll be changing your name to O'Conner." My voice was not yelling but was forceful enough to get the point across. "I will not change my name for anyone. I was born with that name and I will die with that name, and if I ever have children, they will also carry my name." "What? You will do no such thing." "Look, William, I'm very proud of whom I am, and I want my children to be just as proud. It's my legal right, and if I decide to marry again, I will do as I please."

His voice started to get louder, as if he was going to change my mind. "Phil, you have a man's pride. Do you think your father would want that?" For me, his voice started to fade into the Irish countryside; whatever he said made no difference to me. I had made my decision years ago. Even if he raised my father from the dead, they both could not change it.

We visited with his aunt Anne, his father's sister, who lived in a very lovely trailer-type home on the property, not far from the main home. "Phil, let's visit with Aunt Anne today. She wants to meet you." Aunt Anne had worked for a wealthy Philadelphia family and had retired on the family farm. We walked to her home with his brother Seamus, and as soon as Aunt Anne opened the door, I was happy that the home was very warm. I was having a hard time staying warm; regardless of how much clothing I put on, the dampness gave me a chill.

She was a tiny white-haired proper Irish lady who warmly greeted me. "How are you, dear? I've heard so much about you. Are you enjoying your stay?" Before I could say much, she asked Seamus to make a few hot toddies to take the chill out of the bones. As we chitchatted, William, sitting next to me, seemed very uncomfortable as if he just wanted to leave but was forcing himself to be polite.

Seamus mixed away in the kitchen, making the hot toddies, giving each of us one. I sipped, and wow, it was really good, sweet, and it didn't seem too strong. As Aunt Anne walked away for a moment, William whispered, "Phil, don't drink too much of that stuff. You're not used to it. It will knock you on your ass."

I sipped a bit more and then motioned to him, asking what I should do with it. He grabbed the glass from me, switching with the glass he had already finished. In one gulp, he downed the rest of mine. "Well, Aunt Anne, it was good seeing you. We'll pick you up for Easter dinner. Phil is taking everyone out." "How nice of you, dear." "Oh, it's the least I can do. Everyone has been so nice to me." With that, I started to get up. William noticed it immediately—as I started to sway, he grabbed on to my arm. My legs felt rubbery, and my head was spinning. He put his arm around me, helping me walk out the door. "Phil, are you OK?" "No, not really. What was in that drink?"

Seamus had followed us out and seemed a bit amused; both brothers looked at each other. "Damn! Seamus, what did you put in that drink?" "Sorry, just the usual." It seemed that the usual was fine for little old aunt Anne and the Irish brothers, but this Italian was wiped from drinking a quarter of the drink. "She doesn't drink. She not used to it." "Sorry, Phil, I didn't realize."

William held on to me until we reached the sofa near the fireplace, helping me sit down. Seamus walked away, apologizing again. I put my head down on William's chest, while he softly rubbed my cheeks with the back of his hand. "Are you OK?" "Yeah, I think so, just a little dizzy." Ever so softly, I heard him say, "I love you, Phil. I really do."

Early in the morning, I found him at the side of my bed, again rubbing my cheeks and brushing away the hair from my face. "William, what are you doing here?" "I'm freezing in that back room. Let me slip in to warm up." "No, William, your mother doesn't approve of us sleeping together." "Oh, for God's sake, I'm not going to do anything. I just want to warm up. My mother gave you the electric blanket. I'm freezing my ass off back there."

"OK, but keep your hands to yourself." He slipped into bed, and he really did feel very cold. "Can't your mom put up the heat?" "Are you kidding? This is fine weather for them." His hands went from my face down to my breast, trying to undo my nightshirt. "Forget it, William. This is your mom's home, and we're going to follow her rules." I got out of bed. With a poor-me voice, William complained, "Where are you going? I need you to warm me up. We wouldn't tell her." I walked out of the room and into the kitchen, where his mom was preparing breakfast.

The Irish bacon was frying; the eggs were sitting on the counter, ready to be cracked; and the homemade bread with butter and jam sat on the kitchen table. "Good morning, Filomena, did you sleep well?" "Yes, I did. It smells great." "We're off to the Giant's Causeway today. You best get William up so we'll get an early start." I stood there motionless, not sure of what I should do. She stared at me as if saying, "Well, are you going or what?"

I should have turned left to the back room bedroom, where William should have been sleeping, but I had to turn right to the front bedroom, where he was actually sleeping. We stared at each other for a few seconds, and then I decided that being honest was best. "*Ah*, Mora, William is in my bedroom." Her eyebrows raised a bit in protest. "No, really, he just came into the room this morning. He was cold, and we didn't. He was just cold."

Seamus had been standing in the doorway, listening to my excuse, and quietly snickered, walking away. Her stern look told me she didn't believe a word I had said, and for a moment, I thought she was going to start lecturing me on Catholic law. "Well then, you best go and get him out of your bed so we're not late."

I was so embarrassed, and when I walked into the bedroom, there was William, not sleeping, but with both hands reaching out. "Are you going to warm me up now or what?" "William, I had to tell your mother you're in here. I'm so embarrassed, and she looks upset." "Oh, for God's sake." He got up, walked into the kitchen without saying a word, sat down, and his mother served us a hearty breakfast.

While we had breakfast, his sister Mora started to iron a pile of clothes in the kitchen. William, without even saying please, orders her, "Iron those pants and shirt so I can wear them today." This beautiful young lady started to iron his clothes without saying a word. I had tried my best to keep quiet in his mother's home, but I just couldn't take it anymore. I had to say something.

I truly wanted to say, "Why don't you iron your own fucking clothes?" but controlled myself and said, "William, *please* and *thank you* are two important words. You should try using them." "What, every time I need something done, I should say 'please' and then 'thank you'?" "That would be so nice, William. You know you get more bees with honey than with vinegar."

His sister started to giggle, while his mother turned around from the sink, telling him, "William, I'm so glad you finally met your match." I enjoyed my breakfast as he cursed under his breath. The day had gotten off to a very good start. Before we left for the causeway, I walked into the very large bedroom where he was dressing, and as we spoke, I saw both our breaths. I realized how cold it was back there. "William, it's freezing back here." "Yeah, I know." Joking, he put out his arms, "You need to warm me up." "William, let's go. Your mom's waiting."

William drove to the Giant's Causeway, and it was truly a spectacular sight. I enjoyed hiking on the hexagonal steeping stones and raced ahead. The view to the ocean was breathtaking, and I took deep breaths, trying to imbed the scents and sights into my memory. William caught up to me, complaining, "Damn, Phil, slow down. Are you trying to kill us?" "Sorry, William, but you know I love to hike." We waited for his mom to catch up, and I noticed how she was smiling at me. "Filomena, you seem to be in the best of health." I thought, *She's probably happy that her son is with a healthy prospect for a wife. After all, health is important to having healthy grandchildren.* I found it very endearing and decided to slow down.

We walked on the farm that evening, and this time, our conversation became so hurtful I wanted to cry at his insensitive behavior. "Phil, how long would it take you to get an annulment from the church?" "Why?" "I like to have a church wedding, and we can't do that because you're divorced." "William, I really don't care about that, and it would take years."

"Well, I told my mother that you got divorced because you were married to a lazy Puerto Rican that didn't want to work." "*What*! Why did you make up such a story? You know that's not true. I left my husband because he was sick, and my presence was not helping him get better." I was so furious that I wanted to scream and punch his face but controlled myself.

"What's the big deal anyway? Fuck him." "William, sometimes you're so cruel. As long as you get what you want, you don't care about anyone else. My husband worked very hard. He took great care of me, and we had a beautiful home." I walked away and almost started to cry.

William followed me, and his words made me realize how little he understood of what had occurred to my marriage. "*Oh*, for God's sake, what did you want me to tell her? That you left your husband because he was sick?" "*No*, William, the truth that the marriage was not making him any better." I clearly understood that this was not only about us but also about him trying to please his family; that made me want to cry even more.

"William, the church process takes years. It's never going to happen, so let's forget about it." I went to bed that night feeling so much emotional turmoil. I really didn't care about the Catholic Church; what I cared about was how his family perceived me. I knew that William and his family would never understand the depth of emotional pain I had endured to leave a husband for his own good.

One of the most emotional events of the entire trip was when William asked me to go and visit his father's grave. On one of our walks on the farm, we wandered into an unkempt graveyard. I was shocked at him just mulling through without giving it a second thought. "William, this is a cemetery. Maybe we shouldn't be here." "Phil, it's OK. This is our family cemetery. My ancestors are buried here." "You're full of it." The headstones were all caved in, some leaning to one side, the names hardly visible. "Who's buried here?" "I'm not sure. This graveyard has been here for generations, and if you stay past dark, they all come out to greet you."

"Cut it out. Let's get out of here. It's spooky." As we started to walk away, I asked, "Why isn't your father buried here?" "He's buried at the local church. He was very loved in the community." His voice started to fade away. "William, you didn't get along with your dad, did you?" I reached for his hand and sensed a great sadness in him.

"No, not really. I was different from my brothers, not able to keep my head in the books, always causing problems in school. I guess he tried to beat me into studying, but that didn't work, and I was always in fights." "William, for immigrants like us, it's important for parents that their children study and do well. It's one of the main reasons they leave their homeland. The main reason my parents immigrated was for us to be educated. It was a way for your father to show his love. Maybe beating a child is not the best way to get him to study, but my parents didn't hesitate in giving us a good ass-kicking. I think it's the immigrant way."

He started to laugh, pulling me closer to him, putting his arm around my waist. "Listen, when we get the chance, let's forget about my head, and let's take care of other parts of my body. I'm starting to go crazy." I gave him a shove, and he pulled me close.

We did visit his father's grave. I stood close to him as he looked down at the black granite stone with his father's name on it. For a moment, I thought he might shed a tear, show some unmanly emotions; but the Irish are trained from birth to keep emotions under control, and he didn't flinch. I stood quietly, trying not to cry for him. I sensed such deep regret, until he turned and walked away. We walked a few feet. I reached for his hand. "William, did you make peace with your dad?" He whispered, "I tried."

On Easter Sunday, William ran into my bedroom and was very flustered. "Phil, we need to get ready for Easter mass. If we don't go, my mom wouldn't come to dinner with us." "OK, let's get ready." Everyone else had already gone, and we rushed to get dressed, but by the time we got there, the mass had already started. William refused to enter, fearing that the priest would reprimand us in front of everyone for being late.

"William, I've never heard of such a thing before." "You've never been to Ireland before." We stood outside for a while, and I could not convince him to go in, so we just went back home. As soon as his mother came home, she seemed furious, informing us that Easter is a holy day of obligation and that she was not coming to dinner unless we went to mass.

Seamus tried telling her that it was a man-made law and not God's law. William started to chime in about the priest. I felt so guilty that I had to step in. "Mora, I'm sure there's another mass we can attend." She seemed to calm down a bit, telling us where there was another mass. "OK, great, we'll go to that mass, and then everyone can go out for Easter dinner."

She seemed happy with that solution, so off we headed to mass. We walked into a typical Catholic church that was not only preparing for Easter mass but also had a coffin in the middle aisle, getting ready for a funeral. "William, should we attend this mass? It's someone funeral we don't even know." "Oh, for God's sake, what difference does it make as long as we attend mass?" "OK." We both sat in the back pew and tried not to laugh out loud.

I was happy that his mother and the entire family came out to dinner with us. The restaurant was nice, but the food was just edible. As we started to eat, Aunt Anne started vomiting. William, who was sitting across from her, noticed and yelled to his mother, "Ma, Aunt Anne is throwing up!" "That's because she drinks too much. Margret, take her to the bathroom." Margret grabbed her by the arm, and off they went.

If my life depended on it, I could not put another morsel of food in my mouth. Everyone else continued to eat, and William's mother complained that if she found out who was bringing Anne liquor, she was having it out with them, and they could take care of her. The Irish are definitely a strong group of people; they can stand the damp and cold, have hot toddies without dizziness, and finish a complete meal after watching an elderly lady spewing vomit from her nose and mouth.

William noticed that I was not eating and asked what was wrong as if nothing had occurred. "I'm fine, William. I'm just not hungry." His mother was also concerned that I didn't eat enough. I just wanted to pay the bill and have homemade bread in front of a fire. As soon as we arrived home, without me even asking, his mother sliced her homemade bread, put butter and cheese on the table, and made me a cup of tea. This Italian felt much better.

As an Italian, I never understood the concept of going out with friends, having drinks, and getting into a fight. Fighting to me was something one did to protect oneself, not as a sport. It seems that for some Irish, barroom fighting is a pastime event. We had gone out with his sister Mora and some of her friends to a local pub. I sipped a wine cooler, while everyone else did some serious drinking. William never drank heavy in my presence and seemed to be watching the crowd very carefully. I just chitchatted with friends until William said, "OK, Phil, we're out of here. Mora, let's go." She gave the slightest protest, and William raised his voice. "Mora, I said now." I looked at William, asking, "What's going on?" "There's going to be a brawl in a few minutes, and I'm not risking staying here with the both of you. Let's go." As we started to walk out, I saw a group of young men in a corner engaged in a pushing match; I knew that fists would start flying within minutes. I was so happy that William had the common sense to get us out. Having survived the South Bronx without getting my teeth knocked out, I didn't have any intention of doing that in Ireland.

For the remaining portion of the trip, we traveled to Belfast with Seamus and stopped at the university he was attending. We shopped and had lunch at a pub, and I didn't see any signs of violence between Catholics and Protestants. I commented at how peaceful it was, and they both said, "Yes, for now." On the following day, William drove to the south of Ireland, and as we passed large open fields, I noticed two soldiers walking back to back with guns in hand. "William, why are those soldiers walking that way?" "Oh, those British fucks are afraid of getting shot in the back."

"I just don't get it. This place seems so peaceful." We drove to the checkpoint that separates Northern Ireland from the south of Ireland, and as we stopped, I went for my passport. "Phil, don't bother. They'll just take a photo of the car." We traveled around for two days just being tourists. William tried to make up for lost time at night. "God, William, give it a rest." "Phil, I missed you. It's lonely in that back room." I had to laugh. "William, it hasn't been that long."

We went back to the farm and started packing to head back to New York. I noticed that William had started to speak with a slight brogue; when I mentioned to him that I thought it was adorable, he said, "Please,

Phil, don't call me adorable in front of my family." I started to laugh, while he informed me, "Don't worry. I'll lose the brogue after a few days in New York." "That's a shame. I think it's sexy." "Oh, well, I can fake it whenever you like." We both laughed.

His sister Mora offered to do my washing so I didn't need to fuss when I got home. I told her not to worry, that it's no big deal. She admired all of my clothing, and I truly liked her; she was so sweet. She was even having a friend knit a typical Irish sweater for me, telling me that the one I was ready to purchase was too dear, meaning too costly. I still have that sweater, wearing it often, especially on Saint Pat's Day.

I had purchased a few new kitchen items for his mom. She, in turn, gave me beautiful china cups, along with two Celtic pins, all which I still have. She packed a bag full of her homemade jam, along with teas, biscuits, and cookies for us to take. I truly liked them all and worried that if William and I didn't formally marry, it would be a disappointment to them. I mentally vowed to do my best to get along with him. On the day we were leaving, I kissed them all; I guess, as an Italian, I like to show my feelings.

I would love to insert the recipe for William's mother's homemade bread and jam to complete this chapter; unfortunately, I did not have the foresight to ask for those recipes. Instead, I will share an Irish soda bread recipe given to me by an Irish immigrant that worked with me for many years.

Kathleen Driscoll was the kindest soul I've ever met; after many years of living in the United States, she still spoke with a beautiful Irish brogue, her voice barely above a whisper. In all the years I worked in the same schools with the same employees, she was the only one that never complained or spoke ill of other coworkers. I admired her hardworking quiet personality and enjoyed listening to her as she spoke of arriving in the United States as a young girl to work as a chambermaid for the very wealthy descendants of the Vanderbilt family in Rhode Island.

Kathleen brought this recipe with her from Ireland, and every year, during Saint Patty's Day, she would bring this wonderful cake for us to enjoy with our coffee. One year, while enjoying Kathleen's cake, I asked her for the recipe, and I now share it with you. This is a copy in Kathleen's own handwriting. Kathleen passed away many years ago, and whenever I prepare this cake for my family on Saint Patty's Day, I think of her and say a silent Irish prayer—"May the Lord hold you in the palm of his hand."

This is a photocopy of Kathleen's recipe.

For clarity's sake, I have rewritten this recipe.
Kathleen's Own Irish Soda Bread
Ingredients:
1 can of beer
1 lb. of raisins
½ lb. of margarine or butter
1 cup of sugar
2 cups of flour
1 tsp. of baking soda
1 tsp. of ginger
1 tsp. of nutmeg
1 tsp. of allspice
3 eggs

Kathleen verbally told me that, if you like, you can add "a few shots of whiskey or such."

Boil raisins in the beer for ten minutes until soft, and set aside to cool. Sift flour, baking soda, ginger, allspice, and nutmeg. Set aside. With an electric mixer, cream margarine by slowly adding sugar, adding eggs one at a time, and beating well after each egg. Slowly pour flour into the margarine mixture, alternating by adding raisins, mixing well. Pour batter in a buttered nine-by-six-inch loaf pan or two round nine-by-nine-inch or a single-fluted Bundt pan. Bake in a preheated 350°F oven for about an hour and fifteen minutes or until a toothpick, when inserted in the middle of cake, comes out clean and dry.

If you've baked this cake in two round pans, you can frost the top of one with cream cheese frosting, placing the second on top of the frosting and then icing the entire cake. You can also drizzle this cake, regardless of the shape, with an icing mixture of confectioners' sugar, vanilla, and milk or, as Kathleen did, a simple dusting of confectioners' sugar, having plain cream cheese available for spreading.

Irish Soad Bread

1 can Beer
1 lb Raisins
± lb margarine or butter
1 cup sugar
3 cups flour
1 teaspoon Baking soda
1 teaspoon ginger
1 - nutmeg
1 - all spice
3 eggs

Boil beer + raisins for 10 minutes
Combine flour - soda - ginger - all spice
+ nutmeg.   Cream margarine +
sugar, add eggs one at a time, add
flour mixture + raisins into beer.
      Bake 350   for 1¼ hours

Chapter 8

Getting Along

Back in New York, we continued our routine of seeing each other almost daily. William hinted that he should move in with me, but I hesitated. His demanding, arrogant behavior worried me. He was also prone to bouts of drinking binges when he hung out with friends. He never overdrank when he was with me, but I started to see a dangerous pattern of self-abuse.

As I shopped for a new car, William mentioned to me not to bother looking. His oldest brother was the attorney for a motor company, and family members were offered a car at a very low cost. "William, that's great, but I don't feel comfortable with that. I'm not family." "Yes, you are, Phil. We consider you family." He did call Owen, and within a few weeks, a car was waiting for me at a local dealership.

The drinking problem was taking its toll on the relationship. William did everything to extreme. He worked to the point of exhaustion, and when he wasn't with me, he partied for days. The phone call came from his brother after I hadn't seen William for days.

"Hello, Filomena, this is Owen, William's brother. How are you?" "Oh, hi, Owen. I'm fine, thanks." "Is William there with you?" "No, I haven't seen him in a few days. You know, he does this often."

"Yes, I know. Is everything OK with you? The dealership called and told me that you still haven't picked up the car." "Didn't William call and let you know that we're waiting for the weather to improve before we pick up the car?" "No, he didn't." "I'm so sorry, Owen. I hope I didn't cause a problem for you." "No, it's not a problem. I was just concerned."

"Owen, he does this often—stays out with friends—and I don't hear from him." "Yes, I know. If you hear from him, please ask him to call me." "OK, I will, and I'm sorry if I caused a problem." "Filomena, it's not a problem. Just take care of yourself." "OK, thanks for your concern. Bye," and I hung up the receiver feeling very embarrassed. I sat on my bed, wondering where William could be, and told myself, *You can't live this crazy life. It's not who you are.*

The next day, I was home, and William knocked on the door. I wasn't expecting him. As soon as I opened the door and took one look at him, I knew what had happened. "William, you're getting to old for this. One day, you're going to get killed." His face was bruised and scratched, his hands swollen and scrapped. He walked into the living room and flopped onto the sofa. "I know, Phil. You're right. I was out and . . ." He stopped in midsentence, not knowing what to say. He didn't need to say anything. I knew exactly what had happened. Drinking and fighting.

"Your brother Owen called. He was looking for you." "Yeah, I know. I spoke to him." I ran into the kitchen, where I had been making chili. "Phil, what smells so good?" "I'm making chili. You're hungry?" "Yeah, I am." "OK, when it's done, we'll have dinner." "Great." I walked into the living room, where he was dozing off. I let him be until I finished cooking. I had made white rice to pour the chili over and a tossed salad.

We sat and ate without much conversation. I looked at his swollen hands while we ate and thought to myself, *What if you were married and had children? How would you explain to them that their father had been badly hurt or, worse yet, killed in a barroom brawl? What if you had small children and their father didn't come home for days? What would you do then?* I started to feel claustrophobic; the stress of his crazy lifestyle was starting to affect me. I knew I had to get away and clear my head.

"Phil, this is really good. Where did you learn to make chili like this?" "From my Puerto Rican husband." He looked up at me and didn't say a word. While we had dinner, I mentally decided to take a monthlong trip to Italy. I needed to fill my being with my own culture, my own people. He helped me clean up the kitchen and apologized, putting his arms around me. I looked up at him, asking, "William, now the fucking starts?" "Come on, Phil, you know that's not true." "William, the drinking and fighting has got to stop." I gave him a hug and a kiss, asking him to leave.

I made a call to my aunt Pina in Naples, asking if I could visit for a month. "Of course. Whenever you want to come, this is your home." I asked if I could first visit her daughter Ana Maria in Milan. "You don't need to ask. We're your family. You're always welcome here." She gave me Ana Maria's phone number. I called and asked if I could visit with her for a few weeks. "Yes, of course, who are you coming with?" "Just me." "You're not afraid to travel all that way by yourself?" "No, not at all." I made travel plans without telling William. I called my cousin and gave her all the info. She with her husband would pick me up at the airport in Milan.

I called a friend in Long Island and decided to drive my car to her house and leave the car in her garage; she'd drive me to the airport. Finally, I had to tell William I was leaving for Italy for the entire month of July. "What? You make plans to be away for a whole month, and you don't even ask me first." "Ask you? Ask you for what? I'm not a child." William was furious; his male ego was being challenged. In a raised voice, not quite yelling but loud enough for me to know he was extremely upset, he said, "Is this what you're going to do when we're married? How do I know that you wouldn't be with someone else?" "William, when I make a commitment, I don't turn away from it. I don't lie, and if I'm going to start seeing someone else, I will let you know. I hope you show me the same respect."

I knew that he was incapable of understanding that I would do everything for a husband out of love, but nothing for a husband that demanded everything and did not hold himself by the same standards. I almost questioned him if he ever thought of asking my permission when he went into a bar and I didn't hear from him for days. I quietly wondered how many times had he taken some half-drunk bimbette home. I thought it would be better not to even start the conversation. I wanted to save my energy for my vacation.

As soon as I saw my cousin Ana Maria, we hugged and kissed, holding back tears. I had always missed them so much. I was tired from the flight but energized to be in my own country. I woke up the next day extremely late, and when I walked into the kitchen, I knew I was home. The smell of coffee, the table set with morning cookies, and the sight of such a clean and organized home made me understand who I was. As I drank my coffee, I watched my cousin, and I could anticipate her next move. The manner she kept her kitchen, her sense of hospitality, her cleanness, and her fussiness in preparing food reminded me of myself. I wasn't sure if it was genetics or a lifestyle handed down from mother to daughter. I was absolutely sure that it was a lifestyle I completely loved.

For lunch, she made pasta with pink sauce, asking me if I had ever eaten it before. I said no, and I watched how she mixed heavy cream into red ragù sauce, turning the sauce into a delicate pink creamy mixture. The meal was fantastic. We traveled north for the first two weeks. We toured Milan, Florence, Venice, Siena, and Lake Como. I could not take in enough of my own culture. It was like needing a blood transfusion; I had been culturally anemic for years and needed to fill my veins with who I was.

After two weeks, I asked Ana Maria to check the train schedule to Naples; I wanted to visit with our family. She was concerned that I was traveling alone. I told her not to worry, that I was accustomed to taking care of myself. The six-hour train ride was beautiful; as I stared at the landscape filled with sunflowers, grapevines, and olive trees, a feeling of harmony and peace came over me. I told myself that I needed to maintain that feeling in New York.

As soon as I saw the sight of endless clotheslines, I knew I was in Naples. The sight warmed my heart. My uncle picked me up at the train station, and when we reached Bagnoli, I inhaled deep breaths of sea air. The recall of my childhood was instantaneous. Most of my family was at my aunt Pina's house, and they greeted me with hugs and kisses. We had been separated for so many years, but the connection was never severed. We had pasta with very tiny clams that can't be found in New York for our afternoon supper.

The freshness of the sea filled my senses. The next day, I awoke to the sounds of church bells, wondering whether they were the same bells that I had heard as a child. The aroma of coffee called from the kitchen, and as I walked in, my aunt gave me a mug of hot milk and coffee along with melted dark chocolate to pour over cookies. I walked outside onto the balcony and saw shadows of myself as a young child, sitting on the floor playing with my cousins. I had been absent from this beloved place for too long. There was so much energy from this country, from this ancient culture, and from my family inside of me that regardless of how far away I was and how many years we spent apart, it always swirled in my being. How I wished that I could live in two places at once. The land of my birth that I still loved so much and my adopted country that had given me so much, forever reshaping who I was. I loved them both and could never give up one for the other.

My cousin Monica walked with me throughout Bagnoli, showing me the building I was born in, the home we lived in near the train tracks; my grandparents' home; and then down the hill to the waterfront and beach area. I held back tears, wishing to relive those simple days when my only worry was making sure I wiped all the sand from my hands before lunch. I had endured such devastating crises since leaving this place, and I knew more would follow. I stayed a few days in Naples and then called friends on the island of Ponza. They were expecting me to visit. I took the three-hour hydrofoil boat ride with the intention of staying only two days, but the beauty of the island and hospitality of my friends kept me there for four.

We walked to the beach daily, ate fresh seafood at the outdoor restaurant, and took the evening passeggiata, listening to local artists playing Neapolitan music and reciting poems. Everyone seemed to know me as Ugo's daughter; most of the locals had lived near my dad's shop in the Bronx and returned to vacation on the island every summer. They had been asking me to visit for years; I was so glad I finally had.

I returned to Naples, stayed a few more days, and tried not to cry as I said good-bye to my family. I had only a few more days in Milan; finally, I decided to call William. While we spoke on the phone, I sensed a change. I wasn't sure if it was within myself, that I had subconsciously made a decision to distance myself from him, or was there something different about him.

William asked if I wanted him to pick me up at the airport. I told him, "No, I'll drive home and call you when I'm settled." I was leaving with a heavy heart—not only because I knew I would miss my family and the land of my birth, but also because I finally admitted to myself that I could not live the lifestyle that William offered. The month I had spent living in my own country, inhaling my own culture, reinforced that I could not live any other way. It had nothing to do with being Italian or Irish but everything to do with the quality and style of life.

After I returned from Italy, I noticed a change in William. He wasn't as attentive; we didn't see each other as much, and I instinctually knew he was seeing someone else. What was hurting me was not so much that he was seeing someone else but that he never told me; he was being dishonest, and I had always been honest with him. I was being treated like a fool, and that thought was infuriating me. I decided to drive to his apartment and, as childish as it may sound, give back all the gifts he had given me. Every time I looked at them, I became enraged; my sense of harmony was completely destroyed, and I became furious, not so much at him but at myself.

I rang the bell, and as soon as he opened the door, I punched him in the jaw. I knew that I could not physically hurt him, but it made me feel better. "Phil, calm down." I went to punch him again, and he blocked the punch with his wrist. Casually, he said, "Phil, don't throw any more punches. You're going to hurt yourself." My wrist was already hurting. He mockingly rubbed his chin and, laughing, said, "Phil, your right hook is not bad. If you were a man, I'd be afraid of you." He plodded in a chair, and I noticed how bad he looked.

"Everything is a joke to you. You look like crap, and you live like shit. Why didn't you tell me you were seeing someone else? Can't you even show me that much respect?" I looked at him and knew he been out all night. I wasn't even sure if he was listening to anything I was saying. "Phil, don't lecture me. What about that fuck you were seeing?"

"That was different. I was always honest with you, and we didn't have a commitment then." "Yeah, well, that makes me feel a whole lot better." In a louder voice that was filled with pain, he continued, "You know what? I don't think you ever stopped thinking of him."

For a split second, I was taken aback by what he was now after almost four years, willingly verbalizing, but refused to let him have the upper hand and control of the emotionally charged exchange. "Don't try to justify your behavior, and I hope she knows what a hypercritical bigot you are." With a sarcastic laugh, he responded, "Phil, we don't exactly discuss politics." "Well then, I'm happy for you. Just what you need, a dumb piece of ass."

"Phil, I'm really wasted. I'm going to lie down." I should have walked out the door, but I didn't. Instead, I walked into the bedroom, I guess to make sure I wasn't the last person he cheated on. He wasn't that wasted.

I ran down the stairs, telling myself that it was better this way. *I'm glad it's over. It never would have worked out between us. We were just too different. Let someone else deal with his crazy behavior. Better her than me.*

I started the car and put my head on the steering wheel to calm myself. Tears started to flow, and I pounded on the dashboard to stop myself from crying, but the tears took over while my inner voice spoke to me. *It's not that you were so different, but so much alike. Two hard-ass, opinionated immigrants incapable of compromise.* I drove away crying and never saw him again.

In retrospect, I think William was deeply hurt by my lack of love in our relationship. He, in his anger, tried to turn the tables on me by seeing someone else. As I tried to walk out of his apartment that day, he came after me, trying to hold me in his arms. I, not wanting to cry in his presence, pushed him away, running down the stairs.

I now realize that I should have thanked William for demanding I defrost my frozen heart and start to love again.

Ana Maria's Pink Sauce

First, you need to prepare ragù sauce. Follow the instructions in part 2, chapter 2.

Remove all the meat from the sauce, placing it in a large bowl. While the sauce is still hot, slowly pour about a cup of room-temperature heavy cream, stirring constantly until the sauce becomes a creamy pink. Serve over your favorite cooked pasta.

Often, we also use ricotta cheese to mix with ragù sauce, making it creamy pink. Place about a cup of room-temperature ricotta in a bowl, and with a ladle, slowly pour ragù sauce into it, stirring until well blended. Add your favorite cooked pasta to the creamy sauce in the bowl, mix well, and enjoy with grated Parmesan cheese on top.

Chapter 9

It Was Meant to Be

For days after the breakup with William, I worked myself to exhaustion. I was at work before 7:00 a.m. and worked at the *gym* until 9:00 p.m. My stomach was telling me how emotionally distraught I was; trying to push down a few morsels of food became a challenge again. I cursed myself for letting anyone upset my inner balance and vowed not to let it happen again.

It wasn't more than three weeks after that breakup as I sat at my desk that the phone rang, and I picked up, expecting a work-related question. "Good morning, PS 83 kitchen." I didn't hear the usual "Ms. Abys, we need . . ." but "Hi, Phil, it's Pete. Remember me?" I froze for a few seconds and didn't say anything. I finally forced my lips to form the words, "Oh! Hi, yes, I remember you."

We had not seen each other for almost three years, and the only contact I had with him was through coworkers that felt inclined to tell me, "Pete is always asking about you. He wants to know if you're OK." I avoided the comments, not even asking how he was doing. Of course, they would tell me who he was with and that she was a no-good bitch just using him for money. My heart broke every time, but I pretended not to care. I told myself not to care. In reality, deep down in my heart, I had never stopped thinking of him. William must have felt it before I even admitted the undeniable fact to myself. He must have sensed the shared love I had for both of them.

Peter continued to speak. "I called you last week and left a message. Didn't the staff tell you?" "No, they didn't tell me you called, Pete. How's it going?" "I'm OK. I've heard that you finally broke up with that other guy." "Yes, I did. It just didn't work out between us." Peter was honest in his response. "I can't say I'm sorry. Phil, let's have dinner. I need someone like you to talk to. I've had a rough few years since we'd last seen each other, and I really need your type of company."

As I listened, I held on to my forehead. I was so torn between not wanting to get involved with anyone again and the memory of how much I cared for him. I knew he had lived a drug-crazed life since we had last seen each other, and I didn't want to take on that burden. I didn't speak for a minute, trying to sort out my emotions. I told myself, *Don't be crazy. Don't start this again. Keep away from the Irish. You'll find a well-adjusted man when you're ready. Don't do it.*

I started to say no; my lips formed the words "No, I can't," but, if one believes in forces beyond oneself, those forces took over, and I said, "I guess dinner is OK." I literally put my hand over my mouth, not believing what I had just said. "Great, Phil, I need to talk to you again." I sat in a daze listening to Peter giving me details about our date. While I listened, I told myself, *You need to guard your heart.* I wanted to place my heart safely in that frozen pond, where I need not feel, but those forces outside of me were in control now, and I just agreed to the day, time, and place.

I put down the receiver and walked out to the staff. In all the years I had worked with the same employees, I had never raised my voice; this time, I did. "Who took the call from Peter Smith last week?" The staff looked at each other, not accustomed to this new tone in my voice.
"*Oh*, I did."
"Why didn't you tell me or leave a message on the desk? You know better. The next time it happens, I'll write you up for not performing your job, do you understand?" The entire staff stood motionless as I walked away. I sat at my desk, realizing that I had started to melt for him already.

After I had some time to calm down, an employee that I was very friendly with came in with a tray of food, speaking to me in Neapolitan. "You know why she didn't tell you he called?" "No, why?" "Well, remember when she was showing us the pictures of her family, and she kept pointing to her son?" "Yeah." "She was trying to set you up with that mamaluke of a son. Can you believe it? She kept telling us how she would like for you to date that tub of lard." I started to laugh and had to cover my mouth so no one else would hear. "Ms. Abys, don't worry about it. Eat. You're too thin. Everything is going to be OK for you."

We had planned to meet in front of Saint Raymond's Church on East Tremont Avenue in the Bronx. Peter was now living in a halfway house in that area after a monthlong drug rehab program. I drove to the church and almost passed by without recognizing him. I took a second look at a man that kind of looked like him, and then I was shocked that it was really him. I pulled over and opened the window, calling his name. He glanced, smiled, and opened the car door. "Hey, how's it going? It's good to see you again, Phil." "Hi, Pete. I almost passed you by." "Yeah, I know I put on a lot of weight." "And your hair is long." Peter with a shy smile placed a hand on the back of his male ponytail, whispering, "I'm thinking of having it cut off, come on, let's get something to eat." He told me where to drive, and we went into a quiet tiny restaurant.

At first, we sat, not saying much, not knowing how to start the conversation. It took about five minutes until we started to feel comfortable; after that, the words poured out as if we had never been apart.

"Phil, I'm sure you heard about my drug abuse and living with . . ." He stopped in midsentence. "Pete, I know all about it. It was all over the district, and for some reason, everyone was always telling me what was going on with you." "Yeah, I know. I always asked about you and knew what was going on in your life. I never forgot about you." I looked down, not wanting to look into his eyes, and started to cry.

Peter's words continued to flow out of him as if an overflowing dam had been released. "When you decided to only see that donkey f—" And then he stopped, correcting himself. "The other guy. I was so hurt that I went on a frenzy of drinking, drugging, and . . ." He stopped again. "Pete, I know. Living with something like that—Jesus."

"Phil, it was so hard for me to keep away from you that when I heard Kenny G music playing on the radio in the boiler room of the school, I flung the radio, smashing it into the wall."

Peter continued releasing his long bottled up emotions and I looked down at the table or straight ahead not having the courage to look into his eyes. "Phil, you know, after I hurt my back and you refused to come over, I called her." I stopped him. "Pete, I can imagine. She came with instant relief and the easy way out." "Phil, I'm not blaming you, but that's what happened. I lived with that whore until I knew if I didn't walk out, I was going to die."

He explained, "The relationship was mostly she gave me drugs and sex, and I gave her money." "Pete, don't call that a relationship. That was prostitution." "I know. That's why I'm asking for your friendship. At this point, you're the only well-balanced, clearheaded person I know."

I finally got the courage to look into his eyes and realized the luster he once had was gone. I wasn't sure what I was feeling—guilt, sorrow, or love. All I knew was that I could not deny him my friendship. I said a silent prayer. *God, why me? I'm not strong enough for this. I've been through hell in the past few years. Why me?* I found my answer in his words. "I really missed you, Phil. I need your company."

I talked about my relationship with William and how we just didn't get along. "It's not that we didn't care for each other. We were too different or maybe too much alike. I'm not sure, but it's over now." He seemed very happy with that. We had dinner, and then I drove him back to where he was staying. He had given up his apartment to live with the whore and had left behind all his belongings with her. She had never even made him a sandwich. I felt rage at that thought, telling myself not to let that guide my relationship with him. *Just give him sound, levelheaded advice, and don't get involved beyond friendship.* We just simply said good night, and I drove away.

During the week, we talked on the phone, and I tried to encourage him to live a healthy, drug-free lifestyle. I told him about my great dislike for drug addiction and how, in the South Bronx, I had watched so many lives fall apart. Not only did I dislike drug addicts, but they disgusted me. "Well, Phil, I hope I don't disgust you too much." "No, Pete, you don't. I think God's trying to teach me a lesson with you." We both laughed.

On the next date, we decided to go see a movie. Peter picked me up at my apartment, and as I opened the door, he handed me a coconut. I stared at him in disbelief. "Why did you bring me a coconut?" "Phil, I remember how much you liked it, and I always felt so bad about what happened to your dad." I looked down at the coconut, telling myself, *Don't you dare start to cry.* I forced the tears back, but when I looked up,

I'm sure he saw the glaze in my eyes. I walked into the kitchen and put the coconut in the basket of fruit on the counter. "Thanks, Pete. I can't believe you remember that." "Phil, I didn't forget anything about you." I didn't answer; I wasn't ready for an emotional conversation. I just wanted to go to the movies. "OK, let's go before we're late."

If one believes in poetic justice, it happened as we walked into the movies. I noticed a couple sitting in the last two seats of the aisle we walked through staring at us. Peter, looking the other way, didn't notice them at all. After we sat, I looked back, and they continued to stare. I asked Pete, "Why are those people staring at us?" "Who?" and he turned around to look. As he realized who they were, without saying a word, he got up, taking a few steps forward. The couple quickly ran out.

I didn't need to ask. The anger in his face told the story. "That's the whore I was living with and her new bank account." The tension in his body was as if someone had placed a spring coil in his back, his hands gripping his knees so hard that his knuckles started to turn white. I waited a few seconds and then reached for his hand. "Pete, don't let anyone else control your behavior. You can gain back everything you lost. You just need to stay healthy. Let's enjoy the movie." The tension slowly started to dissipate as the movie started. I thought to myself, *There's a reason they ran out.* I knew she and the new bank account had seen the not-so-mellow side of Pete.

We watched *Sleeping with the Enemy*, and throughout the movie, I asked myself, *Why are you here with him? You're not a drug counselor. You're not responsible for his behavior.* I searched inside myself for a logical answer, but I could not find one. When he offered me a sip of his drink, I refused, not wanting to put my lips near where his lips had been. We hadn't discussed if he had been tested for any diseases, and I was not willing to put myself at risk.

In addition to that, I was a bit disgusted with the idea of him being a drug addict. I told myself not to be so righteous, that drug addicts are people too. After the movies, he drove me home, and we said good night. We didn't even give each other a kiss on the cheek. I was happy with his gentlemanly nonaggressive behavior. I knew he didn't need sex but just friendship, and that was just fine with me. As I walked up the stairs to my apartment, I told myself, *It's so much better this way. Just be friends.*

We dated for months, much in the same manner. We would go out to dinner, movies, and walks without even holding hands. He started to look healthy, the sparkle in his eyes returned, and I started to see the man I had met years ago. I'm not sure why he mentioned it, but one day, as we had dinner, he said, "Phil, you know, I've been tested for all types of disease. I'm fine. Would you like a written report from my doctor?" I looked down, not knowing what to say, choosing to say nothing.

Peter called me at work on a Friday. "Hey! What are you doing tomorrow? Let's have dinner and maybe a movie." I had started to feel selfish that he never let me pay for anything and realized that I had never cooked for him or even made him a cup of tea. As I listened to his voice, an intense urge to cook for him came over me. "Pete, I'll cook for us. Come over, and we'll have dinner at my place." "Are you sure it's not too much trouble, not too much work for you?"

I smiled to myself, realizing that I had never mentioned to him how many parties I had hosted at my home in Long Island, at times cooking for as many as forty guests. "No, Pete, I think I can handle cooking for two people. Just come over, and don't worry about it."

I called my mother, asking her," Mom, do you have salted capers, pine nuts, and Gaeta olives?" "Of course. I always have them on hand. Why, you cooking for someone?" "Yes, and I don't have time to drive to Arthur Avenue to buy them. I'll be over and pick some up." The next call I made was to the *gym* and told them to remove me from the schedule. I was tired of working out and teaching classes.

After work, I stopped at my mother's home to pick up the items I needed. While I placed the items in containers, she asked, "So who you cooking for?" "A friend." "Oh, another friend. Nice you meet a lot of friends. What, you go around, making eyes at men?" I almost started to laugh and thought, *If she only knew that I did more than make eyes.*

I was thirty-five, and she was worried about me making eyes. As I walked out, she yelled down the stairs, "Watch your step!" I laughed all the way home. I stopped at the supermarket and purchased a pork loin, red potatoes, broccoli, lemons, fresh fruit, and fresh Italian bread that I wasn't crazy about, but it had to do. The remaining items I always kept at home.

I got up extra early on Saturday and made sure the house was spotless. I prepared a sauce that we've been making in my family for years. A red tomato sauce spiced with capers, pine nuts, and Gaeta olives. I made it early so that it sat for a while and picked up extra flavor. I spiced the roast with fresh garlic, salt, pepper, and rosemary, placing spiced potatoes and onions around the roast. All was placed on a cast-iron pan and into a hot oven. I steamed the broccoli until tender, adding fresh garlic, a sprinkle of salt, and drizzling olive oil and lemon juice over it. I set the table, placing the fruit in the middle. Peter called, asking when he should come over. "I'm going into the shower now. Give me about an hour." "OK, you need anything?" "No, just come over."

I primped more than usual and asked myself, *Why are you being so fussy?* I put the thought out of my head, reminding myself that just being friends was best. I was slicing bread when he knocked, and as soon as he walked in, he wrapped his arms around me, asking, "Wow, what smells so good?" He walked into the kitchen and opened the lid to the saucepot, "What kind of sauce is this? I've never had this before." "I know most Americans don't really understand Italian food. They think it's all like lasagna."

He put his arm around my waist whispering, "Maybe you can teach me." I could smell his cologne and his body scent, and with my mother's words resonating in my head, I told myself, *Watch your step.* While I cooked the pasta, I told Peter to go watch TV; he seemed a bit nervous, asking, "Don't you need help?" "Help for what? To cook pasta?" I started to laugh, "I don't think so, Pete. Go watch TV."

When the pasta was ready, I called out, "OK, Pete, come eat." He again seemed agitated, as if he needed to help. "Pete, just sit down." I physically pulled him by the hand and made him sit. As I started to serve, he almost didn't seem comfortable with someone fussing over him. "Phil, I'm not used to this. I'm usually the guy who did everything." "I gather that much, Pete, but it's time you let someone fuss over you a bit. It's not that painful, is it?" We both started to laugh.

With the first forkful, he looked up at me almost embarrassed. "Phil, why didn't you tell me years ago when I made that crappy chicken dinner that you could cook like this?" I smiled back and repeated his own words from years ago. "Phil, I can cook. Can you cook?"

When we finished the pasta, I asked him to thinly slice the roast, which he did very well. I asked him to sit down while I served. "You sure you don't need help?" "Pete, I'm fine. I don't need help." I served the roast, potatoes, and onions on a large plate and placed it in front of him. I was about to serve the broccoli salad on a smaller plate when he immediately waved his hand, "Phil, I'm not much of a vegetable eater."

"Pete, did you ever have broccoli this way?" "Ah, no, my mom usually boiled the shit out of the vegetables and then just plopped them on our plate." I didn't want to laugh, but I had heard about the Irish method of boiling just about everything to death. Smiling, I asked him, "Why don't you just try a forkful?" "OK, I'll try it just for you." He picked up a very small portion, placing it fearfully in his mouth. As he chewed, he smiled, "Phil, I can't believe it. This is really good."

"Thank you, Mr. Smith. I'm glad you like it. Dunk the bread in the dressing. It's really good that way." He ate everything with such gusto that, for some reason, I felt I had succeeded at a major task. At the end of the meal, I picked up a pear, washing and slicing it for him. As I handed him a slice, I wasn't sure what he was feeling. He seemed surprised, thankful, grateful, but mostly uncomfortable. "Phil, you know, I'm not used to all of this. You didn't need to fuss so much." "I know, Pete. I wanted to. Remember, I'm Italian. This is how we start to make love." I remembered his sexual stare from years ago and caught myself staring back. I inwardly smiled, telling myself, *Great Freudian slip. Watch your step.*

Peter helped me clean up, and while I was putting away the dishes, he put both hands on the counter, trapping me in his arms. "Thanks, Phil. That was really great." I reached for his face, my palm caressing his cheek. "You're more than welcome. I enjoyed—" Before I could finish the sentence, he bent down and kissed me softly on the lips.

I reached up, kissing him back. We continued to kiss with such passionate hunger that, somehow, I found myself in the bedroom. I knew there so no turning back. I didn't want to turn back.

He held my arms over my head with his hands in mine, his blue eyes penetrating my being. As his lips softly kissed my lips, cheeks, and neck, he whispered to me, "This time, I'm not sharing you with anyone. This time, you're all mine. This time, I'm never going to let you go."

His lovemaking brought tears to my eyes, and the realization that I had for years been trying to run from my destiny, but that destiny had never been far away. I gave in to my destiny. I held on to him, arched my back for him, and exploded from pleasure.

As I lay in his arms, I asked, "Why did you ever let me go?" "Phil, I didn't want to stand in your way. I knew you needed to live your life. Don't think it was easy for me. I could never get you out of my mind no matter what I did. Did you ever hear that saying, 'If you love someone, set them free. If they come back to you, it was meant to be'? Well, I guess it was meant to be." I buried my face in his chest and cried, telling him that this time, I was never going to let him go.

After that night, I felt as if I had emerged from the confinement of that frozen pond and finally stood in the glow of sunshine. I was ready, truly ready, to love again.

"Let's Make Love" Sauce

Ingredients
2 35 oz. cans of tomatoes (if possible, use San Marzano)
4 cloves of crushed garlic
¼ cup of oil (you may use vegetable or olive oil)
A handful of pine nuts
⅛ cup of salted capers (do not use capers that are jarred in brine)
¼ cup of depitted Gaeta olives

Toss the pine nuts, capers, and olives together in a bowl.
Crush tomatoes by hand or in blender. Set aside. Place oil in a large skillet or pot, and heat over a medium flame for a minute. Add the capers, olives, and pine nuts; mix well, allowing them to sauté over a medium-low flame for a minute or two. Add the crushed tomatoes, mix well, and let cook over a medium-low flame for about fifteen minutes. Lower flame to a simmer, and cook for about another fifteen minutes. You may add salt

and pepper to taste, but be very careful as the capers and olives are already salty. If you like it spicy, you may also add red pepper flakes to the skillet when you are adding the capers, but I prefer the clean, fresh taste without too much spiciness.

It's best to prepare this sauce at least two hours before serving or a day ahead, keeping it tightly sealed in the refrigerator; as the sauce sits, it will pick up great flavor. Serve over cooked spaghetti or linguine. Do not use short pasta with this sauce. My mom always added the caper, olives, and pine nuts after the tomatoes, but I find if you sauté them in the oil, the flavor is better.

"I Never Eat Vegetables" Broccoli Salad

Ingredients

Steamed broccoli (the amount depends on how many people you are cooking for.
¼ cup of olive oil (again, adjust according to the amount of broccoli)
3 cloves of fresh garlic, finely diced
Juice of 1 freshly squeezed lemon
Salt to taste

Steam broccoli until just tender (not mushy). Place broccoli on a platter, sprinkle with diced garlic and salt, drizzle oil and lemon juice on top, and toss very gently. You can mix the oil and lemon juice first in a bowl and then pour over the broccoli, but we just drizzled on top.

I have also stirred fried broccoli for Peter in a mixture of Gaeta olives, salted capers, and pine nuts, and he really enjoys this as a side dish. Heat about a quarter cup of vegetable oil in a skillet; add a quarter cup of pitted Gaeta olives, two tablespoons of salted capers, and a handful of pine nuts; and stir-fry for a minute. Add broccoli florets, and mix well with the oil. Add about four tablespoons of water, toss again, and cook covered over a low flame until tender. Fast and easy.

Chapter 10

A Wife Again

From that night on, we were committed partners. We spent so much time together that I finally asked Peter to move in. His mellow, compromising personality made me feel that we could live together without too much adjustment. When I first asked if he'd like to move in, he hesitated, "Phil, this is such a nice place. I don't want to change anything. I don't want you to be uncomfortable." "Pete, I can't stand the thought of you living in that place. Whenever you're ready, just move in. We'll work things out." "I need to talk to my sponsor and see what he suggests." "OK, do that, and let me know what he thinks."

The next day, Peter called me at work, laughing. "Hi, Ms. Abys. I spoke to my sponsor, and he wanted to know how much drugs you do. I told him you've never been drunk, you don't smoke, and never taken any kind of drugs. He doesn't believe me. He said that's impossible." I started laughing myself, "Well, Pete, God only knows what type of females he's been with. I'm not sure how you can convince him. Just let him know that my body and home have always and will always be a drug-free zone." "Phil, I don't care what he thinks. I'm tired of this place. I'd like to move in." "All right, give me a few days." "Thanks, Phil. You've been a big help to me. I can never thank you enough." "I don't need thanks. Just stay healthy."

I bought him his own dresser and had it placed in the bedroom. I purchased new clothing for him, placing them neatly in the dresser. I made sure we had plenty of healthy food on hand and even purchased male vitamins for him. I finally asked him, "Are you ready for this next step in our lives?" "Yep, never been as ready for anything as much as this."

"OK, Mr. Smith, bring over whatever stuff you have. We're officially living together."

He was shocked when he walked into the bedroom and saw the new dresser filled with new clothes. "Phil, you're crazy. You didn't need to do this." "I know. I wanted to." I started to refold and place the clothes he had brought over into the dresser.

I had a split-second flashback of attempting to have William move in; it was a disaster from the first few moments. William had walked in, carrying his clothes with such an aggressive, arrogant attitude, that although I had rearranged closet space for him, he started to shuffle my clothing around, instructing me as to how things were going to be. His behavior made me think that he must be, in some way, "just plain crazy." I saw the shock in his face when I pulled his clothing out of the closet and told him, "William, this is never going to work. Get out." Peter's personality was the complete opposite.

"Phil, I'm not used to this." Laughing, he continued, "Wow, socks in the sock spot and underwear in their own spot. I've never been fussed over like this before." "Get used to it, Mr. Smith. This is what a loving relationship is all about, taking good care of each other." It seemed, once again, I had a husband who demanded nothing, and I was willing to give him everything.

That week, he started to give me his paycheck, "Here, Phil, take it and pay for whatever we need." I started a bank account in his name, placing his money into the account. I couldn't believe that he had worked from the early age of twelve and never had a bank account, didn't own a credit card, didn't have any investments. He had made more money than me by far but had nothing to show for it. I refused to have him piss away any more hard-earned money.

After a few months of putting his paychecks into the account, I handed him the bank statement. "Pete, I have a gift for you." "What's this? Where did this come from?" "From your hard work. This is what you should have been doing for years." He sat, staring at the bank statement for a minute, and then almost in a whisper, said, "Phil, I gave you the money to help pay for the bills. Now I feel like a freeloader." "Pete, I didn't need the money, and think of it as an investment." "Phil, an investment in what?" "I'm investing in the most important asset of all—in you."

I wasn't sure if he was going to laugh or cry; he just stared at me for a few seconds and spoke with heartfelt words that almost made me cry. "Phil, I knew when I met you years ago that you're a very special chick." I sat on his lap, both of my legs wrapped around him, holding his face in my hands I whispered, "You're very special to me."

In the first year of living together, we loved much and argued very little. As different as we were, our personalities flowed very well together, and we became, in every sense, husband and wife. The first argument I recall having with Peter was about his absentminded behavior of not locking the house door. I came home from work and found the door not only unlocked but wide open. I was furious, and as soon as he came home, I let him have a piece of my mind.

I spoke, not quite yelling but in a very raised voice, "Pete, I found the door wide open. Do you have mental problems that you can't remember to lock a door, or is it that you just don't give a shit?" "Jesus, Phil, calm down. It's not like we live in the South Bronx." The remark made me see red. "What, you think only people in the South Bronx get robbed? From now on, don't forget to lock the door. You know what your biggest problem has been your whole life?" Peter, yelling back, responded, "No. What, Ms. Abys? Enlighten me!" His sarcastic tone was making me crazy. "Your problem is that you never placed value on yourself and what is yours." I pointed to myself and our surroundings. "It's about time you start." "OK, I get it. Can I take a shower now?" "Yeah, and wash good."

He walked away, muttering, "Why don't you wash my nuts?" As mad as I was, the comment made me laugh. I waited for him to start washing and then climbed into the shower with him. His eyebrows rose, and a devilish smirk appeared on his lips. "Well, Mr. Smith, I'm here to wash your nuts." I started to soap him up. He pulled me closer, whispering, "Ms. Abys, let's argue more often."

Peter's absentminded behavior drove me a bit crazy, especially in the morning before work. He would give me a kiss, saying, "OK, Ms. Abys, have a good day. See you later." No sooner did he walk out the door than he walked back in, searching for his keys and wallet. Finally, I just started standing near the door with keys in one hand and wallet in other. "Here you go, Mr. Smith—keys, wallet, and I believe your nuts are in place." He laughed every time while grabbing his crotch, "Yep, nuts are still here." "Great, we can't afford to lose those."

After a few months of that routine, I just asked him to put a shelf and hook in the hallway closet. "Sure, why?" "The shelf is for your wallet and all the junk in your pockets, and the hook for your keys. Now when you come home, remove your boots outside the door, put boots in closet, keys on hook, and all pocket stuff on the shelf. Can you remember to do that?" Peter, while laughing, replied, "Hum, I'm not sure. I might forget." I gave him a shove, and he pulled me close, kissing me and telling me he was starting to feel like a pussy-whipped husband. I reminded him it's better to be pussy-whipped than not know where your wallet is and spend fifteen minutes looking for it, especially before six thirty in the morning.

I had stopped teaching at the *gym* and only exercised for myself about four times a week. My life had started to change, and I was becoming a wife in every sense. Busy with domestic concerns that I had, years prior, sworn never to be burdened with again.

Peter seemed to enjoy domestic life very much, and as unbelievable as it may sound, he relished the thought of being in a clean, well-organized kitchen, playing at being chef. The days I would work out, he'd run home to start dinner and, for the most part, was really very good. My favorite meal Peter prepared was a lemon sole fillet stuffed with sautéed shrimps. The only problem was that, with the extra shrimp, he had also prepared a shrimp cocktail, which he placed uncovered in the freezer to chill.

He beamed with pride when I walked in, and he proudly announced, "Phil, sit and relax." Pointing to the freezer, "Have a few shrimps." I opened the freezer and wasn't sure if I should laugh or cry. "Pete, the shrimp looks great, but next time, please cover them. The whole house is going to smell like a fish market." He immediately became insulted. "Jesus, Phil, can't I do anything right in the kitchen?" "Peter, it all looks really good, but just be careful, especially with fish. I like my house to smell fresh, not fishy." "*Oh!* For God's sake, Phil, you have a nose like a bloodhound. I hope you enjoy dinner," and placed a hand on his hip mocking me. "I slaved for hours over this." I gave him a hug and went to take a shower. Dinner was really great, but dessert was better.

I spent a good deal of time in the kitchen, trying to help Peter get over what I call his food phobias. He had been traumatized as a child by poorly prepared meals with certain food items such as vegetables and eggs, making him extremely anxious. When he'd come home and find me preparing vegetables like spinach with white kidney beans, he'd back away from the kitchen, waving a hand, saying, "*Oh,* I hate spinach. My mom boiled frozen spinach and just popped the wet stuff on our plates. It was torture trying to eat that crap."

"Pete, remember these Italian crackers I told you about?" "Yeah." "Let's see. Maybe you'll like spinach prepared this way." I had sautéed fresh baby spinach in olive oil, garlic, and hot pepper flakes, adding white kidney beans to it, letting it sit for a while until all the flavors came together. I slightly soaked a *frezzile* under cold water, breaking it into bite-size pieces in a bowl, placing the hot spinach and beans over the top, adding extra hot liquid from the pan to the bottom and top of the dish.

"Pete, just try this." While I sliced the meat loaf that I had stuffed with three different cheeses and sprinkled Parmesan cheese over the top, I watched him from the kitchen. At first, he took a miniscule bite, carefully chewing. I didn't bother to ask if he liked it; he just kept eating, and as I served him his meat loaf, he looked up, smiling, "Phil, I can't believe it. This is really good."

Teasing him, I asked if he was with me for the food only. "Ah, well, there are a few other things you're good at, but the food really keeps me here." "Pete, just promise me you'll never tell my mother that I used canned beans. She'll give me hell, telling me, 'What does it take to cook a bag of beans?' You know, after working all day, I should be able to start soaking and boiling beans." We both started to laugh.

I was preparing a potato and onion frittata for dinner one day, and as he walked into the kitchen, he gave me a hug and a kiss, asking, "Wow, Phil, what smells so good?" "I'm making a frittata. It's like an Italian omelet." I noticed that concerned look on his face. "Don't tell me you have childhood trauma with eggs." "Yeah, well, my mom made us eat runny undercooked eggs that at times I just put them in my pocket instead of eating them and then spill my pockets outside." "Pete, I don't believe that you stuffed your pockets with runny eggs." "Believe it. I'd rather have eggy pockets then eat those eggs."

"Well, this is what we're having for dinner, and maybe you can help me flip the frittata over. I'm not strong enough to flip a large skillet like my mom does. You can do that." He watched as I beat the eggs—to which I had added salt, black pepper, and a generous portion of Parmesan cheese—until frothy then poured the mixture over the cooked potatoes and onions. I explained that after the bottom cooks and the sides are a golden color, he was going to take this plate that fits right over the skillet and flip the omelet onto the plate then slide the omelet back into the pan to finish cooking it. "No runny eggs in this house, OK."

He smiled, watched, and flipped very well. "Pete, take a quick shower while the omelet finishes cooking, then we'll eat." "Phil, what would you do if I wasn't here to flip?" "I'd just place the skillet into a hot oven, maybe sprinkle a mixture of Parmesan cheese and breadcrumbs on top to make it extra crispy." "*Oh!*"

After his shower, we sat down to have dinner, and he ran to the refrigerator to look for catsup. "Phil, where's the catsup?" Oh, sorry, Pete, I never use catsup." "You're definitely not a real American." "Next time we go food shopping, I'll buy catsup, but what do you need it for?" "To put on the eggs." "For God's sake, Pete, that's just as disgusting as drinking milk with your dinner. How can you possibly taste the food with your taste buds covered by milk or catsup? Just try it this way." He ate the frittata and didn't stop eating until it was completely gone. I didn't even ask if he liked the omelet; with the last bit still in his mouth, he walked into the kitchen to cut himself another slice. I just smiled to myself.

As a side dish, I had served fried zucchini slices in olive oil and fresh mint dressing which my mom had prepared a few days earlier and stored in a mason jar for us to have. He picked up slices of bread and put spoonfuls of the zucchini salad on top. With every mouthful, he commented, "Wow! This is really good." I nodded, placing my chin on my hand, watching him enjoy his meal, and wondered if he enjoyed me as much as the food.

It was during one of our dinnertime conversations that I asked the question that had been on my mind from the day I climbed to the rooftop of the school to view his compound bucket-grown tomatoes. For over five years, I had wondered why he had made that crazy comment—"Yeah, when the wind blows, my dick gets hard." I had always assumed that he wanted to see what type of reaction I would have to such an off-colored remark, but I wanted to hear his reasoning. This was his explanation. "Well, Phil, I was told by the staff that you were a very proper person, but somehow, I knew you were no prude, so I figured if you met my stare after that comment without smacking me in the face, I had a good chance of getting you in the sack." I started to laugh, asking him, "Well, Mr. Smith, did I meet your expectations?" "Phil, I saw a slight smile on your lips, and you met my stare head-on. I knew I had you halfway in the sack." "Well, Mr. Smith, I knew I had you there too." We both howled with laughter.

We started to discuss legal marriage; the word in itself gave me a queasy feeling in my stomach. I knew and had told him many times that I loved him, but why spoil a good thing? We were enjoying our lives so much together. We discussed having a wedding on a yacht out on the water. That sounded so romantic, but neither of us pushed the issue. We didn't see the point. Peter still had not asked me to meet anyone in his family, and from the brief conversation we had about them, I really didn't want to.

In less than a year of living together, I realized that I needed to see my gynecologist. I was feeling great but had missed two menstrual cycles. At first, I thought that age was taking its toll but decided to make an appointment. "Pete, I have an appointment with my gynecologist." His face immediately beamed. "You feel OK?" "I feel fine, but I think it's a good idea for me to see him." I noticed the smile on his face. "OK, great. I'll see you later."

I had been seeing the same doctor for ten years and knew all the nurses in the office. Some had taken my classes at the gym and knew me well. I explained why I was there, and they asked for a urine sample. I waited in the reception area with other women showing baby bumps and noticed that most were much younger then I was. While sitting, I started to get waves of panic attacks. I didn't want my life to change that much. *We're happy. Why spoil it?* I told myself. *It's probably the start of menopause.*

The nurse called my name, and as I walked into the doctor's office, I noticed the smile on her face.

My doctor sat across from me, and he knew I was not legally married. "Filomena, you're entering the third month of pregnancy." I sat so still, trying to absorb the reality of my situation. The doctor noticed my blank stare and asked, "Are you and your partner going to be happy with this pregnancy?" I fumbled for words. "I'm not sure. I think he's going to be happy. I'm . . . I'm a bit overwhelmed." "I understand, but at this point, you really need to discuss and let me know what your intentions are. Please make an appointment for next week, and we'll take it from there." I stood up in a daze, and as I started to thank him, he smiled, and congratulated me." I said, "Thanks. I'll see you next week" and walked out to make an appointment.

I drove home in disbelief, telling myself, *Maybe they made a mistake. I feel fine. I don't feel pregnant.* Peter found me slumped in the armchair in front of the TV, which was on, but I was not watching. "Hey, how did it go at the doctor's?" I didn't answer immediately, and he knelt down next to the chair, holding my hand. "Are you OK?" "Yeah, I'm fine." He continued to stare, looking for an answer, but his smile already told me he knew what was going on. I turned off the TV and slowly started to tell him the most important news of our lives. My emotions were on a roller coaster; I wasn't sure if I was happy or sad. I just knew that I was really scared.

He shook my hand, "Hey, Phil, come on. What's up?" "Pete, I'm three months pregnant—" and I didn't finish the sentence. His face beamed with happiness. "That's great!" he said, and he kissed my hand. He looked at my blank expression and asked, "Phil, don't tell me you're not happy. This is great. It's what I always wanted to have, a child, and I'm so lucky to have that chance with you." I didn't know what to say, but his happiness made me happy. "Pete, it's not that I'm not happy. It's just that everything was going so well. I'm so afraid that this will upset our relationship." "Phil, listen to me. This is the right time for both of us. If not now then when? You'll be thirty-seven by the time this baby is born. This is a godsend." Everything he said made me feel safe. I reached for his face and placed my forehead on his, telling him, "I'm just so scared."

"Don't worry, Phil, everything is going to be just fine. What did the doctor say?" "He said we should discuss it and let him know what our intentions are." "What is there to discuss? We're having a baby. Did he say everything is OK with you?" "Yes, Pete, I'm fine. I have an appointment for next week. You know, the usual testing et cetera—"

He pulled me off the chair and into his arms, "Thanks, Phil. I couldn't ask for a better mother for our child. I know it's all going to work out." "Peter, when we first met, I thought it would be great to just be friends. Now we're having a child together." Laughing, he responded, "OK, we'll be friendly parents." He made me laugh, and as I sat back down, I asked him, "Who's telling my mother?" "*Oh* shit, yeah, your mother. OK, I'll tell her this weekend."

"That's a very good idea. You tell her. She likes you better than me and calls you the pearl. She's forever reminding me of how lucky I was to find a pearl of a person like you." From the first day my mother met Peter, they somehow understood each other. Peter had worked his diplomatic charm on her, and whenever we had gone out to Long Island, he would bring her fish, calms, and fresh vegetables. The first time we had stopped at her home on our way back from Long Island, I ran up the steps to give her a bag full of fresh fruits and vegetables. Peter waved to her from the car, and she asked me if he was Sicilian. "Sicilian? Ma, he's Irish." "*Oh!* He's so dark for an Irish. He looks Sicilian to me." "Ma, he spends a lot of time in the sun." "OK, this weekend, you bring him over for dinner. I like to meet this dark Irish."

She had liked him immediately, and he felt so comfortable with her that from the first day they met, he also called her *Ma*. She had prepared a usual Sunday meal of pasta with ragù sauce; from the saucepot came out a plate full of meatballs and *bragoli*, which she placed in a large bowl and on the table. Fried broccoli raab with sausages was also placed on the table, along with a basket full of fresh bread. Peter's favorite was still in the oven, eggplant parmigiana. When my mom pulled out the eggplant, Peter charmed her with, "Ma, how did you know that this is my favorite Italian meal? I could eat this every day." My mom smiled, and I translated whatever she didn't understand. Peter continued to charm her by complimenting her motherly skills, "Ma, I really need to thank you for teaching your daughter how to cook so well."

In Neapolitan, she asked what he had said and told me to tell him that I was OK but still needed to learn more. He got a kick out of that and started to laugh. I could see the instant connection and thanked God for small favors. We sat down, and I watched Peter eat without any reservations; he didn't need convincing to eat the broccoli raab. He enjoyed it on bread with sliced sausages on top. This Irishman was starting to eat like a Neapolitan. I watched my mother watching Peter enjoying his meal and saw her smile; it filled my heart with love for both of them. During dinner, I had to translate often, but the language of good food was helping to bridge that gap.

That evening, after many hugs and kisses from Peter, I finally admitted to myself that we were expecting a child. We decided to celebrate by going to our favorite Chinese restaurant, and for some strange reason, everything tasted so much better. I ate more than usual, Peter closely watching me, almost speaking to himself. "Thank God." "For what, Peter?" "For what, Phil? You're three months pregnant and haven't been sick one day. You didn't even know you were pregnant. Let's hope it stays this way." With my right hand, I made the sign of the horn, imitating the old-fashioned Italian symbol for keeping the evil eye (*malocchio*) away; we both busted out laughing.

I called my mother and asked her if we could go over for Sunday dinner. "Sure, I make Pit's favorite, eggplant parmigiana. That Sunday, before going to my mother's home, we stopped at Conti's an Italian pastry shop on Morris Park Avenue and purchased an assortment of miniature pastries. As soon as we walked in, Peter gave my mother a big hug and kiss, asking her, "Ma, what smells so good?" "I make parmigiana just for you. I know you like." I kissed my mother, placed the pastries in the refrigerator, and went to sit on the sofa in the living room.

Peter looked at me, and I smiled, nodding my head, insinuating. "Well, are you going to tell her?" He shrugged his shoulder and, with a broad smile on his face, started to work his magic on my mother. I watched from the living room and told myself, *Don't start laughing just yet.* "Ma, I have a special surprise for you." My mom looked up and waited. "Your daughter, we're going to have a baby." Without saying a word to him, she immediately came to the doorway of the living room and, in a harsh voice, asked me in Neapolitan, "You're pregnant?" I nodded and said, "Yeah." "You're not even married." "I know, Ma. We're thinking of that, but—" She didn't let me finish the sentence. "You thinking of doing other things first."

Peter asked, "What did she say?" I told him, and he continued to soften my mother. "Ma, you're absolutely right, but don't worry, we're going to get married real soon, and by next Christmas, it's going to be great. You'll have your first grandchild. You know, this family needs some children. I know you're going to be a great grandmother." I couldn't believe it. She must have gotten the gist of what he was saying and smiled. "Come, Pit, I make this just for you." Bringing the food to the table, she wanted to make sure the pearl was well fed.

She came over to the doorway and, in a stern voice, asked, "Hey, you going to eat or what?" I got up and wondered if she thought that I had gotten myself pregnant. As we sat eating, I asked Peter if I could have some of the parmigiana my mom made just for him. With a smile and teasing me, Peter said, "OK, I'll share but only a little bit." My mom turned to me and asked how many months. When I told her three, she replied, "*Ah*, well done. Did you see a doctor? Is everything OK?" I told her, "So far, so good" and that I was having testing done next week.

Peter spoke and put a smile on my mother's face again. "Ma, you know, we're so lucky your daughter, she never gets sick." "My daughter, she just like me when I'm pregnant. I never get sick, I eat everything, I work all day, and never get sick." "Yeah, Ma, thank God your daughter is just like you." I had to hand it to Pete. He had a special talent. I turned to him and told him, "You should have been a diplomat. I can't believe it, Pete. My mom is angry at me and smiling at you." "*Ah*, don't worry, Phil. It's that old-fashioned Italian bullshit. You know, it's OK for a man to fool around, but not for a female." I responded, "Did you ever wonder who all these men are supposed to go to bed with if a female isn't allowed to fool around?" Peter shrugged, and we both started to laugh.

The following week, I went for my first visit, and the usual testing was done, along with a sonogram. I watched as the images appeared on the screen, wondering if everything was OK. I asked the technician. She said, "Yes, everything is fine. After you get dressed, the doctor will see you." Again, I sat across from my doctor as he started to tell me, "Well, Filomena, you're full of surprises. You're pregnant with twins."

I sat in complete disbelief as he continued to explain that the sonogram revealed two fetuses but only one heartbeat. I had images in my mind of conjoined twins sharing one heart and started to sweat. The doctor continued to explain that at times it's hard to pick up a heartbeat and that if one didn't develop soon, the fetus will probably be miscarried.

I summoned the courage to ask, "What happens to the other fetus?" "Don't become too alarmed. This is not that uncommon. The fetus with the heartbeat is completely fine. The other will simply disburse back into the placenta, and you may have some spot bleeding." He saw the worried look on my face and reassured me that everything was OK. "Just go home and continue with your daily routine. Unless something happens, I see you in four weeks."

As I drove home, I realized that, in a brief amount of time, I had become very attached to the child inside of me and hoped that at least one was well. I almost started to cry thinking of miscarrying both and disappointing Peter. I felt an enormous pressure to have a healthy child for him. I knew how very much he wanted to have a son.

He found me slumped in the chair again and knelt down next to me. "How did it go? Is everything OK?" "I'm not sure. I'm pregnant with twins, and . . ." I didn't finish the sentence. "Twins? What do you mean twins?" "Peter, what does *twin* mean? Two, double, more than one." "Holy shit, I can't believe it. Twins don't run in my family." "They don't run in my family either, but, Pete, listen. They only picked up one heartbeat, and they're not sure if the other fetus will develop." I saw the immediate concern on his face and tried to explain what the doctor had told me.

For the next two weeks, we continued to live our daily lives, becoming extremely attached to our child. I had already slowed down on my exercise and didn't perform the countless number of abdominal crunches and stopped stretching myself into pretzel-like positions. Peter, forever the diplomat, very carefully asked after I came home from the *gym*, "*Ah*, Phil, I'm not trying to tell you what to do, but maybe you should slow down on the exercise." I had to smile at him in understanding of his feelings, and with a sweet kiss on his cheek, I whispered in his ear, "I already have." He whispered back, "Thank you."

It wasn't more than two weeks after I had found out about having twins that I started to have a small amount of bleeding. I immediately told Peter, and the concerned look on his face was overwhelming, but he remained calm. I called my doctor, and he sensed the concern in my voice. "Filomena, there's no reason to panic. All your test results are perfect. As I told you on your last visit, this would probably happen. The bleeding will dissipate in a few hours." With my voice still in a bit of panic, I asked if I should go over to see him. "It's not necessary. If the bleeding does not stop by tomorrow, come in for a visit." As Peter held me, I prayed. I had not prayed in years, but this time, with all my heart and soul, I asked God, "Please don't let me lose this child. We both love it so much." In less than an hour, I stopped bleeding, and when I told Peter, I saw the relief on his face.

We had to start discussing legal marriage, and at first, I didn't see the sense in it. I still was not comfortable with the term *legal marriage*. Peter made more sense than I did on this issue and kindly but firmly reminded me of practical issues, such as claiming each other and the child on our medical forms, pension, and most important, my mother's request for legal marriage. He always had the ability to make me laugh. "Phil, don't tell me you just want to be friends." I had to admit to myself that we were already husband and wife in every sense and needed to take the final, legal step.

We went to the White Plains office and filled out all the necessary papers. We wanted to just simply get married and go home. The clerk asked us if we were bringing our own witnesses, we looked at each other and said, "Sure, we'll bring two witnesses." I decided on my sister, and he decided on his brother.

I thought to myself, *Fine, that should be easy enough.* As soon as the families found out of the set date for the wedding, everyone wanted to come. The only problem was that I still had not met Peter's family. "Phil, I guess before the wedding, you should meet my mother and father." "Pete, I think that's a good idea." From the short conversation we had about them, in which Peter vented with great bitterness, I felt a bit anxious but decided to meet with them on a positive note.

"Phil, after my parents got divorced, my mom moved into an apartment, and my dad moved in with his girlfriend. We'll go over to see my mother this week and then my dad next week." "OK, fine." As I met with both parents, I sensed the nervousness in Peter. I did my best to be cordial and as friendly as possible. I thought it went very well, and when I told Peter, "That wasn't so bad," he said, "Thank God, and give it time. Things change in my family in an instant."

Pete's "I Can Cook" Stuffed Lemon Sole

Ingredients

1½ lb. of lemon sole
½ lb. of medium-size shrimp (cleaned, deveined, and cut into small bite-size portions)
¼ cup Chopped scallions
1 stick of butter
Juice of 2 lemons
1 cup of unflavored breadcrumbs

In a large hot skillet, melt half of the butter; sauté scallions until wilted. Add remaining butter, melt, and stir; add shrimp, mix well, and cook for about three minutes. Add half the lemon juice, toss well, add breadcrumbs, and toss very well. Remove from heat. On a large piece of wax paper, place fish fillets and add about two tablespoons of shrimp stuffing in the middle. Roll into a tight cylinders, skewer each piece with toothpicks, and place seam down into a butter casserole dish. Add tiny pats of butter on top of each fillet; drizzle the remaining lemon juice on top. Bake at 375°F until fish is flaky or about twenty to twenty-five minutes. Do not overcook.

"I Never Eat Vegetables" Spinach with Cannellini Beans or Escarole with Cannellini Beans

Ingredients

6 tbs. of canola oil or olive oil
2 15-oz. cans of white cannellini beans
24 oz. of washed baby spinach
4 cloves of crushed garlic
Salt and red pepper flakes to taste

In a skillet, heat four tablespoons of oil, add garlic and red pepper flakes, sauté garlic until it gets a slight golden color, add spinach, toss well, and cook on a medium-low flame until it softens. Add the cannellini beans (without rising), toss well, add a bit of water to the cans, and slouch around, adding the water to the skillet. Add salt to taste. Simmer for no more than ten minutes. Serve over toasted Italian bread or *frezzile*. This recipe can also be made with escarole. Wash two heads of escarole, cut off the back end, and discard. Cut the escarole into small portions, and sauté in oil, garlic, and hot pepper flakes. Add a bit of water if needed (four tablespoons), and cook until tender. Add beans, toss well. Slouch the cans with a bit of water, add to escarole, toss well, add salt to taste, and cook for about ten minutes. When serving, place toasted bread or *friselle* in a bowl, and spoon spinach-escarole with beans over the top, adding the liquid from the skillet. Drizzle olive oil over the top.

A Neapolitan Patty Boy's Broccoli Raab with Sausages

Ingredients

2 lb. of Italian sausages (you may use whatever type you prefer, sweet or hot)
2 heads of broccoli raab, washed and coarsely chopped
4 cloves of garlic
4 tbs. of oil
Salt and red pepper flakes to taste

Heat a large skillet with a tablespoon of oil; brown sausages on all sides and remove onto a plate. In the same skillet, add three more tablespoons of oil, heat over a medium-low flame, add garlic and red pepper flakes, and sauté for a minute or so until the garlic has a bit of color. Add the broccoli raab, toss well, add salt to taste, and cook covered over a medium flame until almost tender. Add browned sausages to broccoli, toss well, and cook over a medium-low flame for about five minutes or until sausages are completely cooked. (If you prefer less bitterness in the broccoli, you can blanch them first in salted boiling water.) Broccoli raab and sausages make a great sandwich with crusty Italian bread.

Fried Zucchini with Fresh Mint Dressing

Ingredients

½ cup of vegetable oil for frying
¼ cup of Olive oil for dressing
¼ cup of White vinegar for dressing
Fresh mint
Salt to taste
4 zucchinis, washed and cut into thin slices

Place vegetable oil in a skillet over a medium flame. When oil is hot, fry zucchini slices until they reach a slightly golden color. Remove zucchini slices with a slotted spoon, place in a bowl. Sprinkle salt, drizzle olive oil and vinegar on top of the zucchini slices, shred mint by hand into the zucchini slices, toss well, and serve. You can place the zucchinis into a mason jar and add a bit more olive oil and vinegar to cover the zucchinis. Store tightly covered in the refrigerator; this salad keeps for about a week and is great for picnics.

Chapter 11

The Wedding

I'm not sure how all the wedding fuss started, but what I was trying to avoid happened, and the simple signing of papers snowballed into a wedding. I found out that at least sixteen family members would be attending the courthouse signing of papers with a short service and that Peter's oldest sister very kindly arranged a beautiful restaurant dinner for everyone to attend. I understood that this was Peter's first marriage and was happy to have the celebration. I purchased a beautiful white satin suit to wear, and although I was well into the fourth month of pregnancy, I didn't look pregnant at all. Peter purchased a new suit, and we were happy and ready to be a legal husband and wife. *There,* I thought, *not too much stress.*

That is, until the phone calls started from his mother. "If your father is bringing that woman to the wedding, I'm not coming." You could have cut the nervousness in Peter with a knife, and at times I physically held his hand down in trying to stop him from pulling out his mustache. I tried to remain neutral, but as a female, I understood a woman not wanting to be in the same room with not so much her ex-husband but with the woman that had been one of his mistresses for years. It was like rubbing salt into an old wound. I told myself, *Don't take sides. Just focus on staying healthy. All this other stuff is bullshit.*

The back-and-forth bickering was taking its toll on Peter, and I worried about him going off into his old habits. I understood that a good portion of his drug abuse was connected to him not finding comfort and serenity with his own family; I desperately tried to compensate for them.

The day finally arrived, and everyone was there at the courthouse; even Peter's mother came, and I thought she displayed great fortitude to be in the same room with her ex-husband's mistress. I was very happy that everything went well.

It wasn't until years later that Peter told me his brother had pulled him over just before the courthouse service was about to start, lecturing him, "You know, you don't have to marry her. We can walk out of here right now." In a fit of rage, Peter vented to me, "First, that son of a bitch taunted me when you decided to only see that donkey fuck. 'What happened to that nice Italian girl? You fucked that up too?' And then when I'm finally happy and ready to get married, he's asking me to walk out on you. I told that son of a bitch that I was sound and sober and had been waiting to marry you for years. Just like him to try and burst my bubble."

I thought, *This is where the problem lies—the lack of understanding that families are meant to comfort each other, not taunt one other.* Peter continued in a cleansing rage to spew out, "That selfish bastard married his wife, who already had two children with two different husbands in a drunken state, and managed to glom the Long Island house for himself, and he tries to give me advice."

I sat listening, allowing him to release his frustration, and then simply told him, "Forget it. It's not worth the energy you're using. Let it go. When you're ready, we'll have dinner. It's one of your favorites." Peter pushed his head back onto the sofa whispering, "Thanks, Phil. I don't know what I would do without you." I gave him a soft kiss on the cheek, telling him, "Pete, I don't know what I would do without you." With both of my hands holding his face, I continued, "I'm so happy we're husband and wife. You were so right when we got back together. It was meant to be."

With the stress from the wedding over, we were both basking in the glow of not only being newlyweds but from the anticipation of waiting for our first child. How can one describe complete shock and disbelief? When one evening, no more than two weeks after our wedding, I picked up the receiver that stood on the nightstand in the bedroom with Peter lying next to me and heard William's voice. I became dizzy, anxious, and speechless. I guess I was completely shocked to hear his voice.

"Hey, Phil, it's William." Peter heard his voice and immediately jumped off the bed and walked out of the house. I stood there motionless, not knowing what to do. William continued, "Phil, I heard through the grapevine that you got married. I didn't believe it. I want to hear it from you." All I could manage to say was "William, I can't talk now."

"Oh, why, is he there? I'll call you tomorrow." With those words ringing in my ears, I placed the receiver down and walked out of the apartment to look for Peter. I found him sitting in the dark on the bench in front of the building. I sat next to him and, without turning around to look at me, staring straight ahead into the darkness, he spoke, "If that donkey motherfucker ever comes near you again, this time, I'll put a bullet in his head." The calm coldness in his voice frightened me, and I understood that this was no longer just about me but about the child he so much wanted.

I reached for his hand, telling him, "Pete, that's not necessary. Come on, let's go upstairs. It's cold out here." He got up, taking me by the hand, and as we climbed the stairs, I knew I needed to make one last phone call when my husband was not around.

After work the next day, before Peter came home, I took a deep breath, picking up the receiver to call William. "Hi, William. It's Phil." "Hey, Phil, how's it going? I heard—" And before he could finish his sentence, in a voice filled with emotional stress, I asked, "Why did you call me after all this time?" "Phil, I just wanted to hear it from you. Are you really legally married?"

"Yes, I'm really legally married, and I'm five months pregnant." With my voice cracking and shaking, I continued, "I can't afford to get upset." "I'm sorry, Phil. Please don't get upset. I just wanted to make sure that everything was OK with you. Your husband didn't yell or get mad at you yesterday when I called?"

"No, William, my husband is a gentleman. He just walked out of the house to give me some space. William, please don't call me anymore. I don't want to have problems with my husband, and I really can't afford to get upset." "Phil, your husband is good to you?" "Yes, he's very good to me." "OK, I promise I'll never call again. Please apologize to your husband for me. Tell him I'm sorry for upsetting his household." "OK, William, I will. Bye." We never spoke to each other again.

In no more than a few seconds after that conversation, my whole body started to shake. My legs felt wobbly, my hands sweaty and trembling. I felt as if I was going to start crying but held back the tears. I became so frightened that I lay down on the bed and placed my hands over my eyes to stop the tears from flowing. At first, I wasn't sure if William was being sincere or sarcastic, but as I lay there, I realized that it was his old-fashioned way of withdrawing from the four-year-long tug-of-war and that he was truly a caring gentleman.

I pulled the blanket over myself, hoping that the extra warmth would stop the shaking, and prayed that William find happiness. The concern over having another miscarriage was forever present, and I forced myself to close my eyes and meditate on all the positive good things in my life. I slowly started to take deep breaths, relaxing my whole body.

When Peter came home, he found me in bed and immediately became concerned. "Hey, are you OK? I've never seen you lay down at this time." "I'm OK, just a little tired today. Pete, I didn't cook today. We can have the leftover beef stew." As he rubbed my cheeks with the back of his hand, I saw him smile, and he softly said, "Phil, you don't have to cook every day. Just stay there. I'll take a quick shower and get everything ready for dinner." I was happy for the help still extremely afraid to get out of bed.

While we had dinner, I noticed that Peter was unusually quiet; I knew what was on his mind. I searched for the right words to put him at ease. "How was work?" "Same old crap. How was work with you?" "Same." With increasing nervousness and while twisting my napkin into a tightrope, I summoned the courage to speak. "Umm, I called William today." Peter didn't look up but spoke in a cold manner that I had never heard before. "Yeah, what about?" "I asked him why he called. He said he wanted to hear it from me that I was legally married. I told him yes and that I was also expecting and to please not call here anymore. William also wanted to know if you were good to me and asked me to apologize to you for upsetting your household." Peter never looked up while I spoke. His response was short in words but very clear in meaning. "I think that's a really good idea." We never spoke about William again.

"You Don't Need to Cook Every Day" Beef Stew

Ingredients:

2 to 4 tbs. of vegetable oil for browning beef and vegetables
1 medium-size onion, finely diced

4 cloves of garlic

½ lb. of London broil cut into tiny bite-size portions (you may use chuck or other stew meat)

4 medium-size potatoes, peeled, washed, and cut into bite-size portions (if cooking for an Irishman, add 2 more potatoes)

3 medium-size carrots, scraped, washed, and cut into bite-size portions

1 cup of defrosted peas

4 Italian-style canned tomatoes (crushed by hand with all the juice)

3 cups of boiling water or beef stock

Optional: If you prefer a spicy stew, add a finely diced hot pepper such as jalapeno or red pepper flakes or a teaspoon of chili powder. You may also add about ½ cup of good table wine, red or white.

Salt to taste

Add oil to a large stockpot, heat over a medium flame, add the onion and garlic, and cook until slightly golden; if using hot pepper, add at this point and mix well. Add the beef and toss well, seasoning with a small amount of salt and chili powder. If using wine, add at this point, mix well with the meat, and allow alcohol to foam and dissipate. Add the potatoes and carrots, mixing well with the meat; allow the vegetables to brown for a few minutes. Add the tomatoes, mixing well, and season with a bit more salt. Add hot liquid (water or stock), just enough to cover meat and vegetables. Cook covered for about an hour over a medium flame. Add peas, and cook over a low flame for about forty-five minutes or until meat and vegetables are tender.

I understand that most recipes for beef stew dredge the meat in flour before browning, but I used this method once, and we did not enjoy the results as much as just plain browning the beef. Of course, you can use beef stock instead of water, but be careful with salting the stew. At times, I have spiced the meat while browning with a combination of chili powder, paprika, or Goya Latin spices with good results. Make sure the pot is large enough for the beef and vegetables to brown well before adding the liquid.

We enjoy this stew over a bed of cooked rice or egg noodles.

Chapter 12

Our Son

After the call from William, I made sure to give Peter extra attention to reassure him that I was in love with him and looking forward to the birth of our child. I fussed over his clothes, prepared daily meals that he always seemed to enjoy, and heated up the bed as much as possible with a baby bump that was finally starting to show. One evening, I realized that I had never told him I still had the Hawaiian shirt he had given me years ago.

The shirt had been placed at the bottom of my drawer, and while I solely dated William, I had several times walked over to the garbage with the shirt in hand, ready to dispose of it. I could never bring myself to discard that shirt, again hiding it safely under other garments. In the recesses of my being, I must have had a deep connection with the sentiment attached to the shirt and felt love for the original owner, now my husband.

I decided to put that shirt to good use and, without anything else on, walked into the living room, where Peter was watching TV. His eyes immediately widened, and that devilish look appeared on his face.

"Well well well, Ms. Abys. I can't believe it. You still have that shirt."

"Mr. Smith, I tried many times to get rid of it but could never bring myself to doing it. I guess I was in love with you from the start but never admitted it to myself."

Peter, pulling me by the hand, bringing me closer to him, softly said, "Then why don't you show me how much in love you're still in?" As Peter spoke, he ever so gently lifted the shirt and rubbed my round belly. I still use that shirt on occasions to show him my love but have never forgotten my mother's only love advice that in order to keep a husband happy, a wife must heat up the kitchen first. A rough translation—"first take care of a man's belly, and everything else will take care of itself."

Although Peter always claimed to be just an American, his Irish roots spoke loud and clear when it came to foods like potatoes, bacon, and beef. On one occasion, I had prepared roast beef with a potato *gatto*, and he claimed that it was the best shepherd pie he ever had. I started to laugh, telling him, "Patty Boy, this is called *gatto*. It's from the French word meaning 'cake.' I guess when the French ruled Naples, they introduced French words into the Neapolitan language, and *gatto* was used to describe a potato pie that can be stuffed with sliced mozzarella, diced salami, and whatever else you like."

"Well, Phil, I don't care what it's called. It's great." I knew that I could even get him to eat Brussels sprouts if I sautéed them in bacon, garlic, and hot pepper flakes. When he walked into the kitchen, I didn't let him say a word; I just put my hand up, stopping him. "Pete, don't worry, I didn't boil the shit out of them." The Brussels sprouts went along fine with fried chicken cutlets, and I didn't need to ask if he liked them. The whole bowl was finished, and he jokingly said, "Phil, I'm only eating them to please you."

Peter relished looking at my growing belly and breasts. While we watched *Jeopardy*, he would cup his hands over my belly and pretend to talk to our child with silly comments. "Hey down there, can you hear me? I'm kicking your mom's butt in *Jeopardy!*" Or "How did you like the meditation music your mom listened to today?" As for the breast, well, he had always enjoyed them, but the enjoyment was enhanced not so much by the size as by the thought that they would one day feed his child.

Luckily, I was able to work a full day, exercise, and keep up with our household without too much effort. After the miscarriage of the twin, Peter came to every doctor's appointment that a sonogram was scheduled for. He would hold my hand while watching the screen and beam with happiness. We were asked if we wanted to know the sex of the child, but we both refused, wanting it to be a surprise.

How did I sense that my husband wanted a son? I'm not really sure. Maybe it was from the deep connection we had developed, or was it that I wanted to have a son for him? Was it the old-fashioned comments I had heard so often that every man wants a son? To be very honest, I had always considered myself a liberated feminist and surprised myself for wanting a son. Was it a cultural trait, or was it that I just simply wanted to please my husband? I hoped for a boy.

As we lay in bed one evening, Peter told me he had decided on a name for our child if it was a boy. I was taken by surprise; this was very unlike him to just tell me what he had decided. "I'm naming him James Joseph. You can pick the name if it's a girl." I smiled and nodded in agreement. "OK, I like the name, but the last name will be Abys-Smith."

Even my very forward-thinking compromising husband went into defense mode. "I don't know about that, Phil. I'm the father. The child should have my last name." "Says who?" I responded. "Who made up that rule but a male-dominated society. It's not fair. A woman puts in a good deal more in having a child, and in the end, the child carries the father's name. That's bullshit. It's as bad as when a woman marries and is forced to use her husband's name. First, she carried her father's name, and then like the transfer of property, she carries her husband's name. *Bullshit*." I guess he sensed an argument brewing and placed his arm over his head, taking a deep breath.

I continued with my debate, "and in addition to that, I'm very proud of my name. There're very few of us that carry Abys as a surname, and I don't intend on losing my name. Smith is so common. I don't want our child lost in the shuffle of millions of other Smiths." With that, he turned around and, with a soft smile, said, "You're absolutely right."

Peter continued speaking as he held me close and I inhaled his male scent, "By the way, did I ever tell you the story of when I was a young boy visiting my Nana Smith out on the Jersey Shore and decided, for entertainment, I'd walk under the boardwalk, poking people in the ass with a sharp stick?" I started to laugh, snuggling even closer to him, ready to listen as he continued. "Well, I got caught by a guard who grabbed me by the arm and asked my name. I told him, 'Peter Smith.' He started to shake my arm, yelling, 'Don't play games with me, son! What's your real name?' I got so scared that I started to cry and kept telling him my name is Peter Smith. Thank God my nana came looking for me. When she realized what was occurring, she told the guard, 'You ass, his name is Peter Smith.'"

He continued, "Phil, you're absolute right. Abys-Smith is a better last name. No one will forget that name." I snuggled very close to him, placing my lips near his ear, thanking him. He placed his lips on my neck, thanking me, and we spent a good portion of that evening thanking each other.

We, of course, followed all the standard instructions for expecting first-time parents and attended Lamaze classes. We both tried our best not to look at each other and start to laugh, but when the very overweight instructor started imitating the proper breathing, it was just too much, and we both convulsed from laughter.

Before the next class, I firmly told Peter, "Look, we can't keep disrupting the class. Don't make me laugh." "OK, OK, just don't look at me and practice *shshsh*." He already had a smirk on his lip. The next class was going along just fine until the instructor, while sipping soda and belching a bit, informed us, "That when your water breaks, it will have a fruity smell." I turned to Peter, whispering, "Gee, I hope mine smells like a bowl of fresh strawberries."

His body started to vibrate from trying to hold in the laughter. I placed my hand over my mouth so as not to disrupt the class, but we both had such uncontrollable fits of laughter that we quickly walked out of the class. In the last class, the instructor congratulated everyone on how well we did and handed us a video of different types of actual births to watch at home.

Peter told me, "Forget it, Phil. Don't watch it. What difference does it make?"

"Pete, we're supposed to watch it. You know it gets you ready."

"*Oh*, for Christ's sake, do you always need to follow rules? Fuck it, it's going to upset you."

"No, it wouldn't."

We sat nice and comfy on the sofa, Peter asking me again, "Are you sure you want to watch this?" "Yes, it will prepare us. That's the reason they gave it to us." Peter rolled his eyes, muttering, "They're a bunch of assholes." When did I start to have waves of panic attacks along with crying fits? I can only guess halfway through the video. With a stream of tears and a bit of gasping for breath, I told Peter, "I can't do that. I don't want to do it." In an even louder voice, "I'm not doing it."

Peter, with an I-told-you-so smirk on his face, held my face in his hands softly speaking, "Come on, Phil, it's going to be just fine. Women have been doing this forever, and besides, you're seven months pregnant. I don't think you have a choice." He had already turned the video off, and his comforting hands calmed me down. "Yeah, well, it's not fair. Men say they have children. Bullshit. They don't do a damn thing." "Phil, if I could, I would do it for you." "You're so full of it. You're just saying that to calm me down." "Yeah, well, I'm not equipped for the delivery, just for the insertion." With that, I started to laugh through the tears. He laughed with me, kissing and holding me tight.

The arrival of our child became ever so real when we had to start shuffling around furniture and placing a few pieces in my mother's home. In the bedroom, where my armchair stood to watch TV, a crib was placed, and in the living room, where a curio stood filled with trinkets, a changing table was placed. For whatever reason, even in a slowly shrinking space, we were able to work as a team and never got into each other's way; our personalities flowed in unison. After an elaborate baby shower, which my mother gave me at a catering hall, I had more than enough baby stuff. We both laughed as we rearranged our home. With a little organization, which I had always been very good at, our home looked very cozy and ready for the new arrival.

I had planned on working until only two weeks before the due date. On Monday, May 18, I worked my usual Monday routine of going to all four schools, picking up the necessary paperwork to bring to the office. As I entered the office, the staff started to tease me. "Ms. Abys, you're finally starting to look pregnant, and by Friday, you'll be a lady of leisure. Use those two weeks to get some rest."

I responded, "I'm going to sleep past five thirty and enjoy taking my time shopping." I finished handing in all the papers with these final words: "OK, ladies, talk to you tomorrow. Have a good day." I drove to the gym, exercising my usual pregnant routine. I was just about to walk over to the desk to chitchat with friends when I passed the ballet bar; I stood there and felt an urge to lift my leg onto the bar, which I did very easily. *There,* I thought, *I can still do that. I'm happy with myself.* And after chatting with friends, I went home. Peter was frying lemon sole. I had eaten large quantities of fish throughout the pregnancy, and as I walked in, Peter, while putting up his hand, automatically stated, "Phil, I'm being careful not to splash or get anything smelly." I gave him a kiss and went to take shower. After enjoying dinner, we sat to watch *Jeopardy*, and as the familiar tune came on, I felt wet and, without saying a word to Peter, went into the bathroom to check.

I told myself, *Don't panic. You're leaking fluid. Just tell your husband, and call the doctor. Stay calm.* I surprised myself by remaining calm as I walked into the living room and told Peter. "What? You're not due for another three weeks. You feel OK?" "I feel fine, Pete," and went to call the doctor. He asked me to come into the office.

As my husband drove, I blamed myself for lifting my leg onto the ballet bar. Maybe that caused the water to break, but I didn't mention it to him; not wanting to upset him further. In the examination room, the doctor informed me that I was in labor and to go to the hospital. In disbelief and cursing myself for lifting my leg onto the ballet bar, I responded, "What? I didn't even pack a bag yet." I should have listened to myself and packed one weeks ago but didn't want Peter to make fun of me for being so nervous. I asked the doctor, "Are you sure it's only a little fluid?" He smiled and, in a soft voice, told me, "I've been doing this for a long time. You're in labor." As I stood up from the examination table, the fluid gushed out all over the floor. The nurses ran to help, reassuring me, "Don't worry, you have plenty of time. Go home, pack your bag, and the doctor will meet you at the hospital."

As we walked across the lawn to reach our apartment, Peter turned to me, asking, "Are you in any pain?" I was feeling completely fine. I shrugged and replied, "No, not at all." He grabbed me by the hand, "Ms. Abys, are you ready to be a mom?" "Do I have a choice?" "I don't think so. Ready or not, here we go." We quickly packed and headed for the hospital. A very kind nurse led us into a delivery room; she helped me get into a gown and then into bed while asking, "Do you want to watch *Murphy Brown*? She's having a baby too." Peter sat in a chair next to me, ready to watch TV and have a baby. I mentioned, "Gee, Pete, this is not so bad. I hope it stays this way." "Yeah, me too."

As the show started, an intense pain shot from my lower back into my legs, and I moaned in pain. Peter turned to me, placing a hand on my forehead, "Are you OK?" "No, not really. My back feels like it's going to split open." A series of spasms followed, and as I winced from pain, Peter's face turned pale. "Pete, turn off the TV. I don't want to watch anyone else having a baby." "OK, I'll get the nurse," he said, and he ran out of the room.

The nurse came running in with Pete cheerfully announcing, "We're busy tonight. It's a full moon." She examined me and told me, "You're doing great" and walked out of the room. I saw my pain in Peter's face, and every time I winced, holding on to the bed rail, his jowls tightened. He placed a cold compress on my forehead, held my hand, and rubbed my back, but the pain became so intense that I cursed in Neapolitan and English. After a few hours, the doctor came in and told me, "I know you're in a lot of pain, but I'm not going to give you any medication. It will slow down the labor. The baby's head is in the birth canal. It wouldn't be much longer." I nodded. "OK."

Peter, placing ice chips on my lips, spoke softly to me. "Phil, you're doing great. I can see the baby's head." I asked him, "How long has it been?" "About four hours, not bad for the first child." I held on to his hand, yelling from pain, with my legs shaking uncontrollably. The nurse and doctor ran in, waiting for the delivery, but as hard as I pushed, the baby just would not budge.

They placed monitors on the baby's head, and the doctor again reassured me, "It wouldn't be much longer." From sheer exhaustion, I dozed off, waking up to the smell of coffee and bagels. My husband had taken the opportunity while I dozed to buy a bit of breakfast and was munching away. "Phil, I had to get something to eat. Is it bothering you?" "Pete, after this, not too much is going to bother me, but when I get out of this mess, I'm going to cut your balls off." He almost choked on his bagel as he started to laugh, and regardless of the pain I was in, I also managed to laugh, along with the nurse that was checking the monitor. Chuckling, she asked, "Are you two this funny all the time?"

I'm not sure how long I was in labor before my husband started to lose his temper, but I guess he could not take any more of watching me squirm, shake, and yell from pain. He walked outside the door, where the doctor was, and I heard him raise his voice. "You need to do something. My wife has been in labor with the baby's head in the birth canal for ten hours. She's exhausted. You're the doctor. Do something." "Mr. Smith, I can assure you that your wife and child are not in any danger." "I don't give a shit. Do something. She's been up for almost twenty-four hours. Do something to get the baby out." With that, they came in and moved me into the OR.

I asked Peter if they were going to give me a C-section. "Honey, listen, I'm not sure, but soon, it will be all over. Look, I need to leave for a few minutes to scrub and put on a gown. I'll be right back." I only nodded, not wanting to use any more energy. I was surrounded by a team of nurses and my doctor; Peter stood near the doctor as he examined me. "Mr. Smith, I don't know what's stopping the delivery, but the baby is far down into the birth canal. I haven't done this in many years. We usually don't use forceps, but this is the best option."

I saw the look of shock on Peter's face as he looked down at the forceps. "Mr. Smith, please go and hold your wife's hand and shoulder." With that, Peter walked over to me. A nurse came to my other side and held my shoulder. Peter, with a very shaky voice, spoke to me. "Phil, it's going to be very quick. Just look at me." As they started to give me local anesthetic and I screamed from pain, I thought my husband was going to cry. I felt the coldness and pain from the forceps going in and then the release of the head and shoulders of our child. I should have passed out but was fully conscious. The miracle of birth for me was that among the pain, blood, and exhaustion. My sole focus was on our child.

"Mr. Smith, you have a son." I saw complete joy on my husband's face, and I felt a happiness and pride that I cannot describe. "Mr. Smith, I think the reason your son was giving us a hard time was the way his umbilical cord was wrapped. This little guy was playing bungee jump. Your wife pushed, and the cord was wrapped in such a way that it pulled him back."

I tried to force my head up to see what was going on. With glazed eyes, Peter walked over to take a first look at our son. The doctor asked him if he wanted to cut the cord, but he declined. The nurse came over, placing the baby on my chest; as I looked down, I was in complete awe.

It was as if I was looking into a mirror. He looked exactly like me, same lips and chin. I looked up at my husband. "I'm sorry, Pete. He looks just like me." Peter bent down, kissing my forehead and cheeks. "I know. He's beautiful just like you. I'm sorry it was so hard for you," as he kissed me again and again. "Thank you, thank you." He was holding back tears.

A nurse came over and told me, "I need to take the baby. Don't worry, he's fine. I just need to clean him off and dress him up a bit." I spun my head around as she walked away with him; she again reassured us, "Your son is fine. He just peed all over me." We both smiled at each other, and although the doctor was still working on stitching me back together, I asked my husband, "Did you call my mother?"

"No, Phil, I didn't." One of the nurses came over, giving me a cordless phone. "Here you go. Call your mom." I dialed the number and spoke in Neapolitan, explaining that I had gone into labor and had a boy. She yelled in joy asking, "How did the labor go?" I explained that the doctor used forceps, and she yelled, "Just like when I had your brother. They used forceps on me too."

I started to feel so tired and weak and told her that they were still working on me and handed the phone to Peter. I looked up at Peter, asking him, "What time is it?" "It's 10:30 a.m., Phil. Why?" My voice barely in a whisper, "Oh my god, I didn't call the office. They're probably looking for me." Peter started to laugh. "I think they guessed why you didn't call." "Pete, please call for me and tell them I had a baby boy."

He called and then held the phone for me to hear the cheers and well-wishes. After that, I must have passed out or fallen asleep because I don't remember anything else until much later in the day, when I woke up in a room with Peter sitting next to me. "Pete, you're still here. Go home and get some rest." "You're sure it's OK? I could use a shower." "Yes, go home. We live only five minutes away." "OK, I love you," and kissed me good-bye.

I fell asleep again and woke up in the middle of the night with an intense urge to see my son. I took a deep breath and held onto the railing, lifting myself out of the bed. I sat for a few seconds, steadying myself, and then walked into the nursery. The nurse came over to me, and I told her

I wanted to see my son. She helped me sit in a rocking chair and carried my little boy to me.

I sat looking at his face, admiring how beautiful he was, and became alarmed by the tiny black and blue marks on his face. I called the nurse over, "Are these marks from the forceps?" She must have noticed my concern, quickly reassuring me, "Don't worry, they will disappear in a few days." While I counted his fingers and toes twice, checked his ears, and made sure that all his body parts were in the proper place, a love so deep filled my being that tears streamed down my cheeks. I knew from that day on, my main focus would be on his well-being. I sat staring at him until I became tired and, afraid of dropping him, called the nurse over to place him back in his crib. I went back to bed, wanting to be well rested and healthy to care for my son.

The next morning, before Peter arrived, a clerk handed me papers to fill out for the birth certificate. I wrote in Name of Mother, Filomena Abys; Name of Father, Peter Thomas Smith; Child's First Name, James; Middle Name, Joseph; Child's Last Name, Abys-Smith. The clerk asked if I was done, and I said, "No, I need to wait for my husband." He was already on his way, and I wanted to make absolutely sure he felt comfortable with the last name.

The tower of feminism I had built around me was slowly collapsing under the weight of love I had for my husband and son. I wanted Peter to see and approve of the last name; I wanted to show him my love and respect. Peter walked in looking very happy, but also very tired. He had already stopped at the nursery and, after hugging and kissing me, plopped into the chair. "Peter, didn't you get any sleep?" "No, not really. I tossed and turned all night with excitement and worry for you and Jamie." He was already calling our son Jamie.

I handed him the papers, "Take your time. Make sure the last name is what you want also. I don't want this hanging over our marriage." "Phil, we've already discussed this. I'm fine with it." As he read the form, he smiled at me, "Phil, you're absolutely right. With a name like that, Jamie will never get lost in the shuffle like I did. No one will forget his name. You're a very sharp mom." "OK then, you hand the form in. Make it your decision."

It was only my mother that scolded me on the last name. Peter had picked her up, and as he drove to the hospital, she must have asked for her grandson's name; she was fine with the first, but the last name gave her shame. As soon as she walked into the room, without even asking how I was feeling, she laced into me. In Neapolitan, she spoke, "Whey, tu a maritet c e fatt fa na brutta figura." In rough translation, she was telling me that I made my husband look bad, made him lose face. Peter noticed the heated exchange of words and stepped in, "Phil, what's the problem?" "My mom is upset that I used Abys in the last name. She thinks I'm showing you disrespect. You know, the old-fashioned Italian bullshit. I stepped out of my place."

Peter, for the first time using a firm voice, spoke to my mother. "Ma, listen to me. I'm fine with the last name. Your daughter is absolutely right. It's a better name. No one will forget your grandson with that last name. Ma, it takes a real man to admit that his wife is right." As usual, my mom was happy that Peter the Pearl was happy and even if her daughter had stepped out of line, she made him happy, and that was all that was important. The nurse brought Jamie in for grandparent time, and with one look at her first grandchild, all was forgotten.

My Patty Boy's Potato *Gatto*

Ingredients

8 to 10 large cooked potatoes (cook potatoes in the skins; you can peel the skin off or just put them through a ricer after they're cooked)
1 stick of butter cut into small parts
4 whole eggs, slightly beaten with a bit of Parmesan cheese
¼ cup of milk
½ cup of grated Parmesan cheese and a little extra for sprinkling on top
8 oz. of mozzarella diced into bite-size portions (make sure the mozzarella is dry)
Salt and black pepper to taste
Optional: tiny bite-size pieces of salami

In large bowl, rice cooked potatoes; add butter, eggs, and milk, and mix very well with a wire whip. Add Parmesan cheese, mozzarella, salami, and salt and pepper to taste. Mix well until all ingredients are uniformed.

In a large casserole dish that has been buttered and sprinkled with breadcrumbs and Parmesan cheese, add the potatoes and spread evenly with a spatula. Sprinkle the top with breadcrumbs and Parmesan cheese. Bake at 375ºF until bubbly and golden. Let the pie sit for a while before serving. It can be served hot, as a side dish, or even at room temperature.

I have cut this pie while at room temperature into bite-size square portions and served them on a platter as an appetizer.

"I Didn't Boil the S—out of the Vegetables" Brussels Sprouts with Bacon and Hot Red Pepper Flakes

Ingredients

2 tbs. of vegetable oil
2 qt. of brussels sprouts, washed and cut in half
4 to 6 slices of bacon cut into bite-size portions
Salt and red pepper flakes to taste

Place oil and red pepper flakes in a large skillet over a medium flame; when hot, add bacon; cook until almost crispy, adding the brussels sprouts and tossing well. Salt to taste. Cook covered until sprouts are tender but a bit crispy; you may need to add a few tablespoons of water.

Chapter 13

Parenting

When I arrived home with Jamie, the front of the stairs to the garden apartment I had lived in for over eight years never looked as welcoming as it did on that day. Peter had decorated the front steps with balloons and a large sign, all in blue and white, to announce the birth of our son. I was truly touched by his display of love and knew he would be my biggest help in the coming months. As I started to climb the stairs, Peter took the baby from me, "Now, Phil, don't get upset when you go inside. I didn't have time to clean up, and it's a bit messy." Still feeling very tired, I just nodded and hoped for the best.

The bed was unmade, the kitchen counter had crumbs and stains on it, the sink was filled with dishes, the bathroom needed cleaning, and the wash was piled high. I could not blame Peter; he himself was exhausted from not being able to sleep and from running around. I was looking forward to just being in my clean home and holding my little boy; instead, I had to mentally coach myself, repeating, *Don't cry. You're accustomed to hard work. Get on with it.* I jumped right into being not only a new mother but a very busy housewife.

Peter had to work; I, on maternity leave, never worked as hard trying to keep up with a new infant and our household, all the while trying to heal from the difficult birth. Regardless of how hard we worked and the exhaustion of new parenthood, we enjoyed our new lives, falling deeper in love with each other but most of all with our son.

Peter was as dawdling a parent as one could imagine. For a man that had been accustomed to a wild bachelor life, he was, by nature, a skilled father, not hesitating to help with every child-care task. Of course, we did occasionally clash over child-care ideas; Peter was always willing to read up on the latest concern we had for our son in, as he called it, "The Book." He would carefully review in "The Book" everything from proper burping to the correct color of baby poop, at times pointing to a chart of baby poop colors for me to look at. I, feeling no need to constantly use "The Book," told him to shove it. He responded, "I tried. It doesn't fit."

We both laughed through the exhaustion and somehow even managed to make love before the proper amount of "healing time." After that first spontaneous lovemaking, we realized that we had not been very careful, and I, in a bit of a panic, told Pete, "If I get pregnant again, this time, I'll really cut your nuts off." He responded, "Don't worry, you won't need to. I'll cut my own balls off."

Peter, deciding to take the responsibility of birth control into his own hands, came home with an assortment of condoms, "Here, Phil, I have a present for you," tossing the package to me. I was very amused and, giggling, asked, "When are you planning on using these?" He rolled his eyes, seriously stating, "Come on, Phil, don't make fun. The industry of getting laid has come a long way. Wait until I put these babies on. You're going to go nuts." I just laughed and threw the package back at him. Needless to say, the very fancy condoms decorated the bedroom walls as Peter tossed them in frustration, complaining, "These things suck. I hate using these fucking things." I rolled over in laughter as Peter held me down, telling me, "Now you're really in trouble."

Peter, from the day we met, had an unbelievable ability to make me laugh, and that talent served us both well when we were so tired that laughter was the best cure for what I call "new parenthood syndrome." The syndrome was a combination of great love and concern for our son. We worried about everything from my breast-feeding method to concern about Jamie pooping too much or too little. The new parent syndrome was also sprinkled with lack of sleep, hormonal changes, and the need to start screwing around again without getting pregnant.

While I breast-fed Jamie, I confided in Pete that I worried my breasts were too large and the baby's mouth too small to suckle out enough milk. He noticed I was close to tears, so to alleviate the stress, he bent down, placing his mouth on my breast, taking a good taste, very cheerfully stating, "You know, Phil, it's sweeter than regular milk, not bad at all. Now if you can give me an eight-ounce glass so I can have some with my cookies later, that would be great." Instead of crying, I laughed, "Peter, now I know you're just plain nuts. How about getting me a breast pump?"

Maybe it was the Italian in me, but I constantly worried about our son being well fed. I breast-fed as much as possible, used the pump when needed, and introduced formula in small portions to make sure he was growing well. After the first three months, I stopped breast-feeding. Peter jokingly complained, "Now how am I supposed to enjoy my cookies?"

I was determined not to let motherhood turn me into a frumpy-looking old housewife. I was up early every morning to put my house in order and out with Jamie in the stroller by 11:00 a.m., walking for miles to stay in shape. In less than three months, I was back to my usual five/six size. I planned lighter healthy meals, which Peter seemed to enjoy. Lentil soup, chickpeas and pasta, white kidney bean and rice soup, and spicy broccoli and pasta were his favorites.

I steamed thick pieces of codfish, shredding it into bit-size pieces, topping it off with olive oil, green olives, chopped parsley, and lemon juice. Occasionally, Peter, using his very diplomatic skills, would say, "Ah, Phil, I'm not complaining, but can we eat something not so healthy for dinner? Maybe fried chicken cutlets with mashed potatoes?" I could never refuse him anything and happily prepared what he wanted, adding healthy desserts of banana chocolate chip bread or fresh strawberries soaked in a bit of lemon juice and sugar, which I placed in a tall glass topped off with vanilla ice cream and crumbled amaretto cookies. Peter seemed to bask in the glow of the much-needed care that he had desperately, for many years, searched for. In disbelief, I laughed at myself that I had once again fallen so in love, becoming the overcaring wife that I had vowed never to be again.

To make up for the small wedding, we planned an elaborate christening for Jamie. Catholic law requires all parents to attend a series of short classes before a child's Christening day; we, along with two other couples, sat and listened as the pastor lectured us on the meaning of baptism. At the end of the classes, the very nice pastor brought out cookies and small glasses of liquor to celebrate. When he noticed Peter not taking a glass, he again offered. Peter very casually stated, "Father, it's best I don't. If I start, I may use up all your reserves." The priest smiled and nodded in understanding. I realized that Peter's down-to-earth, this-is-the-way-I-am attitude was the main reason I had fallen in love with him so many years ago.

We invited sixty guests to attend the celebration at the Glen Island Casino catering hall. As a special surprise for Peter, I hired Irish bagpipers, hoping this would show him how much I cared and how content I was in the marriage. When we were called up to the stage by the DJ and the bagpipers marched in, I turned to Peter privately, whispering in his ear, "Thank you." He held back tears.

After the christening, I knew I had to get back to work. It's not that we couldn't make ends meet with Peter's paycheck, but I wanted to make sure we had enough for extras, and personally, I didn't want to feel like an old-fashioned stay-at-home mom. We visited and interviewed too many child-care centers and, each time, looked at each other with the "I don't think so" look. I agonized with Peter as to what we should do until my mother, not being able to bear the thought of her grandson in the care of strangers, offered to babysit while I worked. I probably would have stayed home if she had not offered; I just didn't feel safe with Jamie in anyone else's care.

I was fortunate that on many occasions, my mom had home-cooked meals for me to take home for dinner. Chicken soup with tiny pastina was Jamie's favorite. Chicken cacciatore was easy to heat up, and placing it over cooked rice made a quick meal. Her minestrone soup was a special treat as it was too fussy for me to prepare after work. The homemade *taralli* that my mom's landlady Tina made for Jamie to chew while he was teething kept him content.

On weekends, I often cooked double meals so as to have ready cooked meals for the week. I would make extra spicy red sauce, keeping it in the refrigerator, and only had to poach eggs into it after work, telling Peter that my family had been calling this meal "eggs in purgatory." It was so easy to place the eggs and sauce over cooked rice or pasta. Kielbasa sausages with plenty of onions, potatoes, and hot cherry peppers was one of Peter's favorites, and it held up well for a Monday or Tuesday meal.

Soups were always great to prepare, and I often cooked lentils with pasta, mixed bean soup made with a porket or beef barley.

I told Peter that I never understood why families purchased frozen TV dinners as they took just as long to reheat in the oven and tasted like crap. He responded with a wide smile, "That's why I hooked up with you. I could tell you knew your stuff when it came to housekeeping and cooking." "Well, Pete, at least you're honest. You checked me out like a prized mule." He cracked up, "Yeah, kind of. What man wants a useless slob for a wife? But I like other things about you too." "Hmm." I shrugged him away. He pulled me close, telling me he loved me with all his heart for all that I was. His honest charm always made me melt, and many times, the cooking was put to the side.

The exhaustion increased as we both were up by 5:30 a.m. Peter was out the door by six, and I, with Jamie dressed, diaper bag and all other essentials packed, walked down the stairs, across the lawn by six thirty. It was only by the strength of youth or maybe the deep passion we felt for each other that we managed to spend time fooling around. Even with the crib in our bedroom, we managed to get our groove on. On one of those occasions with Peter on top of me, passionately grooving away, I looked over his shoulder and was stunned to see my little boy standing up, holding on to the crib with one hand and with the other arm waving at us, trying to get our attention. I did a double take to make sure I was seeing correctly while telling Peter, "Stop, stop, the baby is watching us."

Peter, not accustomed to being stopped in midpassion, simply said, "*What?*" "Pete, the baby is watching us." He spun his head around, and as soon as Jamie saw his father's face, he started widely swigging his arm, trying to get attention. Peter fell over with laughter, "Phil, he wants to be part of the action," and he started to move forward to pick up the little intruder. I stopped him. "Pete, wait. Let me take a few photos. This is the first time he picked himself up." Peter, with his head on one hand and the other waving at Jamie, beamed with pride. I took two quick shots with Peter urging me, "Hurry up, Phil, the poor kid wants to get picked up." I saw the deep love Peter had for our son; it was so clear by the manner in which he picked Jamie up, hugging and kissing his cheek. The bond between father and son filled our bedroom as he placed Jamie on the bed, making a kissy sound on Jamie's belly and cheeks; I thought my heart would explode from love for both of them.

I placed my head down on the pillow next to them, enjoying watching Jamie reach for his father's face, Peter kissing his fingers, making his son giggle. I asked Peter, "Do you think he'll remember seeing us? I'm really not comfortable with that thought?" Peter, laughing, responded, "Come on, Phil, he's only six months old. What do you think they did in the old days? Not everyone had a separate bedroom." I nodded, realizing that my wild single days were definitely over. I knew that, soon, I needed to place this apartment, where I had spent so much time reshaping my sense of self, up for sale. Smiling, I further realized that I had been reshaped exactly into what I instinctively knew I would eventually be, "a mother and a wife."

Lentil and Rice Soup (*Riso e Lenticchie*)

Ingredients

4 tbs. of vegetable oil
4 to 6 slices of bacon or about ⅓ cup of pancetta cut into bite-size pieces
1 small onion, diced
4 cloves of garlic, crushed
2 medium-size carrot, finely chopped
2 stalks of celery, finely chopped
2 medium-size potatoes, peeled and diced into tiny bite-size portions
4 plum tomatoes crushed by hand with all the juice
½ lb. of dried lentils rinsed under cold water
6 cups of boiling water or 6 cups of stock (you may use beef, chicken, or vegetable)
1 cup of cooked rice
Salt and black pepper to taste
Optional: You may add a diced hot pepper to spice up this soup, sautéing it with the bacon bits. You may also add chopped parsley at the end of cooking.
Place oil in a large stockpot, heat over a medium flame, add bacon, and cook until slightly crispy; add vegetables, sauté for a few minutes or until they start to soften a bit. Add the lentils, mix well into vegetables, add water or stock, and mix well. Cook covered over a medium flame

until all the vegetables and lentils are tender. Just before serving, you may add the cooked rice to the soup or pour soup into individual bowls, adding spoonfuls of rice into the bowls of hot soup. If adding the rice into the soup pots, add slowly, stirring well.

Nonna Fortuna's Chicken Cacciatore

Ingredients:

4 lb. of washed and trimmed chicken parts, trimming off excess loose fat from the breast and thighs (pat dry and add salt)
¼ cup of oil
Red hot pepper flakes to taste
1 large onion, thinly sliced
4 cloves of garlic, crushed
2 35 oz. cans of crushed tomatoes (if possible, always use San Marzano)

Place oil in a large stockpot; heat, brown chicken on all sides; remove the chicken, place in a platter, and set aside. Add onions, garlic, and red pepper flakes to the same pot; sauté until onion is wilted and garlic has a bit of color. Add tomatoes, mix well, cook for about fifteen minutes or until the sauce bubbles, and add salt to taste. Place chicken back into the sauce, and cook until chicken is completely cooked through. At times, I watched my mother add a small glass of white wine to the chicken after it was brown on all sides, and she allowed the chicken to cook in the wine for about five minutes then removed the pieces and added the remaining ingredients to make the sauce. We enjoy chicken cacciatore with spaghetti, so the best method is to move the cooked chicken onto a serving platter and toss the cooked spaghetti with the sauce into a large bowl. A great deal of crusty bread is needed for this meal to sop up the sauce.

Pete's "I'm Not Complaining" Banana Bread

My husband forever teased me about being overly health conscious and often called me Mrs. Granola. I converted many recipes to disguise healthy ingredients, making sure that we ate healthy without too many complaints.

Ingredients:

2½ cups of sifted all-purpose flour
3 tsp. of baking powder
½ teaspoon of salt
1 cup of sugar
⅓ cup of softened butter or a healthy type of butter spread
2 tbs. of oil (canola or olive)
1 egg
3 small ripe bananas, cut up
½ cup of milk
Optional, healthy type: ¾ cup of chopped nuts (whatever kind you prefer), ¾ cup of dried cranberries, ½ cup of raisins, ½ cup of flax seeds, ½ cup of wheat germs, ¾ cup of grated zucchini, ¾ cup of grated carrots, or a combination of each (make sure not to add too much of the optional ingredients into the banana batter as it will make the batter too heavy to rise)
Optional, not-so-healthy type (Pete's favorite): ¾ cup of mini chocolate chips, ¾ cup of shredded sweetened coconut flakes, ¾ cup of chopped peanut butter cups.

In a large bowl, mix together flour, baking powder, and salt. Set aside. In a blender or food processor, put in sugar, butter, oil, egg, and bananas. Blend together until smooth. Pour banana mixture slowly in flour, mixing well with a wire whip into a smooth batter. You may pour batter into a buttered loaf pan or muffin pan. This recipe is very versatile, and when apples are in season, I layer the bottom of a buttered loaf pan with apples that have been dipped in sugar then pour the batter on top, layering more apples on top of the batter, and bake at 350°F for about one hour. You can also make a crunchy topping of a quarter cup of oatmeal, a quarter cup of flour, and half a stick of softened butter, placing all three ingredients in a bowl, mixing uniformly together by hand, and sprinkling on top of the batter before baking.

Chapter 14

The Challenges of Being a Family

We had become so accustomed to being a family living in a tight but cozy apartment that we put the search for a new home on the back burner, opting to enjoy our son's first year in what Peter referred to as "our love nest." Jamie started to walk on his own by nine months, and we scrambled to secure every part of our home. Child locks went on all the lower kitchen cabinets; the coffee table with brass decorative spikes, along with houseplants that Jamie seemed to love, went to my mother's home.

The living room had an array of toys ranging from an activity gym mat to plush cars, jingly keys to noisy interactive let-me-torture-my-parents gadgets. This was nothing compared to the new assortment of toys that were given to him after his first birthday party. I had arranged a birthday luncheon for thirty guests, along with a very annoying insecure clown that kept asking us if she was doing a good job of entertaining the kids. A full-size toddler's car came into the living room, where Jamie climbed into and walked all around the now very scaled-down love nest.

We now seriously discussed that after our Cape Cod vacation and visiting my family in Long Beach, New Jersey, we definitely had to start looking for a larger home. This very serious conversation took place in the living room with Jamie disregarding all the expensive toys while placing the smaller boxes on his head and climbing into the larger ones.

On our Cape Cod vacation, I again realized that I had missed two menstrual cycles, and after confiding in Peter, he, with a slight smirk on his face, said, "Hey, what do you want from me? I'm trying my best." So much for leaving birth control up to a male. To use one of Peter's expressions, "it has a mind of its own." We discussed how urgent it would now be to have a larger home with another child on the way. I was happy to have one more child, and then that would be it; at my age, I was already pushing my luck. Peter had a panicked look on his face, and this time, I didn't see the happiness of the first pregnancy, and I understood why. The love nest had been great for a single chick looking to just fool around; it was just fine for a lovey-dovey, hot-in-the-pants couple and cozy with the joy of the first child, but a new addition was pushing the limits of what an eight-hundred-square-foot apartment could hold.

After our Cape Cod vacation, I immediately saw my doctor, who confirmed with a smile, "Congratulations, you're entering the third month of pregnancy." I went home to tell Peter, who was on the floor playing with Jamie, the living room holding more toys than both of us ever had in our entire childhood combined. He didn't jump up for joy; he seemed concerned and anxious. I, on the other hand, this time, felt more secure and happy to have a sibling for Jamie.

We drove to Long Beach to vacation for a few days with my brother, his wife, my mother, and aunt, all in a very beautiful home which my brother had rented for the summer. As everyone was having morning coffee, my sister-in-law and brother proudly displayed a copy of a sonogram; she too was pregnant. I motioned to Peter not to say anything about us; this was their first child, and I wanted them to bask in all the attention.

We both went back to work, and the heat of the summer, which could reach over ninety-five in the school kitchens by eight in the morning, was starting to affect me more than usual. I was now thirty-nine years old and felt lucky to get pregnant so easily but also understood the dangers of older motherhood. I told Peter that after this child, we needed to take a permanent course of action for birth control. He jokingly said, "Shall I cut my nuts off?"

At work, in the middle of a very hot day, I started to bleed heavy and immediately called Peter and my doctor. I told myself not to panic, but with the amount of blood I was losing, I was close to tears and only controlled myself so that the staff didn't realize what was occurring. Fortunately, both Peter and the doctor were only a few minutes away; Peter, sprinted into the school and drove us to the doctor's office. As the nurses helped me into a gown, I miscarried, the complete fetus falling out of me and onto the floor. I felt dazed, and as the nurses helped me lie down on the examination table, I cried out for Peter. My doctor walked in with Peter at his side, who immediately sat next to me, holding my hand and stroking my forehead.

The doctor spoke not so much to me but to Peter, whose face displayed my very own anguish. "Mr. Smith, your wife is bleeding too heavily. I think it's best I give her a D&C." I started to shake and cry pleading, "I don't want it done." The doctor again looked at Peter, telling him, "She really needs to have it done to stop the bleeding." Peter, holding my face in his hands and coddling me, softly said, "Phil, just look at me. It's going to be over very quickly." I felt an IV being inserted as I slowly passed out and awoke later with Peter by my side, holding my hand.

I was physically and emotionally drained as I slowly slid onto the sofa in our living room, Peter placing Jamie on the floor next to his toys. I placed my head on the pillow, tears soaking my cheeks as I watched my little boy's face, who seemed to realize that something was wrong. The sadness on his little face made the tears gush out harder with Peter sitting next to me, softly speaking, "Phil, please don't cry. I can't stand to see you cry. It's all going to be all right. When we're ready, we'll have another one, don't worry." I waved a hand, choking on tears, feebly saying, "No no, I don't want to get pregnant again. I'm too old. I need to be able to care for Jamie." I used the last bit of energy to tell Peter, "I'm fine with just one child." As I started to doze off, I heard Peter's voice whispering, "You're right. One is just fine for me too. We'll be extra careful from now on."

Within two weeks of that miscarriage, we started a serious search for a larger home. I placed the apartment on the market with the same realtor that I had known from years prior when attempting to sell. I then becoming too busy for the hassle, and deciding to just stay in the apartment. Peter now met this very nerdy nervous fellow who had always been extremely kind to me. He was so nervous in my presence that when I handed him a cup of tea while we sat in the living room, conducting an open house, the cup and saucer rattled with earthquake thunder.

Peter towered over him as they shook hands; I took one look at the smirk on Peter's face and knew what he was thinking. I whispered to him,

Be nice. He's a very nervous guy. Peter rolled his eyes, holding back laughter. With Jamie in our arms, we searched for the perfect home. Needless to say, that first search brought only exhaustion as we took turns with Jamie. For the next home search, Peter gave a big sigh and said, "Phil, you know what? It's too much of a hassle with the baby in harm's way. Go on your own. I think you can handle that nerd." I asked, "Are you sure?"

"Phil, if that nerd had to watch you stretch out in your short-shorts like I did in Southold, the poor bastard would have had a fucking heart attack. Go ahead. If I ever had to worry about a nerd like that, I'd really cut my own nuts off." As I started to walk out the door laughing, he yelled, "Don't give that poor bastard a heart attack before we find a house!"

After many months of searching, I can't say we found the perfect home, but it was large with beautiful sunny rooms and a large backyard for Jamie to play in. The only problem was that it needed a complete renovation. I hesitated, having been a homeowner before knowing the hard work that goes into making a house a home. Peter was fed up with looking and, in an unusual stern voice, said, "Phil, for God's sakes, you'll never find a perfect home. I'll remodel the whole fucking house for you, but let's get on with it." I yelled back, "OK, but don't blame me when it's too much work!"

The home did have a perfect location, an easy twelve-minute commute to work and my mom's house. Close to all the shopping, parks, and a hospital. The biggest problem was that the pervious homeowner was, as Peter phrased it, "a master butcher." The home built in 1924 would have been better off if "the butcher" had left it alone. Before we even moved in, Peter was at the house with a crew of five men, ripping up smelly rugs, tearing down six layers of cigarette-stained wallpaper, having the original hardwood floors refinished, and painting the whole house. Of course, I would have liked new bathrooms and a kitchen, but we needed to move in; the remaining renovations would be completed later. We both thanked God that Jamie was a very easy-to-handle toddler that seemed to understand when he was told not to touch or go near dangerous tools, considering there would be tools as well as renovating materials around the house for the next seven years.

The home renovation continued for years, similar to this first scenario with Peter getting fed up of walking into the door with Jamie in the stroller and not having enough space to maneuver because "the butcher" had placed two useless closets where they didn't belong. In frustration, in a manner so unlike him, he ordered me to take Jamie for a walk. I raised my brows in protest, and he smiled, saying, "Please take Jamie out. I'll have a big surprise for you when you come home." I smirked, wondering what kind of surprise he was talking about, but decided a brisk walk would do me good. Placing Jamie in the stroller, I told Peter, "This better be good."

No more than an hour later, I pushed the front door that was already slightly ajar open to find the useless closets gone, a sledgehammer up against the wall and a pile of debris piled neatly in a corner. Peter, standing in front of the opening, smiling, casually asked, "OK, how do you want to decorate?" I stood in shock and motionless. Peter, putting his hand up, continued, "Phil, don't complain about the dust. You now have more space." I did what I've always done and jumped right in to cleaning up and planning how to make the most of the extra space.

The remainder of the home renovation continued in much the same fashion, with one of us getting so fed up with a particular aspect of the butchering that we just started ripping it apart, setting it anew. Where I lacked physical strength and technical skills, Peter took over; where Peter lacked cleanup and decorating skills, I took over.

I didn't hesitate to get my hands dirty, and he never found it unmanly to help with household chores. We became a renovating team, often joking with each other, calling ourselves the Honey-Do Couple. From the very start of our relationship, I often asked Peter, "Honey, can you do this or that for me?" Peter, replying in a whippy, pussy-whipped husband voice, would say, "Sure, honey, can you do this for me?" pointing to his male anatomy. I just smiled, shooing him away. "How about you settle for a good bowl of pasta?" "OK, Ms. Abys, you got a deal, but maybe later we can still share a good dessert."

It was well into the third year of living in our constantly renovating home after we had finished dinner and were both cleaning up the kitchen that an unusual phone call came from my brother. I picked up the receiver in the kitchen, hearing my brother's voice, and immediately became concerned as my brother was always very busy with his work at

Bell Labs, and we usually only spoke during the holiday season. "Hi, Phil, it's Joe. How's it going?" "We're fine, Joe. Is everything OK with you?" I was worried that he was going to tell me that someone in the family was sick, and I braced myself for bad news, hearing the seriousness in his voice. He asked what we were doing, and I gave a quick reply, wanting to hear what he had to say. "Phil, maybe you should sit down. I have something serious to discuss with you." With my hands already shaking, I sat at the chair closest to the phone, saying a silent prayer. Oh, *God, please don't let him be sick.* Peter, who was at the sink, gave a few quick glances and continued with the dishes.

"Joe, what's up? Is someone sick? Are you OK?" "Phil, everyone is fine." I immediately started to relax from his reassurance. Joe continued, "I had a visit from Mike at work today. He said he was in the area and decided to come and talk. When the receptionist called, I met him in the lobby, and we both hugged, becoming so emotional that we had to walk into an empty office."

I sat silent without any type of emotional turmoil at all. Joe continued, "Mike asked about you, and I told him you're married with a son. He asked to see a photo of Jamie, but I didn't have one on me." I thought, *Thank God. I don't want him to know what Jamie looks like.* I wasn't sure what mental state he was in and found the visit very odd. My first concern was for Jamie's safety. I, without much emotion, spoke, "I'm glad you didn't show him a photo. I don't want him knowing what Jamie looks like." My brother further explained that tears were shed by both, and he asked me to forgive Mike. "I responded with the same sentiment that I had carried with me for years. "There's no reason for forgiveness now because I forgave him from the very moment he did wrong. Joe, he was a very sick man, physically and emotionally. I have no ill feelings towards him and always wished him well." "I'm glad you feel that way, Phil. He seems like a very lonely man. He spoke about how he's into music again, but I don't know."

We spoke for a few more minutes, and I think my brother was expecting a great deal more emotions from me, but I had none to give. Maybe I was too tired; I had to finish cleaning up the kitchen, get Jamie ready for bed, finish the wash, and shower. I had been up since 5:30 a.m., working a seven-hour day, and was looking forward to spending a few minutes alone with my husband. When I placed the receiver down, Peter turned to me, asking, if everyone was OK. I explained what had occurred, and the only remark he made, with a bit of a sad smirk, was "Gee, what did he think, you were going to wait around for him all these years?" I just shrugged, and we simply continued with our nightly routine.

In retrospect, I realize how fortunate I was to simply walk away, not caring about all the material possessions and never having wronged Mike. I had been able to fill my life with so much passion, love, sexuality, and excitement. If I felt a bit of resentment, it was never toward Mike but against anyone who had given him such misguided advice. They had wrongly guided him at his weakest point to value things more than self-respect; until this day, I pray that he finds happiness and peace.

No Regrets Peas and Pasta

After explaining to Peter what the conversation with my brother was about, I turned to the stove, holding the skillet with the remaining peas, and cut spaghetti I had prepared for dinner. I didn't have time to dwell on the past—I was too busy living my life in the present—and started to place the leftovers into a bowl.

Ingredients:

4 tbs. of oil
1 16-oz. box of frozen peas, semidefrosted
1 small onion, diced
2 gloves of crushed garlic
Salt and pepper to taste
16 oz. of cooked short cut pasta, such as *tubetti*, bow ties, or cut spaghetti

In a skillet, heat oil, add onions and garlic, cook until light golden, add the peas, mix well, and cook until the peas are tender. Add the cooked pasta, toss well, and serve with a generous amount of grated cheese. This same recipe can be made with zucchini cut into bite-size pieces and sautéed in the onion and garlic until zucchini is tender, later adding the pasta and tossing well. These are a great side dish to hamburgers, which Peter prepares for us with great reviews.

Pete's Cheese-Stuffed Hamburgers

Ingredients

1½ lb. of chopped meats
¼ cup of cubed cheddar cheese or any type of cheese you prefer (we've even used crumbled Swiss Knight cheese or blue cheese)
¼ cup of diced onions
Salt and black pepper to taste

First, I remind my husband to wash his hands thoroughly, then I allow him to place chopped meat into a large bowl, adding onions, cheese, and salt and pepper. Mix well. Shape into burgers, cook on grill. When our children were very young, Peter made miniburgers for them. Now he makes football-size burgers that only he can finish. For whatever reason, Pete's burger always tastes great, and we don't enjoy eating at a burger joint.

Ms. Granola's Favorite Brown Butter Onions

Ms. Granola is another pet name that Peter gave me; when we first started dating, he often teased me when I went hiking with friends and placed an assortment of healthy snacks in my backpack, one being granola bars. "Jesus, Phil, how are you going to survive on that stuff? I'd take an Italian combo hero if I were you. No wonder you're so thin."

My very favorite topping for Pete's burger is his very own brown butter onions. Now as you already know, I dislike catsup and will never ruin a good burger by adding that foul stuff, so my dear husband always prepares these onions for me, and I truly enjoy them. Peter's cooking technique has improved tenfold from that first chicken dinner he made for me in Southold; I still remind him that he was lucky to be good at other techniques in our wild young days because if he had relied on cooking to keep me happy, I would have sent him packing.

Ingredients:

2 very large white onions
4 tbs. of vegetable oil
½ stick of butter

Salt and black pepper to taste

Place oil in a cast-iron skillet, heat over a hot grill; when oil is hot, add sliced onions. Cook until soft, add butter, and add salt and pepper. Mix well. Cook until onions are a bit brown. These onions are great with burgers, meat loaf, and roast beef. Please try a tomato salad on top of a burger, especially garden-fresh tomatoes; it's so much better than catsup.

"You Don't Add Sugar" Tomato Salad

Ingredients:
2 to 4 fresh tomatoes (from your own garden is best)
¼ cup of olive oil
Shredded fresh basil
Salt to taste
Optional: dried oregano

Slice tomatoes into bite-size portions; add oil, basil, salt, and oregano. Add a few tablespoons of ice water, mix well, and let it sit for fifteen minutes. Substitute this salad instead of catsup with a burger; it's so much better. You can also pour this salad over Italian *frezzile* or grill-toasted bread.

Chapter 15

The Demons Within

We were, in every sense, a happy family busy with raising a child, working, renovating a home, and just plain living life to the fullest. When did it all start to go wrong? How did our happiness start to unravel? I'm really not sure, but the changes in Peter were at first very subtle, barely noticeable. The first complaint was of his recurring back problem, which he claimed was making him moody, lethargic, and depressed.

We sought help from an excellent surgeon who told us that Peter had five herniated disks and needed surgery on his lower back. Jamie was was not even four years old, and I wondered how I was going to keep up. I just told myself, *You need to do what needs to be done.* Peter's behavior worried me; it wasn't so much the physical condition but the personality change. His mellow, happy outlook was gone, replaced by anger and irritability. He never tried to make me laugh, never made light of any situation. His usually hardy appetite for food and sex was almost completely gone. Most painful of all was his lack of attention toward Jamie, who he had always adored. I wondered if he had gone back to his old habits but didn't confront him, possibly not wanting to accept that he could at any time.

I told myself that if his personality didn't return to the loving, caring man I had married, I needed to take drastic measures to assure not so much my happiness but that of my precious little boy. I decided to wait after the surgery, hoping that if he felt better, I would once again have a husband and Jamie a father. I was up by four on the day of the surgery and had Jamie dressed and packed to spend the day at my mother's home. Peter seemed extremely calm, and I pampered him until the hospital attendants started to wheel him away. I released his hand and gave him a final kiss as he told me, "Phil, don't worry so much. I'm going to be OK." I smiled, holding back tears, saying a silent prayer. *Please, God, help him feel better. I really need my husband back. It's so hard without him.*

I sat in the waiting room for three hours before the doctor had an assistant call me on the hospital phone. "Mrs. Smith, your husband is doing fine, but the surgery is a bit more complicated than we expected. Please don't worry. It's just going to take a bit longer." I was thankful that I had had the foresight to pack a bag with snacks and coffee since I refused to even go to the cafeteria. I waited three more hours before the surgeon came in to speak with me. "Mrs. Smith, your husband is in the recovery room and is doing well. The surgery took longer than expected because I had to remove a disk that had disintegrated, and a calcification deposit the size of a quarter was sitting on a nerve. I removed the calcification and readjusted the nerve again. Please understand that he may feel a bit better but will always have some level of pain."

I asked, "How do we deal with the constant pain? He really hasn't been himself for months." The surgeon must have seen the look of disappointment in me and reached for my hand, holding it with both of his. "Let's see how he feels in a few weeks. After that, I'll recommend physical therapy with pain management." I nodded, saying thanks, and walked to the room Peter was assigned to. I waited for two more hours before he was wheeled into the room, asking the nurse, "What took so long?" "We had a hard time reviving him from the anesthesia." My first thought was that he was probably taking some kind of drug without telling anyone. I kissed and stroked his cheek; I helped him push down a few morsels of food until, with a very raspy voice, he told me, "Phil, go home. You've been here since 6:00 a.m., and you need to pick up Jamie." I left him with a very heavy heart, knowing almost for certain that the biggest challenge we faced was not so much his back problem but his drug addiction.

After he came home from the surgery, it became so obvious that the back condition was only a very small part of the personality change; where once we had flowed in unison, now we clashed constantly. How many times did I reach out, asking if he had gone back to his old habits? Too many times to remember or admit to myself that I had become a fool in my own home. The more I reached out, the further away he fled.

His favorite outburst was "I want to be left alone. Just leave me the fuck alone."

He just plain lied about everything. He said that the reason he was depressed was because he was not happy with the marriage. When I asked about missing funds, he gave a pitiful excuse that he had to pay back an old debt. He denied using any kind of drugs with such conviction that I almost started to believe him. The words from my counselor from so many years ago came back to haunt me—"Maybe he's taking some kind of drugs." With Mike, I downright refused to accept that possibility; with Peter, I was certain of it. I agonized alone, thinking maybe Mike had in fact been taking drugs. His personality had changed too much, and now I was facing the same dilemma again. Those phantoms with empty eyes that I had tried to escape from were following me; they had now entered my own home, destroying our happiness.

He continued to complain that the marriage was just not working because we never had any time alone, that all we did was work and take care of Jamie. I didn't believe a word of his excuses but decided to make one final effort into collecting the scattered pieces of our marriage. I booked a four-day vacation for couples, only hoping that it would, in some way, help. I was shocked that he even agreed to go. The money would have been better spent if I had burned it in the fireplace; at least I would have received some physical warmth. He was just as uncaring, bitter, and angry that I spent most of my time alone, walking on the beach, hiding my tears. I found the proof that he could not deny safely tucked away in his bag, rolled up into socks—a small prescription bottle containing a liquid with someone else's name on it. With clenched fists, I asked, "Peter, I found this bottle. It's not yours. What's in it?" He became enraged. "Why do you need to go through my things? You're always butting in to my life."

I stood so close to him, my face right on top of his, that I'm sure he felt my spit as I spewed out, "I wasn't butting in. I'm your wife. I'm doing what I've been doing for years, taking care of everything. Do you realize what would have happened to both of us if customs had found this crap? We'd both be in a fucking foreign jail, you asshole." I took the bottle, spilling its contents into the toilet, and, with tears streaming down my cheeks, choked on the words "I made a big mistake marrying you. You don't give a crap about me or Jamie. All you care about is your first true love, drugs." The trip had mended only one thing, my dismembered conviction that I needed to file for a divorce.

As soon as we got home from that disastrous trip, before we even stepped a few inches into the house, Peter started to walk out again. Already filled with such resentment at being treated like a fool, I grabbed his arm with as much force that my now exhausted body could exert. Through clenched teeth, I demanded to know, "Where the fuck do you think you're going? We just walked in, and Jamie needs to get picked up." He looked completely crazy to me, a man out of control. His eyes no longer holding the sparks of love I had so often seen. The demons of drug addiction had taken hold; he had again become a slave to those demons. I tried to pull him back from leaving, but I was no match for his strength; he merely pushed with his arm, and I crashed onto the bench near the front door. I too became completely insane, running after him, throwing a coffee cup at the moving car he was in, screaming at the top of my lungs, "I hope, this time, you take enough to kill yourself! Everyone is going to be better off!"

My sole focus from that day on was to care for Jamie, making sure the turmoil that had, like a thief, entered our lives didn't leave any lasting emotional scars. I cried myself to sleep every night knowing that I had to protect this innocent little boy from his own father, a father that I knew the son idolized. We barely spoke to each other; there was really not much to say that we didn't completely disagree on. His sense of reason was totally lost in the confused mind of what we called in the South Bronx "a junkie."

I had to take a very uncomfortable look at myself and admit I was married to a "junkie." I stared in the mirror, hating myself, asking, "How did you let this happen, and now what are you going to do about it?"

I could not waste any more time. Jamie's well-being was at stake, and I felt like a tiger protecting her cub. My heart was again in shattered pieces, realizing that I had to protect my son from his own father. Where Peter once had been all caring, fussing over his son like a prized trophy, he now barely paid him any attention. I too often saw a blank look on Jamie's face and knew that this very intuitive, smart little boy was trying to figure out what was going on. I didn't waste any more time making an appointment with an attorney, filing for a legal separation. I could no longer stand to look at what he had become; it drained every ounce of energy from me—the energy I now needed to solely care for my son.

Peter very agreeably came to the attorney's office to iron out the details of the separation. Deep in the remnants of Peter's former self, in the deepest part of his being, he held on to hope that we could again become a loving family. It was the struggle with those hateful demons that were ripping him apart making him unrecognizable to the people he truly loved. That never-ending struggle between the insane need for drugs and the need to love his family. A torturous tug of his will. He agreed to all the separation terms.

For some reason still unknown to me, the attorney asked that we have a month long cooling-off period before he officially filed the papers. Did he sense that we still loved each other? Did my brother have a talk with his longtime schoolmate, or had Peter been able to charm even my own attorney? I resented the suggestion, feeling controlled by men, telling myself that if after the month was over I didn't have official separation papers and Peter moved out of our home, I would seek the counsel of a female attorney.

My memory became a swirling maze of angry existence from that day. I cried myself into a restless sleep every night, awaking exhausted and disheartened, only pushing myself to the very limits of my strength out of love for my son. He was the only person that gave me joy, any hope for happiness. I tried to hide all of my sorrow from him and did my best to continue living normal lives.

I would walk up to Jamie's school daily to watch him, from a distance, playing in the schoolyard, holding back tears over the fact that I had such a precious child with a drug addict for a father. I ran to pick him up after work, giving him the attention that was now lacking from his father. While I cooked or did housework, I set up his playroom with an array of educational games. On sunny days, I pitched softballs for him, laughing through my anger, making him laugh at my comical throw. What Peter did was no longer my concern; I only had a few weeks before being freed from the disgust and anger I felt every time I saw him.

Why did Jamie mention to me that the days daddy took him to school he had to first stop at the bank? I can still hear his sweet tiny voice, saying, "Mommy, you know, before Daddy drops me off at school, we stop at the bank." I held him with both of my hands on his arms, asking, "Jamie, what bank?" "I don't know, Mommy. It's a bank. You get this stuff. I sit in a chair, and Daddy goes to the window and gets this stuff." I felt the heat of rage filling every part of my being. I started to feel my legs trembling under me. It was only the innocent look on Jamie's face that quelled my rage, and I controlled myself out of deep love for him. I knew that Peter would never be alone with his son again.

I left work that day speeding home, knowing that the man I now completely hated was there. I was ready to strike in any way, making sure he was out of our home. He saw the rage on my face as I yelled, demanding to know, "Where did you take my son? Where have you been taking him?" Was he calm from drugs or from the decision he had made? I'm not sure. He softly spoke as I wildly started to throw punches. I didn't even have a chance to hit him with one blow before he, with one arm, flipped me onto a chair, holding my hands with one of his and steadily holding my kicking legs between his knees. I was no longer human. I didn't speak my words but hissed them out, demanding to know where he had been taking my son.

Peter spoke above my hissing and kicking, almost in a rehearsed speech. "Phil, I'm going away for a month to a drug rehab. I can't do it on my own. I've been trying for months to get off of the crap I was on. That's where I was going with Jamie in the morning, to Saint John's methadone program." I howled through tears and rage, "What, are you crazy? You were taking my little boy to a place like that?" If I had been strong enough to release myself from his grip, I have no doubt that I would have tried to choke him to death. Again, Peter spoke in a voice so calm that it made me even more furious; he was speaking as if this was all part of normal life. How crazy had he become?

"Phil, you need to calm down. I can't talk to you when you're like this." His casual tone, asking me to calm down after the months of torment he had put me through, only increased my rage, and I yelled, "You're completely out of your fucking mind! Let go of me, get out of my house." "Phil, I'm leaving. I'll call you in a few days when I feel better. I can't stay here feeling like this. It's not good for any of us." "Good?" I cried out, choking on my own tears, "Who the fuck needs you? You've been useless for months, and do us all a big favor—don't come back."

Holding back his own tears, he spoke, his voice cracking from confused emotions. "I'm going to let you up now. Please don't throw any punches. Maybe when I come back, we can start to put our marriage back together again."

As he released his grip, I collapsed from sheer exhaustion. He turned to look at me for the last time, telling me, "I'll call you in a few days." I was only able to whisper, "Don't bother. I never want to talk or see you again. You're nothing but a junkie. I hate you." I managed to raise my voice to let him hear "I hope you drop dead" as he closed the front door.

I don't have recipes for this chapter, only memories of deep sorrow and hate for the man I never wanted to cook for again.

Chapter 16

Dying Embers

I became no more than a walking android, only existing to care for my son. I awoke every morning with swollen eyes and a raspy voice, hiding my sorrow from Jamie as I prepared us for school and work. At work, everyone noticed something was very wrong, and I only completed my work from years of habit. The smiling "good morning" the employees sent my way were returned with a brief nod. The usual daily problems of work were corrected out of sheer need for a paycheck. The vitality I had always given to my work was gone, replaced by bitterness.

It became so obvious that something was very wrong that an employee, who was like a mother to me, came into the glass-enclosed office, shutting the door behind her. She sat at her desk next to mine, speaking in a gentle motherly manner, "Phil, what's wrong? Are you sick?" I spoke in barely a whisper, looking down at the paperwork on my desk. "No, I'm fine." I could see from the corner of my eyes the concerned look on her face as she continued to ask, "Is Jamie OK? He's not sick?" "No, he's fine." "OK, Phil, then what's wrong with Pete? His back is giving him problems again?" The bottled-up sadness poured out of me at the mention of his name, and tears started to soak the order forms in front of me.

I spoke without looking up, not wanting the other employees to see my tears. "Pete's in a drug rehab. I don't know if he's OK." "*Oh* my god, not again." "Yeah, again," I said as I reached for tissues. "What happened? What the hell made him go back to that after all these years?" "I don't know. Your guess is as good as mine. He claims his back pain, but I don't believe him. We had a team of doctors he could have gone to, but you know, old habits die hard. What can I say? I'm married to a drug addict. I filed for a separation. I don't want him near Jamie or me ever again."

She placed her hand over her mouth. "Oh my god, Phil, I don't know what to say." "There's not much to say. It's over," I said, and the tears started again, completely soaking the papers that I knew had to be redone. The phone rang, and as I started to pick up, she, with great intuition, stopped me. "Let me take it. You can't think straight right now." As she answered, she placed her hand over the receiver, telling me, "Go to the ladies' room." I nodded, walking out of the office. I almost ran into the ladies' room, not wanting anyone to see me.

The thought of Peter's drug addiction and of a pending divorce so weakened me that I sat on a stool, placing my head on the sink, sobbing with deep gulps. I cried until I had no more tears, and my inner voice spoke telling me, "Don't shame yourself by being so weak. The woman giving you comfort raised seven children on her own. Her husband died when the youngest was only three, and she's out there now doing your job. Get up, and go back to work. Don't be such a wimp." I washed my face, blew my nose, and went back to work. She walked into the office with a tray of food, ordering me to eat. "For God's sake, Phil, eat. You're starting to look like a skeleton. Eat. You have a son to care for." I nodded and started to push down the food.

Peter did call, and as he spoke, asking how we were doing, I could hear the great strain in his voice. His voice revealed a multitude of emotions, but the most obvious was the battle to overcome drug addiction. I barely responded to his questions, not wanting to use any of my energy on him. I hated him for what he was putting me through and constantly worried what the long-lasting effects would be on Jamie. I told myself over and over, *Don't let him charm you again. Go through with the divorce, and get on with your life.* I hated myself for suffering over a man that had betrayed me after I had given him so much. I felt like such a fool.

The resentment only grew with each passing day, and made worse by the struggle to keeping up with a small child, a hectic job, and a large home all on my own. To make matters worse, my mother called me at work, urging me to rush over, that Jamie had suddenly come down with 105°F fever and was barely able to swallow a few drops of water. I ran out of work, yelling to the staff to call the office and tell them I was gone for the day. I didn't even park the car at my mother's home; looking for a parking spot would have taken at least fifteen minutes, and I just pulled into the neighbor's driveway, running up the stairs.

I took one look at Jamie and didn't bother to even take his temperature, ordering my mother to put a cold cloth on his head while I called the doctor. I had to physically pick him up to carry him down the stairs, tripping on the way down, catching myself by holding on to the railing with one hand, hearing my mother yelling and praying from the top of the stairs. I carried Jamie to the doctor's office, cursing Peter for not being there. His arms were so much stronger than mine; I hated him for not being there to care for a son that he had so much wanted.

I didn't need to wait; the doctor saw my panic and told me to go right in. Jamie started vomiting while the doctor examined him and, with one look, knew it was strep. I ask the nurse to please call my pharmacy and ask that they deliver the medicine to my home. There was no way I could hold him in the pharmacy, waiting for the prescription; I was starting to feel shaky myself and wondered who would care for both of us if I got ill.

That night, after I had cared for Jamie—removing his soiled clothes, washing his face and hands, putting him in his pj's, placing him in bed, and coaxing him to take his medicine—Peter called.

I was beside myself with hate for him. I hissed into the phone, "I don't have any fucking time for your bullshit. I'm taking care of Jamie. He has strep with 105-degree fever." With that, I slammed down the receiver. I slept on the rug next to Jamie's bed for fear that his fever might cause a convulsion. While I checked him every half hour, I cursed the father that had promised to always be there for both of us.

When Jamie awoke the next day, after I managed to give him his medicine and some juice, I rubbed his cheeks, giving him kisses on his forehead, asking, "You're feeling a little better now, right?" He nodded, and although I could see he didn't want to speak, he forced himself to ask, "When is Daddy coming home?" I choked back tears, telling him, "Daddy is busy making a commercial. He'll be home in a few days." I propped him up on his pillow, placed the juice on the nightstand, and ran into my bathroom to throw up bitter bile.

Toward the end of the month, Peter called, sounding better, asking if I could drive with Jamie the two-hour ride to the rehab center for family day. I laughed and hissed my response like a venomous snake. "Wait, let me get this straight, you want me to take my son to hang out with a bunch of drug addicts? Are you out of your fucking mind? Dealing with one junkie is bad enough. I don't need more bullshit in my life. Oh, by the way, did you forget there's this thing called work and school? After that comes cleaning, washing clothes, food shopping, cooking, and most important of all, educating my son." Now yelling in fury that Peter no longer understood everyday life, I told him, "Fuck off, asshole! Life is not only about what you need." I again slammed down the receiver, truly wanting to slam his face.

After a month long absence, Peter very casually walked in as if he had just come home from work. Jamie ran to the door, yelling," Daddy, Daddy!" and then ran into the kitchen to happily inform me that Daddy is home. I clenched my teeth but forced myself to say, "Oh wow, that's great." I heard the exchange between father and son, and if Jamie had not been home, I'm sure my temper would have exploded.

"Daddy, you were gone for a long time." In a very calm voice, Peter responded, "Yeah, I know, Jamie, but I promise never to be away for that long again." I thought, *What a line of shit he's giving the poor angel. What a fuck he has for a father.* Peter walked into the kitchen as if nothing had occurred, very calmly asking, "Hey, how's it going?"

I looked up at him with venom pouring out of my eyes, pushing past him and running up into the bedroom. I slammed my fits into the pillows, wanting him out of the house, but knew if I called the police, Jamie would suffer the consequences. I thought, *How lucky for him I have a son to worry about, or else he'd be out on his ass. What do I need him for? The lying fuck.*

No more than two days had passed when Peter, after having listened to Jamie read before going to bed, walked into the bedroom, sat on the bed, and started talking to me like a loving husband. "Phil, I know you're upset with me. You have every right to be, but my counselor suggested that you should attend Al-Anon. It's this group for family members of addicts. They meet in the evening, and you can talk out your anger."

I placed my face only a few inches from his and, with a hateful look, while clenching my teeth, hissed my feelings at him. "You selfish motherfucker, I work all day, come home to housework and caring for

Jamie, and you want me to use up the precious little time I have for my son listening to other people's bullshit? I don't think so. I've lived a life of strict discipline, and I'm not paying for your lack of it. This is your problem. You take care of it. Get the fuck out of my bedroom." He sat for a few seconds, closed his eyes, took a few deep breaths, and walked out of the room.

I collapsed on the bed and did what I had been doing for months—crying myself to sleep. I had called my attorney, explaining the situation, asking him to file the necessary papers for a separation. He seemed to hesitate, and I became extremely frustrated, telling myself, *He's my attorney, not a family counselor. What's his problem? Had my sweet-talking husband spoken to him, taking control of my life?* I started to look for a female attorney.

For days, I avoided every room he was in, not wanting to be near him in fear that I would either lash out or melt in his arms. When I cooked meals for Jamie, he would just very nonchalantly serve himself and sit at the table. A Neapolitan expression always flashed in my mind, *face e puttan*, the rough translation being "he has the face of a whore," meaning that he knew he had done wrong but was still willing to stand his ground to get what he wanted or that he had no shame.

Peter sat at the kitchen table, eating and softly speaking to Jamie and me like we were the perfect family, even making jokes, beaming as Jamie laughed. In the evenings, he would go out to AA/NA meetings, telling me where he was going and the time he would be back. I would respond, "Ask me if I care," clenching my fist and quickly walking away in fear of punching him. He even told me that his counselor agreed with me that this was his problem, and he needed to take care of it, not me. I sarcastically responded, "Wow, I'm so glad. He's really a smart guy."

Deep down in the depths of my soul, I knew that I truly loved him and feared that this blind love would lead to further mistakes. I forced myself to freeze my heart and harden my resolve. Again, he entered the bedroom, quietly closing the door behind him, and calmly sat on the bed. My face was turned away from him, looking down into a drawer of my dresser, where I was pulling out nightclothes. I refused to turn around, closing the drawer and placing both hands tightly on the edge of the dresser, telling myself, *Don't turn around.* He spoke in a very soft, mellow manner. "Phil, I just want to thank you for the great job you've done with Jamie. I can't believe how well he reads. He's so smart." I clenched my teeth, telling myself, *Here comes a barrel of sugarcoated bullshit.*

I didn't respond, staring down at the lace doilies on my dresser, wishing I could suddenly become deaf. He continued to speak. "I know you have every right to be angry with me. In trying to do right, I did a horrible wrong, but, Phil, please give me a chance to make it up to you." His voice was now cracking with emotions. "Please put the divorce papers away. You know I love you. I loved you from the first day I saw you. I'll try my best to make it up to you and Jamie. If not for us, do it for Jamie. I don't want him raised in a separated home." I almost started to laugh, thinking, *Now he's going to use Jamie to get to me.*

I continued to stare down at the lace pattern, refusing to speak and dignify his presence. I told myself, *This time, you're going to be tough and not give in to his charm.* I stared down, refusing to look up for what seemed to me like hours, hoping he would just leave the bedroom. He quietly sat, and I could hear his breathing, feeling his energy. I stared at the lace pattern until those external forces that had so often guided me placed their hands firmly on my shoulders, slowing turning me around. Refusing to look up, I willed myself to stare down at the wooden floor, but those guiding forces placed a hand under my chin, forcing me to look into my husband's glazed eyes.

Peter's arms reached out for me. I planted my feet firmly on the floor, not wanting to give in. Again, those guiding forces gently pulled me into his embrace, his arms wrapping around my waist. He placed his face into my chest, asking for forgiveness, his tears soaking my shirt. I became helpless, wrapping my hands around his face, kissing his forehead and cheeks until, finally, our lips interlocked, releasing months of bottled-up passion. I desperately tried to resist, but those forces steadily blew on the dying embers inside of me. My clothes faded away, Peter's hands firmly pulling me onto the bed.

He cupped one hand around the side of my face with one knee pressed between my thighs. He kissed my cheeks and neck as I told him, "I hate you," trying to push him away. He whispered, "I know. I hate myself too, but I love you. I've always loved you, and I'm never going to let you go." I spoke, holding back tears. "I still hate—" His lips silenced my anger. I did what I had always done, melted and gave in to him.

Again, in this chapter, I don't have any recipes to share with the reader, only memories of great exhaustion and deep regret at having lost so much time dealing with my husband's drug addiction instead of enjoying the fleeting moments of my son's childhood.

Chapter 17

Hot Corn Cakes

For the first time in months, I fell into a deep sleep, awaking with the thought that I was going to be late for work. I jumped, sitting up in bed, gladly realizing that it was Saturday. "Oh, thank God," I told myself, "I can stay in bed a little longer." I placed my head down on the pillow facing Peter. The internal debate started within me. *You know you love him, but can you trust him? He's always going to be a drug addict. Can you live with that? He can be the most wonderful husband and father, but the drugs make him a demon.* I didn't know what to think or feel but decided to put the divorce papers on hold.

How I wished to stroke his forehead and remove the demons that lurked deep inside, realizing with a stabbing ache that they would always be part of him. For now, all I could do is give my husband and son the best care and let destiny guide our fate. Knowing what a difficult time Peter had always had in falling and staying asleep, I quietly rolled out of bed. While showering, I decided to prepare Jamie's and Peter's favorite breakfast.

Jamie came scurrying out of his bedroom as soon as he heard my footsteps in the hallway. "Good morning, my little boy," I said, and I held his hand walking down the stairs. "Mommy, is Daddy still asleep?" I put my finger over my lips, making the *shhh* sound. "Let's be very quiet so we don't wake him up." Jamie went into his playroom, sitting on the sofa, putting on *Barney*, and I gave him a container of juice while asking, "How about cornmeal pancakes and bacon for breakfast?" He quickly nodded. "OK, that's my favorite breakfast." I placed my hands around his angelic face knowing that I would gladly give my life and soul for him. I mushed him up with kisses, tickling his belly, enjoying his giggles.

I prepared the cornmeal pancake batter without looking at a recipe. I had developed the recipe as part of a college experimental cooking class, and it was imbedded in my mind. In college, I never realized how often I would use the recipe to feed my family. I knew that the smell of frying bacon would awaken Peter, and I asked Jamie, "Is that Daddy?" Jamie ran to the bottom of the hallway stairs, looking up. "Yes, Mommy, he's going to the bathroom." Yelling up, he said, "Hurry up, Daddy, Mommy is making our favorite breakfast!"

Peter came bouncing down the stairs with more energy than I had seen from him in the past year. He walked into the kitchen holding Jamie as he rubbed the top of his father's head the same way he had done from infancy. The sight warmed my heart, and I knew we had to give our marriage a second chance. Peter had been right—if not for us then for Jamie. Peter placed Jamie into his seat and walked over to me, wrapping an arm around my waist, giving me a kiss on the cheek. I smiled, gently nuzzling him with my cheek, handing him a plate for himself and Jamie.

I continued to flip the remaining pancakes in the skillet as Peter ate and spoke, "You know, Phil, these pancakes are so much better than the diner kind. They have more body and flavor. The diner pancakes are all fluff." Jamie chimed in agreement, "Yeah, Daddy, they're hard to stick on the fork." Peter once again beamed with pride and reached across the table to stroke Jamie's cheek.

I sat in my usual seat between husband and son, finally enjoying a meal. Peter turned to me with that familiar devilish sexy smile and said, "Thanks, Phil. Thanks for everything." I smiled back, understanding the meaning in his words, realizing that, for now, Mr. Smith was on the mend. The sparkle was back in his eyes; his appetite seemed to be just fine, and for some bizarre reason, I loved him now more than ever. Sadly, I admitted to myself that I would never completely trust him again. I vowed to be vigilant in guarding our family against his inner demons, knowing that they could strike at any moment, destroying our happiness. I told myself, *You need to love more carefully and trust a great deal less.* As I watched Peter once again eat with hearty gusto, I inwardly smiled, realizing that food and sex are two very powerful cures.

After that first reunion, I can't say that the marriage was completely mended; it was only the first stitch in repairing the torn fabric of our relationship. The strongest fiber that kept us together was woven by the deep love we had for our son. While Peter still had a long journey to becoming the clearheaded, fun-loving person I had married, I had to navigate through a maze of anger and resentment. We would spend months in heated exchanges about what he referred to as an illness and what I considered betrayal and downright selfishness. These were typical scenarios that lasted for months.

Peter often came home from meeting with his sponsor with what I considered bullshit excuses for drug abuse and tried to explain how a family should deal with the problem. I, of course, had a completely different opinion, and the heated debate would start. Peter started the discussion with suggestions such as, "You know, Phil, you really need to start trusting me a little more. I mean, everyone I know agrees that you need trust in a marriage." I just laugh and look him straight in the face with a "you've got to be kidding me" look, responding, "OK, let me get this straight. You lied and betrayed me, put our marriage and our son in jeopardy, and I need to trust you? No, Pete, what you need to do is gain my trust and love again. It may take years, and even then, I'll never completely trust you."

Peter sat for a few minutes, contemplating what I had just said, and blurted out another cock-and-bull slogan—"Well, what about unconditional love? You need unconditional love in a family." I just threw my hands in the air, bringing them down again with clenched fists, telling him in a hissing voice, "What a bunch of bullshit ammunition you've been given to use for a defense. There's no such thing as unconditional love. Everyone wants something in return." Peter, now getting hot under the collar, responded, "What about your son? Don't you have unconditional love for him?"

Becoming furious at him for using Jamie as an example, I yelled back, "No, it's not! I expect a great deal from him. I expect him to become an educated, productive member of society. I expect love and respect from him. I expect him to make me proud to be his mother. I don't think that's unconditional love, and I expect you to make me proud to be your wife and mother to our son." I'd gotten so fed up with the bullshit conversation that I put my sneakers on, ready to walk miles to clear my head while yelling from the doorway, "Tell your sponsor he's an asshole! Even Jesus Christ expected much from his followers. You're all a bunch of assholes."

I walk for miles, having an internal debate with myself, realizing that although, for me, Peter's AA network of friends was like the blind leading the blind, in the end, I didn't care what type of bullshit they use for excuses as long as Peter stayed sober.

I walk into my home completely exhausted, running up the stairs to take a shower with Peter calling from the bottom of the stairs, "Phil, I bought lemon sole and shrimp to have a fish fry. I cleaned and butterflied the shrimp just the way you like them. I'll fry outside on the deck so the house doesn't get smelly. Come down and eat after your shower."

I had to admit to myself that he was trying his best to make amends, my heart melting as it always had. I almost talked to myself out loud, thinking, *You're so dick-whipped, so in love, that even if he fed you bread and shit, you'd appreciate it.* I knew I was going to enjoy a great fish fry, but more gratifying was my husband's attention.

That evening, as I read in bed, Peter quietly placed himself next to me with his head on his hand, whispering, "What are you reading?" Without looking up, I softly whispered back, "Tell Patty Boy I don't believe in unconditional love. I expect something in return." Peter ever so gently removed the book from my hand; leaned over me, placing it on the nightstand; turned off the light; wrapped his hands around my face; and ever so gently whispered in my ear, "This Patty Boy will give you whatever you want." As I placed my hands on my husband's shoulders, inhaling his male scent, I thought, *Ah yes, food and sex, two powerful cures.*

While basking in the afterglow of passion, as I watched Peter sleeping, I had a momentary urge to wake him so I could break his chops by asking him, "How much unconditional love would you afford me if I didn't work all day, come home to care for Jamie, cook, clean, and still give of myself by pleasing you in bed?" My heart would not allow me to wake him. Instead, I closed my eyes, enjoying hearing his breathing, holding back laughter, realizing that maybe that was my unconditional love for him.

Of course, there were many other dinnertime conversations that help mend our marriage; the most vivid in my memory is Jamie complaining about a girl in his class trying to boss him around. We were clearing the dishes from the table as Jamie started to explain, "Mommy, can you believe that? Who does she think she is? She's just a girl, and she's not smarter than me. She can't do that." I don't recall exactly how this girl was trying to push Jamie around, but my response made Peter howl with laughter. "Jamie, don't let anyone push you around, especially not a girl."

I turned to Peter, who was convulsing with laughter. "What's so funny?" "Well, Phil, I always knew that only a son could lower your feminist fist." "What feminist fist do I have? I spend all of my time caring for two men. Boy, I'm really a feminist." Peter continued to stare and smirk at me. I gave him a playful shove; he pulled me closer, wrapping his arms around my waist. "Ms. Abys, let's tell Jamie we're paying bills upstairs. I like to spend a bit of time being the boss." This feminist started to melt, realizing that the day I had my son, the tower of feminism I had built around me had collapsed, and now the deep love I felt for husband and son was paving it over. I yelled to Jamie, who was in his playroom. "Jamie, we're going upstairs to pay bills."

I tried my best to participate in his recovery, even attending an anniversary celebration AA meeting for one of Peter's friends. I'm not sure what I expected; of course, I knew that they would not be offering a glass of wine but maybe a bit of music and a few laughs. Instead, I sat listening to one alcoholic after another telling his tale of woe and how they found a fellowship of hope in AA. I wanted to laugh and cry all at once, not understanding why this was called a celebration. For me, it was more like misery onstage. When I leaned over to Peter, telling him how I felt, he started to laugh, whispering to me, "I know, but it helps us stay sober." I whispered back, "OK, whatever floats your boat, but after this, I'm ready for a drink." We both sat for the rest of the "celebration" trying not to look at each other and laugh. After that, I attended only one more AA celebration for Peter's ten-year sobriety anniversary. He publicly thanked me for all the help and love I had given him. As Peter continued to speak, I inwardly smiled, thinking, *Thank God I know how to heat up the kitchen and bedroom. If it helps you stay sober, I'll cook and . . . until I drop.*

In the first few years of Peter's recovery, we grew closer as a family, Peter becoming a caring, attentive husband and father again. I indulging him with whatever he needed, I listened, loved, cooked, and took care of every detail of family life to ease his burden. We even took on the added burden of finishing the home renovation by removing a small bedroom which we didn't need and adding that extra space to an adjoining bathroom. After all, Jamie was growing at rapid speed, and the two men in our family needed more bathroom space. In the midst of having a crew of men demolishing walls, removing floors, rearranging doorways and closets, I'd come home after work daily to clean up the mess and care for Jamie, while Peter worked twelve-hour days.

I'm not sure how I realized that I had missed menstrual cycles, but this time, I was completely sure that menopause was starting; after all, I was forty-three, and who had the time to—to use a Peter phrase—"get hammered." I told myself, *As soon as you have time, just see the doctor and let him know that you're going through menopause.*

"You Make Me Melt" Cornmeal Hotcakes

Ingredients:

½ cup of all-purpose flour
½ cup of cornmeal
3 tsp. of baking powder
½ tsp. of salt
1 egg
1 tbs. of vegetable oil
4 tbs. of sugar
¾ cup of milk

In a large bowl, sift together the flour, cornmeal, baking powder, and salt. In a separate bowl, beat the egg with sugar, add milk, and whisk until well mixed. Add the vegetable oil to the middle of the dry ingredients. In small amounts, whisk milk mixture into flour until a well-blended batter is formed. On a hot greased grill, pour the batter; you can make the corn cakes as small or as large as you like. I usually pour the batter into a large measuring cup, placing a paper plate under it, and pour the batter onto the grill right from the cup.

You may also spice up these corn cakes by adding a teaspoon of vanilla, nutmeg, lemon zest, or orange zest.

Unconditional Love Fish Fry

Ingredients

2-lb. lemon sole
1 lb. of medium-size shrimp, washed and deveined on both sides
2 eggs with 1 tsp. of milk

Salt and black pepper to taste
1½ cups of unseasoned breadcrumbs
3 tbs. of cornmeal

In a bowl, beat eggs, milk, salt, and pepper together. In a large plate, mix breadcrumbs with cornmeal; dip each piece of fish into the egg batter, and then dredge each into the breadcrumbs set on a platter. Repeat the same method with the shrimp. My husband recommends, if possible, frying fish outside with an electric fryer; the house doesn't get messy or smelly and keeps Ms. Abys, his not-so-feminist wife, happy. Place fried fish and shrimp on a large baking sheet with paper towels, or better yet, cut open brown paper bags to drain fried fish of excess oil. I know that all TV chefs first dredge fish in flour then in an egg wash and then dip into breadcrumbs; we do not like this method as the coating overpowers the taste of the fish or whatever you're frying. Our method of frying is by simply coating with beaten eggs and breadcrumbs, which gives a lighter, crispier product.

Pete's "I'm Just an American" Cocktail Sauce

The only time I consume catsup is when Peter prepares his own cocktail sauce. I must admit that I do enjoy dipping my fried shrimp into this catsup-based sauce with my very American husband smiling and reminding me, "Phil, I think you're finally becoming Americanized."

Ingredients:

¼ cup of catsup
3 oz. of Gold's prepared horseradish
Optional: 1 tbs. of jarred hot sauce

Place all three ingredients in a bowl; mix well with a fork. Enjoy. If you prefer a spicier sauce, use more hot sauce, or if you prefer it mild, omit.

Pete's "In a Hurry" Tartar Sauce

Ingredients:

½ cup of mayo
½ cup of finely diced pickles (any type you prefer)
1½ oz. of Gold's Horseradish

Place all ingredients in a bowl; mix well with a fork. Enjoy.

Chapter 18

I Shook instead of Shimmied

After missing another menstrual cycle, I told Peter, "Thank God I'm finally going through menopause. Who needs that headache every month?" Peter, with eyebrows raised, stared at me for a few seconds and then, with that familiar wiseass smirk, asked, "How many cycles have you missed?" I had to think for a moment, having been too busy with the renovation to even keep track. "I'm not sure, two or three." Peter's jaw nearly hit the ground as he plainly stated, "Phil, you're going through pregnancy, not menopause." "Don't be silly," I responded, continuing to explain, "At my age, it's not so easy to get pregnant, and besides, we haven't even had time to fool around."

As I started to walk out the door, heading off to work, Peter asked, "When do you see the doctor?" "Tomorrow, after work. You'll have Jamie all to yourself." He yelled out the door, "Ms. Abys, you're pregnant again! I can tell. It's in your face." I simply waved my hand, shooing him away.

I explained to the nurse why I was there, and she asked for a urine sample. I asked, "What for?" She looked at me in disbelief and said, "For a pregnancy test." I firmly stated, "I'm not pregnant. This is the start of menopause." She smiled, nodding her head, and told me, "It's standard procedure. We'll have the results in a few minutes, and the doctor will come in to see you." I nervously waited in the examination room, thumbing through magazines, telling myself, *Wow, if you're pregnant, it's like the Immaculate Conception. I don't remember having sex. We're always so damn busy to have fun.*

The doctor walked in with a smile on his face, sitting on the examination stool. He stared at me for a few seconds and then quietly spoke, "Filomena, you're in the fourth month of pregnancy. This is a change of life, but not menopause."

For a few minutes, I could do nothing but stare in disbelief, convinced that they had made a mistake. I stared down at my feet then back up at my doctor, not sure what to think or say. I finally asked, "Are you sure? I mean, I can't believe it. I don't even recall having sex. We're very busy renovating our home."

With that, my doctor of many years started to laugh out loud. "Well, you must have some time because you're pregnant. I've already ordered a series of blood tests and a sonogram." Before I could absorb the change that was occurring in my life, the doctor examined me; the nurse came in for the blood test, and I was told to go into the sonogram room.

I watched the monitor in complete disbelief as the images appeared on the screen, and the beating of a heart was very clear. The technician smiled and told me, "Not to worry, everything looks fine. After you're dressed, the doctor will see you in his office."

As I started to dress, I felt those external forces wrapping their arms around me. They had so often taken control of my life, directing its destiny. Once again, they had taken charge, and I was merely a participant on their stage.

I sat across from my smiling doctor, and I guess he noticed the shock on my face, asking, "Are we looking forward to this pregnancy?" I again fumbled for words, not sure what to say. "I'm not sure. I thought I was going through menopause, and now, all of a sudden, I'm four months pregnant. I don't even know how it happened."

My doctor, with clasped hands, patiently nodded, explaining that with this pregnancy, we should be more careful because of my age. I immediately started to worry about having a child with the many disorders associated with older women. With a shaky voice, I told my doctor, "I don't want to have a sick child. The burden would eventually land on my son's shoulders. I don't want that to happen."

"I understand. This time, please have the amino test. That will tell us for certain if everything is OK." I agreed, telling myself, *This time, you can't be such a chicken. You have a son to worry about.*

I sat in my car before driving home, trying to steady myself, realizing that this must all be part of the external forces' plan. I was forty-three, didn't even remember having had sex, and I was four months pregnant. We had been extremely careful for almost seven years not to conceive another child, and now destiny was in control.

I almost laughed out loud remembering how we discussed removing the extra bedroom. "What do we need it for? Let's make the bathroom larger." As the saying goes, "You plan, God laughs." I drove away, hoping that whatever external forces were controlling my life, they would give me extra strength to go through the rest of the pregnancy while going to work, caring for my son, and cleaning up the daily mess of a major renovation.

Peter was sitting at the kitchen table when I walked in, and without me saying a word, he asked, "How many months?" I plopped into the chair next to him, making sure Jamie was not within hearing distance, then I spoke, "Four months." I shrugged, continuing, "Peter, we've been so busy these past few months. I can't even remember having sex." He, of course, made his usual smart-ass remark. "See what a smooth lover I am? In and out without you even knowing." He was joking but looked extremely worried. "Jesus, we've been so careful. I guess I shook instead of shimmying." With my forehead on my hand, I asked, "Yeah, well, now what are we going to do about a nursery?" "Ms. Abys, I guess you'll just have to give up your personal boudoir and turn it into a nursery."

We both stared at each other for a few seconds and burst out laughing. I, with a nervous giggle, continued, "Pete, I can't believe this. I just finished decorating, as you call it, 'my personal boudoir' the way I like, and now, in a few months, everything needs to be rearranged."

"I guess the desk and the TV will come into the bedroom—thank God we have enough room—and the sofa into the playroom." Peter just nodded, not caring about home décor, but worried about starting over again after almost seven years of contentment with one child. We discussed not telling Jamie about the pregnancy until all the test results indicated a healthy child, and Peter, with another wiseass remark, commented, "Well, looking on the bright side, we can screw around all we want. I can shake and shimmy without being careful."

Pushing his head back, looking up at the ceiling, and with a long-sounding "*Ah*, great," softly whispered, "Come on, Phil, let's tell Jamie we're paying bills upstairs." I extended my leg under the table, trying to playfully kick him in his balls; he grabbed my foot, yelling to Jamie in the playroom, "Jamie, we're going upstairs to pay bills! If someone calls, take a message, and unless it's really important like you're sick or the house is burning down, don't bother us. You know paying bills is serious business."

Jamie, forever the adult child, responded, "OK, Daddy, don't worry. I won't open the door to anyone either." Peter, grabbing my hand, pulling me off the chair, moving his eyebrows up and down, whispered, "Phil, thank God you have him trained like a good soldier. Come on, let's start enjoying this pregnancy."

Regardless of my age and the many hours of work, I was fortunate to again have an easy pregnancy, being able to eat everything and work long hours without too much effort. All the test results were fine, and I very anxiously thought of not having the amino test done, asking myself, "What if there is something wrong? What are you going to do about it?" After we had a pre-amino counseling session and asked if either of us knew of any family members with genetic disorders, we looked at each other, responding in unison, "No, not that I know of." I really didn't want to go through with the procedure after all the warnings of what could happen but felt I needed to forge ahead for the well-being of our son.

On the day of the amino, Peter held my hand, telling me to just watch the monitor, not at the long needle being inserted into my belly. He gently stroked my cheeks, telling me silly jokes until the test was over, and I took a deep breath of relief. Of course, the anxiety lasted until I received a call from the nurse informing me that all was just fine and asking if I wanted to know the sex of the child. I thought for only a few seconds and decided, this time, I wanted to know how to decorate a nursery. I was happy when she informed me, "You're having a girl." I would have been just as happy with another boy; after all, I had plenty of brand-new boy stuff to use, but one of each was great.

As soon as Peter came home that afternoon, we decided to finally tell Jamie. I called him into the kitchen, asking, "Jamie, how would you like to be a big brother?" His inquisitive eyes moved from mother to father, and a slight smile appeared on his lips. "Why, Mommy, are you going to have a baby?" I nodded. Jamie immediately raised his arms in the air, yelling, "Yes, now I get to be the boss! I'm the big brother." We both started to laugh, asking Jamie, "Do you want a brother or sister?" Jamie didn't even need to think for a moment, quickly responding, "A baby sister. I want to be the only boy in my family."

His comment instantly brought a flashback memory of my brother when we found out we had a baby sister; jumping on the bed with arms raised in victory, he shouted, "Yes, the sole king!" Peter, laughing, said, "Son, you're one lucky guy. That's what we're having, a baby girl."

The *woo-hoo* sound went on for the rest of the evening as Jamie excitedly jumped around in his playroom, singing, "I'm going to be a big brother, I'm going to be the boss." He was so excited that he ran into the kitchen where I was preparing my own version of turkey patties, asking,

"Mommy, Mommy, can I tell all my friends at school?" After I responded yes, he ran into the living room, telling Peter, "Daddy, Daddy, Mommy said I can tell all my friends at school. Woo-hoo!"

I heard the sounds of wrestling on the sofa as Peter tickled Jamie and explained that he had to be a good brother and help out with the new baby. "I know, Daddy. I'll be a good brother and help, but not with the poopy diapers." Peter continued to break Jamie's chops, telling him, "Oh, yes, you are. The first thing you're doing when the baby comes home is clean a big shitty diaper." Jamie responded, "Uh-uh. No, I'm not." Smiling, I raised my eyes to the ceiling, silently asking divine providence for extra strength.

I was fortunate with a great pregnancy until the eighth month of pregnancy after I had decided to stop working to enjoy a few weeks of staying home and just relaxing. The most important event outside of the birth of our daughter was to prepare a bowling birthday party for Jamie's seventh birthday. I wanted to make sure he didn't feel pushed aside with the delivery date only a few days before his birthday. On my first day off, I went to shop for the beach buckets along with all the candy and toys that went inside each one for the giveaway goodie bags. We were expecting twenty friends; I made sure to have twenty-five in case someone came unexpectedly. Even if I was unable to make his party, I wanted to make sure that he didn't feel rejected because of the new baby. I shopped all morning and had a doctor's appointment in the afternoon, thinking, *Great, I'll have everything done before the pool contactors start installing a twenty-four-by-twelve-foot pool in our backyard tomorrow morning.* We wanted Jamie to feel extra special, and although he attended camp for the summer, we thought the pool would make the first summer with a baby in the house extra exciting. I, in trying to swell Jamie's ego, allowed him to select a name for his sister. "Mommy, I like the name Nicole. I'll name her Nicole." "OK, big brother, that's a fine name. I like it."

I sat on the examination table expecting the nurse to tell me as she always had before—"Great, everything looks fine." Nope, not this time. With a concerned look on her face, she asked, "Did you have a very busy day?" I told her yes and asked why. She responded, "Your pressure is high." "What?" I almost yelled. "I never had high blood pressure before!" The nurse asked me to sit for a few minutes and then took the pressure again; she softly said, "It's high."

My doctor came in with a concerned look on his face, trying to reassure me that this is very common with older women's pregnancies. *Great,* I thought, *now I'm an old bag having a baby.* He strongly advised me to go home and relax in bed, telling me, "I want you to come in again tomorrow." I almost started to explain that tomorrow was a busy day with the pool installation but thought better of it, afraid that he would send me right to the hospital.

I didn't bother to call Peter, knowing that he was extremely busy working on setting up for a New York sports bar commercial. I plopped on the sofa and, after no more than thirty minutes, had to drive to pick up Jamie at school. Peter came home very late that evening and looked extremely exhausted; I almost didn't tell him but thought better of it. Peter became so anxious that he paced around the kitchen, asking, "How did this happen? You're always in great health." I blamed myself for not eating as healthy with this pregnancy and at times not even going for a walk, being so busy with the home renovation. Peter finally calmed down and with a deep breath told me, "Thank God tomorrow is a night shoot. I'll take Jamie to school and you to the doctor before going to work." I tried to protest, but before a word was released from my lips, Peter put his hand up to stop me, telling me, "Come on, let's get you to bed. You really need to rest more."

We both sat in the examination room the next day with the nurse taking my blood pressure a number of times. It was consistently high. The doctor walked in, looking at the numbers for a few seconds, and began talking to both of us. "This is not uncommon with older women, but I'm concerned you'll go into early labor." "Oh, great, just what I need," I blurted out. The tightness in Peter's jawline revealed his tension, and his unusual quietness spoke volumes of concerns.

The doctor softly spoke, "Filomena, I want you to go home and rest. I'll see you again tomorrow, and we'll make a decision then." I complained to Peter about how much I needed to do and that I was going to go crazy lying around all day long. He just nodded, pulling me by the hand, forcing me to sit on the sofa, handing me the TV remote with a smirk, saying, "Phil, this is the first time I wished for a lazy wife. Just watch TV." As he started to make lunch, I yelled, "Pete, all this TV BS is boring! Do you think I should pack a bag? Remember what happened last time?" Peter helped me pack a bag, picked up Jamie at school, and before leaving for work, warned me not to strain myself, instructing Jamie to help me. I heard him come home in the very early hours of the morning, dropping on the playroom sofa. Later, as I started to prepare Jamie for school, he ordered me up to bed, taking Jamie to school and me to the doctor's again.

This time, the nurse took my pressure once and went to look for the doctor. Both came in, and as the doctor examined me, he looked at Peter, telling him, "Your wife's in labor. Please bring her to the hospital. I'll see you there later." I, looking at Pete, asked, "What about work? Who's going in your place?" Peter, without answering, picked up the phone, called the studio, and told them I was in early labor and he could not go in to work. The response he got from the production company was "Couldn't you have informed us early? Now who are we going to get?" He muttered a few choice words under his breath, ending with "Yeah, like I knew this was going to happen."

Before I knew what hit me, I was in the hospital bed, hooked up to gadgets monitoring all of my vital signs. Peter gently spoke to me as I complained, "I can't believe it, early labor again, and I don't even have my bag." He smiled, stroking my back, telling me, "Don't worry, I'll bring the bag after picking Jamie up at school." He informed me that he had already called my mother. Before Peter left, he cupped my face between his hands, gently speaking, "Phil, I need to leave for a while. I'll be back as soon as I drop your mother and Jamie home. Don't go anywhere." I nodded, asking him to please make sure that Jamie had everything he needed before coming back, reciting a to-do list for him. He whispered, "Phil, you're the best mom and wife in the world. I'll be back soon."

As soon as Peter got back, without me even asking, he told me, "Don't worry, they're both fine. Your mom has him hooked up with more food than he'll ever eat, and he doesn't need to be told what to do." Laughing, he remarked, "He's so disciplined, just like his father was at his age."

Holding my hand, he continued, "Come on, Ms. Abys, let's have a sister for Jamie." That's all he talked about on the ride home. While rubbing my hand, Peter teasingly continued, "Jamie wants to be the boss just like his mother." I had to admit to my husband, "Peter, you always make me feel better when you're near." He softly kissed my hand. The nurse must have heard because she came over, checking the monitor, telling us that when Peter rubbed my hand, my blood pressure dropped.

I was starting to have severe back spasms, squeezing Peter's hand while he clenched his jaw in sympathetic pain.

As the labor progressed, my pressure soared. The only way for me to know that it was soaring was watching Peter's face as he watched the monitor and became increasingly agitated. He, in trying to help, started to forcefully instruct me how to breathe. With his face directly over mine, he almost yelled, "Take deep breaths, Phil. Breathe, breathe!"

After a few hours of listening to his hysterical rant, I got fed up, telling him, "If you don't get the fuck out of my face, I'm going to choke you. Get out. You're making me crazy." I called the nurse over, telling her to keep him out of the room until I was ready to deliver. She kindly said, "Don't worry, we see this all the time. Your husband is just concerned. I'll talk to him."

The doctor came over to inform me that they were going to insert an anti-stroke medication into my IV; the pressure was very high, and this medication would prevent a seizure. I was only able to whisper my concern about the baby's health, telling him, "I've been so careful not to take any medications during my pregnancy." Finally, my water broke, and I knew the baby was ready. I asked the nurse to call Peter into the room; I knew he was pissed off about me asking him to leave and hoped he'd calmed down.

Within minutes of Peter entering the room, the doctor ran in with the nurses. The bottom portion of the bed dropped into a chair-like structure, and I started to uncontrollably push. I turned to look at Peter, who had pulled out a camera and was aiming it right at the birth canal, ready for a photo session. I didn't need to say anything; he just started to explain, "Phil, I know you didn't want photos taken of the birth, but let's face it—this is a girl, and when she turns sixteen and gets frisky like you, just show her the photos. They'll get her back in line." All I could manage to say between pushing and almost laughing was "When I get out of this mess, you're dead meat."

Peter just smiled, nodding his head, continuing with the, "Think twice before screwing around photo album." After Nicole was delivered, I held her for no more than two minutes, kissing her on the forehead and again realizing that she too had my lips and chin. As a mother, of course I thought she was beautiful, but for whatever reason, her eyes were very swollen, and as I went to voice my concern to the nurse, she took Nicole from my arms, telling me that she needed to be examined.

I asked to hold her a few more minutes, but in the distance, I heard voices telling me to rest. I turned to Peter, trying to ask if everything was OK with Nicole, but before I could utter a word, I fell into blackness. I awoke a day later, alone in a private room with my head spinning, not being able to focus on any object without seeing doubles. I searched for the call button, pressing it until a nurse came to my side. The nurse immediately started to explain why I was feeling so dizzy, telling me the medication could take two days before leaving my system.

The tears started to flow as I asked to see Nicole. The nurse very gently told me, "You're not ready to get out of bed. Maybe in a few days." Through tears, I demanded that she bring Nicole to me. She kindly spoke to me while stroking my arm, "Listen, sweetie, you're not ready for that. Just rest for now. I'll call your husband and tell him you're awake." She was back at my side with a photo of Nicole, informing me that Peter was on his way. I held the photo crying, falling in and out of sleep until I heard Peter's voice and felt his hand on my cheeks. Before I could ask, he started to reassure me that Nicole was fine, that the doctors were keeping a close eye on the both of us due to the medication. "I'm going to pick up Jamie at school, and we'll come over. He can't wait to see Nicole."

James was overjoyed, running to my bedside, showing off his big brother button the nurses had pinned on him, telling me, "Mommy, Mommy, I saw my baby sister. She's so small like this," motioning with his hands to show me her size. All I could do was smile and say, "That's great," feeling so sad about not being able to hug him and walk to the nursery as a family.

Within the next two days, I was back on my feet, visiting the nursery a number of times during the day. I was amazed at how much Nicole looked like Jamie, except she had floppy earlobes like her father; I started to fidget with them, laughing to myself.

I was released from the hospital before Nicole as she had been born a month early, and with the increased danger of the medication, the doctors decided to keep her a few extra days. I had asked Peter to decorate the front of the house the same way he had for James's arrival as I was determined to treat both the same way.

The day we picked up Nicole from the hospital was the happiest I had ever seen Jamie; he smiled, oohing and aahing at everything we did. While I dressed Nicole, he gently held her little finger and was in complete awe.

FILOMENA ABYS-SMITH

I asked him, "Jamie, you seem very happy to be a big brother." His loving eyes looking straight at me, "Yes, Mommy, I've been waiting a long time." I looked up at Peter; we smiled at each other without saying a word but in complete understanding that this was another god-sent blessing.

Big Brother Turkey Patties

Out of all the meals I've prepared for Peter, this is his least favorite. I developed this recipe in trying to keep my family on a healthy diet, but of course, every time I prepare turkey patties, my husband starts teasing me with comments like "Jesus, Phil, healthy food again? Don't you know you need to eat a pound of dirt before you die? I'd rather die happy than healthy." I pay him no attention; the kids enjoy them, and Peter, while rolling his eyes, piles on hot peppers and, while suffering, still manages to eat a large-size patty.

Ingredients:

1 lb. of chopped turkey
4 cloves of finely diced garlic
½ cup of finely chopped parsley
¼ cup of sesame seeds
1 egg (beaten with about 2 tbs. of Parmesan cheese)
4 tbs. of grated Parmesan cheese
¾ cup of unflavored breadcrumbs
Salt and black pepper to taste
Vegetable oil for shallow frying

Place chopped turkey in a large bowl; add garlic, parsley, sesame seeds, an egg, Parmesan cheese, salt, pepper, and about four tablespoons of breadcrumbs. Mix well by hand until all ingredients are well blended. In a separate plate, place remaining breadcrumbs, add a few more tablespoons of Parmesan cheese, sprinkle in more sesame seeds, and mix well. Dip hands into breadcrumbs, and start forming patties as small or as large as you prefer. Dredge each patty into the breadcrumbs, and set aside on a platter. When all patties are prepared, heat oil over a medium flame in a large skillet. Place patties in hot oil, allowing a crust to form on the bottom; flip over, allowing a crust to form on that side. Lower flame and cover the skillet, allowing the patties to completely cook through.

Serve on toasted whole wheat buns. I usually serve this meal with an apple-carrot salad, which even my husband enjoys.

Die Happy Salad

Ingredients

2 large apples, washed and sliced thin (I prefer Honeycrisp or Fuji apples, but you can use whatever you like.)

2 medium-size carrots (washed and cleaned, shredded with a vegetable peeler)

¼ cup of cranberries

¼ cup of golden raisins

Fresh juice of 1 lime or lemon

4 tbs. or more of crumbled goat cheese

Olive oil for dressing

Optional: chopped walnuts, almonds, or pine nuts

Place apples into a bowl, add lime juice, toss well; add shredded carrots on top of apples, toss well. Add cranberries and raisins, drizzle olive oil on top, toss well. Add the goat cheese; mix well into the salad, making a creamy dressing; top off with nuts; and enjoy being healthy.

"I Didn't Boil the S—out of It" Porket with Mixed Beans and Vegetable Soup

Peter calls this porket an Irish football because he recalls that it was prepared, as he phrases it, by "boiling the shit out of it." I have reshaped this meal for him in the following manner, and he flatters me by saying, "It takes an Italian to cook a mean Irish football."

Ingredients:

1 porket

1 bag of dried mixed beans, rinsed well

1 medium onion, finely diced

4 cloves of garlic, crushed

2 medium-size potatoes (washed, peeled, and diced into bite-size portions)

2 carrots (washed, peeled, and diced into bite-size portions)
2 stalks of celery, washed and cut into bite-size portions
4 tbs. of vegetable oil
5 cups of boiling water (must be enough to cover top of porket)
Salt and black pepper to taste
Optional: if you prefer a spicier soup, add a diced hot pepper to the onion and garlic while sautéing, or you may use red pepper flakes.

Place oil in a large stockpot over a medium flame; when oil is hot, add the porket, brown on all sides. Add onion and garlic around the porket, making sure they hit the hot oil; after they have a bit of color, add the remaining vegetables, tossing well in the oil, and sauté for a few minutes. At this point, you may add a bit of salt and pepper to the vegetables, but be careful with the salt as the porket is already salty. Add the mixed beans, tossing well with all the vegetables, and immediately add about five cups of boiling water, enough to cover the porket.

Add salt and black pepper to taste. Cook covered over a medium-low flame for about two hours or until beans are tender and a tasty soup is made. If you like, you may add cooked rice to each individual bowl and pour soup on top of the rice. The porket may be served sliced on a platter or shredded and served in the soup.

Chapter 19

Living Life

Life moved very quickly after Nicole's birth; we were all living our lives to the fullest. Peter and I indulged both our children with love and understanding but didn't hesitate at good old-fashioned discipline. We tried to instill in them a great love for learning and were fortunate that both were able to read by the age of four. The love of home cooking was passed on to the children, and if they merely mentioned a food item, we complied. During the warm months, Peter grilled and fried on our deck, sending plumes of savory aromas throughout the neighborhood. Our home became a hangout for friends wanting to have a tasty meal.

Jamie's friends were forever knocking or calling from the adjoining yard, asking if they could come over for dinner. Even if I was cooking indoors, the aroma of stews and sauces yanked them by the nose, drawing them to our deck or kitchen. I knew Jamie understood the importance of a proper meal when he, at five years old, came home after visiting a friend who offered him a hot dog with no bun and a small paper cup of Coke. He came directly to me with a disgusted face, complaining, "Mommy, you know what they gave me for lunch? A hot dog with no bun, not even a vegetable or fruit, and soda in a paper cup. What kind of lunch is that?" Peter, laughing, picked him up, telling him, "Son, now you're starting to understand how lucky you are."

When Jamie didn't enjoy the flavor of chicken marsala, stating, "Mommy, I don't like the taste of this marsala stuff," the next day, I prepared the same dish using lemon juice, joyfully watching him eat the chicken and dunking slices of bread into the lemon sauce. Peter, Jamie, and Nicole enjoyed spicy chili and potato pie (*gatto*), but when I layered the chili in between layers of potato pie, adding sharp shredded cheddar cheese and baking it until the cheese melted, they smiled, informing me, "Yep, this is a *winner*." I realized that my cooking was becoming as American as my husband and children were—a fusion of the many cultures I had been exposed to.

One of Peter's diet's staples was peanut butter and jelly, and when he first moved in to my apartment, I was amazed at how much peanut butter he ate. Pizza was second to peanut butter, and I have never seen anyone enjoy pizza as much as my Irish American husband. I find him making peanut butter and jelly sandwiches for breakfast, lunch, snacks, and if I wasn't around, at times even for dinner. When I would ask him what he had for lunch at work, the recurring answer was always pizza.

I commented on a number of occasions, "Pete, PB and J again? Don't you get tired of eating that stuff?" "Nope. Growing up, it was the fastest and safest food to eat outside of a can of soup." My heart would break hearing him tell stories of how he envied his Italian friends because they always have freshly prepared meals. I could not help myself and, although I was exhausted from work, forced myself to prepare freshly made soups, stew, and sauces for him.

When Jamie and Nicole started enjoying peanut butter and jelly sandwiches as much as their father, I added variety to this most American food by making them grilled peanut butter and Nutella sandwiches on whole wheat bread. I grilled the sandwich until golden and crispy, slicing it in half, adding a dusting of confectioners' sugar.

Peter was amazed that I did not consume an eighth of the pizza that he ate. "Phil, I can't believe it. You're Italian from the other side and hardly ever eat pizza." Laughing, I responded, "I think Americans eat more pizza than Italians. We Neapolitans invented pizza to keep Americans happy." I continued to explain that until I was in my teens, I had never had a store-bought pizza, and when I first tasted one, I was disgusted by the oil mess running off of the soggy slice.

My favorite pizza is fried *pizzelles*, which my mom made for us as a snack. Peter looked at me in disbelief. "Fried pizza? I've never heard of that." The discussion on pizza continued with me telling him, "I also like a type of deep-dish pizza my mom prepared with sautéed escarole spiced with Gaeta olives, pine nuts, and capers." If my husband ever thought of leaving me, I think his love of pizza and Italian food kept him close to home. Of course, being willing and able to heat up the bedroom doesn't hurt.

It was during this whirlwind of cooking, loving, and raising a family that those outer forces took hold of my life again, giving it a new direction. They appeared out of the smelly sewer water that had backed up into our basement from the main drain on our block. We both cursed as we slouched around our basement, mopping and opening storage boxes to examine what had been damaged.

I was opening a box that had been closed for over twenty-five years, realizing that it held long-forgotten items of my childhood and former marriage. My cap and gown from my high school graduation had been soiled with sewer water, and I removed the tassel, placing it on the washer, and decided that the rest was not salvageable, tossing them in the garbage. I tossed out a number of wet high school and college books, along with term papers I had written. At the very bottom, I saw a large grey envelope that should have been wet and soggy from the sewer water, but it sat perfectly dry, waiting for me to reach out and connect with this long-lost friend.

I stared for a few minutes in disbelief as the grey envelope beckoned me to bring it back to life. I had not thought of what lay inside for years. In my frenzy to reshape my life, I had forgotten how I had started to write about my family's past. How, as a very young girl, I would sit watching my mother cook and write recipes on white index cards, hoping they would guide me later as a mother.

After my father's murder, I again started to write recipes and short family memories in hopes that my writing would always keep our spirits alive. I reached into the box, feeling the familiar envelope in my hand, and I spoke to myself, unaware I was speaking out loud. "I can't believe this. I had forgotten all about this journal." Peter walked over to me, looking down at the envelope. "What's that, Phil?" I realized he actually knew so little of me; we had been so busy raising a family that I never really told him much of my past.

I started to explain, "It's a journal I was writing years ago with family recipes and short memories of holidays and how we celebrated them. I called it a cookbook journal. I tossed it in this box when I left my home in Long Island and never looked at it again." Peter, with a serious expression so unlike himself, looked down at the envelope and then straight at me, "Well, I think it's time you start to write again. After all, now you have children. I'm sure they will eventually like to read your journal." I was surprised at his seriousness, telling him, "You know, I think you're right." I ran up the stairs and placed it on the computer desk in the playroom.

Days later, as I sat watching my three-year-old daughter napping on the playroom sofa, her angelic face glazed with sunshine from the afternoon sun, questions were asked within me. "What will she know of you?" "How much of your life will she understand?" Were those questions being asked by those outer forces or by my own consciousness? I was not sure; but I was completely certain that those outer forces were in control again, guiding my hand as I started to write.

Filomena and Lady Liberty

There was once a little Italian girl who sailed on a great big ship away from her native home of Bagnoli, a town in Naples, Italy, you see.

For seven days and six nights on stormy seas, she sailed with her family.

She knew she would soon see her *babbo*, who was her dad, and they would again be a happy family.

The day they finally arrived, the first thing she saw was Lady Liberty standing so proud and tall. She, this Lady Liberty, would now be home to me.

This little Italian girl—Filomena, she was called—wanted to see if America was still the land of opportunity.

Filomena was amazed to see that, sadly, the streets of Lady Liberty were not filled with gold and harmony, but with noise, confusion, and poverty; this made her so sad, you see.

She lived in a place not by the sea like her native Bagnoli, but in a very burnt-out place called the South Bronx by Lady Liberty.

Filomena started to dream of flying away from the streets of the South Bronx to see if Lady Liberty could still be the land of beauty and opportunity.

She would dream almost every night of flying high and far to a beautiful land filled with harmony.

This dreamland was filled with tall, tall trees and, *oh*, such warm blue skies away from the noise and poverty. She flew so high and far until the winds of destiny changed her course and forced her back to the streets of the South Bronx, you see.

In her dream, she was filled with such despair a sense of hopelessness was always there. She awakened every day from her flying dream to say, "I'm here again. Have you forgotten me, Lady Liberty? Are you still the land of opportunity?"

But every day, she professed, "I will do my very best." She tried so hard at school and play; she worked so hard at every task.

Day by day, month by month, year to year, she surely flew away from the streets of poverty. She, this little Italian girl from Bagnoli, has finally reached this land of opportunity.

Through her hard work and steady course, she turned the winds of destiny. Filomena is now filled with great pride that she lives in a fine house with tall, tall trees; bright blue skies; and best of all, a loving family.

Filomena, this little girl from Bagnoli, loves this land of Lady Liberty. Now, in her dreams, she hopes and prays for all the children filled with despair that they too will fly a steady course into the arms of Lady Liberty, for surely, this is still the land of opportunity.

All-American Chili *Gatto*

Prepare the potatoes for the *gatto* according to the recipe in chapter 12, "Our Son." Layer the casserole dish with only half of the potatoes; add the chili con carne on top of the potatoes, adding shredded sharp cheddar cheese on top of the chili; layer the remaining potatoes on top of that; and sprinkle breadcrumbs and grated Parmesan cheese on top of the potatoes. Bake at 375°F until cheese is melted and bubbly. You may use whatever chili recipe you prefer, but this is the recipe I have used for years with good results. You can prepare the chili a day ahead and reheat before adding to the *gatto*.

Ingredients:

4 tbs. of vegetable oil
2 lb. of lean ground beef
1 finely diced onion
4 cloves of finely diced garlic
1 finely diced jalapeno pepper or any hot pepper you prefer (even red pepper flakes will do)
6 oz. of tomato paste
15 oz. of canned red kidney beans (drained, not rinsed, or as my Mom would say, "What does it take to cook a bag of beans?" I leave that up to the reader's discretion)
Chili powder and salt to taste

Add oil to a large skillet; heat over a medium flame; add onion, garlic, and pepper; sauté for a minute or until garlic has a bit of color. Add ground beef, mix well; spice with salt and chili powder, mix well; cook until all meat is brown. At this point, you may add additional spices, such as Sazón Latin spices. Using two wooden spoons, chop meat into a fine mixture. Add tomato paste, mixing well into the meat, making sure meat is well coated with paste. Add the beans, mix well, and cook on a medium-low flame for about fifteen minutes. This chili can also be served over cooked rice, and if you like a soupier chili, do not drain the beans. But if using this chili to layer a *gatto*, drain the beans. Of course, you can also use this chili on top of nachos sprinkled with cheese and baked for a snack or in taco shells.

Filomenas' Favorite Pizza

Fried *Pizzelles* (*Pizzelles Fritta a la Napoletana*)

You may prepare you own pizza dough or purchase some from the supermarket to prepare this recipe. Allow the dough to rise at room temperature while preparing the sauce.

Ingredients: for the Sauce

4 tbs. of olive oil
6 cloves of crushed garlic
48 oz. of crushed San Marzano tomatoes
Optional: ½ tsp. of dried oregano or shredded basil

Add oil to a large skillet, heat over a medium flame, add garlic, and cook until golden. Add tomatoes, and cook for about twenty minutes; if you like, add oregano or basil.

On a floured work surface, roll out dough. You may cut disk shapes with a large cookie cutter or as my mom did; she would pull off a piece of the dough, flatten it by hand into a small pizza shape, and drop it into hot vegetable oil. Fry each *pizzelle* until fluffy and golden, and set aside to drain on paper towels. On top of each fried *pizzelle*, add a large spoonful of hot sauce then sprinkle a generous amount of grated Parmesan cheese on top. For me, this is real Napoletana pizza; it truly reminds me of my childhood.

Escarole Stuffed Pizza

You'll need to prepare or purchase enough pizza dough for two pizzas. Allow dough to rise at room temperature while preparing the escarole.

Ingredients for the Stuffing

2 heads of escarole, well washed (put escarole through a salad spinner to remove excess water) and cut into small pieces (remove and discard the back stalk)
4 tbs. of oil
5 cloves of garlic, crushed
¼ cup of salted capers
¼ cup of Gaeta olives
¼ cup of pine nuts

Place oil in a large skillet; heat over a medium flame; add the garlic, capers, olives, and pine nuts; cook for two minutes or until garlic has a bit of color. Add chopped escarole, toss well, and cook uncovered until tender or for about fifteen minutes. On a floured work surface, roll out pizza dough; place one in a deep-dish pizza pan that has been slightly oiled and sprinkled with a bit of cornmeal. Evenly place escarole in the pan, sprinkling Parmesan cheese on top; place second pizza dough on top, and seal the edges with your fingers. With a knife or scissors, cut slits in the middle on top of the dough to allow steam to escape while baking. Place in a hot 400°F oven to bake until the dough turns into a pizza crust. You may also sprinkle shredded mozzarella cheese on top of the escarole before placing the second layer of dough. This type of pizza is cut like a sandwich wedge and is great for picnics or for bagged lunches; it holds up very well and tastes great at room temperature.

"Mom, It's a Winner" Grilled Peanut Butter and Nutella Sandwiches

Spread peanut butter on one slice of whole wheat bread, spread Nutella on another slice, and put together as a sandwich. On a hot buttered grill, toast sandwich on both sides until golden and crispy. Sprinkle sandwich with confectioners' sugar, cut in half, and enjoy.

Chapter 20

Time to Move On

Peter and I put an enormous amount of hard work renovating our home, and we lived life with great passion; but this was only secondary to focusing on raising our two children into educated, productive citizens.

James, from a very young age, devoured books, reading on historical and current events just for pleasure. Nicole, although seven years younger than James, could easily speak her mind with an extreme practical outlook on issues, all of which I encouraged and delighted in.

I made a point of sitting down to dinner as a family almost on a daily basis and did not allow the current fashion of overburdening my children with too many activities or social events. One sport or activity per child was more than enough, allowing for family time and what I refer to as simply "take-a-deep-breath time."

With our children, we traveled not only to fun sites like Disney but also to historic places such as Colonial Williamsburg and Gettysburg, Pennsylvania; But the most profound trip for me was visiting Lady Liberty with my family. I stood in front of this most American symbol, staring at her in complete awe and admiration. I was transfixed, deep in thought, when I heard my son's voice ask me the most relevant question of my life—"Mommy, are you happy you came to this country?" In surreal slow motion, I looked down at him, up at my husband, who was holding Nicole, and back at Lady Liberty.

With overflowing happiness, I realized I had come full circle; I had journeyed like all immigrants, through struggle, confusion, and reshaping of identity into becoming a proud citizen of this great nation. I looked down at my very American son, suddenly feeling very euphoric. "Yes, I'm very, very happy. This is my home, and I love you, Nicole, and Daddy more than my life."

At that time, we were living very comfortable lives in our totally renovated home when, unfortunately, new neighbors moved next door with drastically different views of the American Dream. Whereas we cherished peace and quiet for reading, studying, and meditation, our neighbors enjoyed loud music, belonged to a motorcycle club which brought dozens of roaring motorcycles to the front and sides of our home, where they had set up a repair shop, and our street became a parking lot for cars that constantly had their plates changed.

I could write a short novel on the drastic change to our once-quiet neighborhood, but it will suffice to say that Peter was afraid that I would one day, to use an inner-city term, go ghetto crazy, and I worried that he would one day lose his mellow personality, getting into a street brawl with one of the "motorcycle club members."

We both knew it was time to move on; yes, we hated the thought of leaving a home we had put so much sweat and love into but realized that it was just made of bricks and cement. A house becomes a home by the efforts of the people that love and live in it; I knew I needed only to have my family with me to transform any house into our home.

We placed the house we had lived in for eighteen years on the market, luckily selling it in less than a month. Peter and I were concerned but happy to be able to take this great leap of change at such a pivotal time in our lives. James graduated from Iona Prep and was heading off to George Washington University in DC only two days after we moved in to our new home; Nicole was ready to enter middle school, and we looked at each other, asking, "Where did the time go?"

It was in the frenzy of packing eighteen years of our lives as I placed dozens of beloved books into boxes that I reached the top shelf of a book case, removing the carved wooden box where I had kept coin mementos of my travels that I told myself, "You have too much stuff. It takes up too much space. Get rid of it."

I opened the wooden box, knowing that I was not going to toss it out, but wanted to lighten the load of what I was carrying. The Christmas note Mike had written so many years ago sat on top of all the coins with the same paper clip holding it closed. I removed the clip, reading the note that I could recite by heart for the last time, telling myself, "What do you need this for? It takes up too much space." I tossed the paper clip in the trash and then ripped the note into tiny pieces, tossing them in the trash. I tossed out all the phone books, postcards, and letters from my life in Long Island, continuing to tell myself that they took up too much space.

In looking back, they weighed no more than a few ounces; I could have carried them in a small shopping bag. In the recesses of my being, I knew I was trying to erase the memory of a tragic end to a beautiful love. The Christmas note is now gone, but the bittersweet memory of that first love still lingers in my heart; it lingers and engulfs who I am, just like all those other scattered memories that will forever be part of me.

Forever in My Heart Recipes

My Irish American husband, Peter, loves potato salad just about as much as pizza but not quite as much as peanut butter or bacon.

Forever in Love Potato Salad

Ingredients:

3 lb. of cooked potatoes cut into chunks (I suggest using Yukon Gold potatoes and cooking them in their skins, peeling them after cooking; I find when cooking a potato after peeling, they don't hold as much flavor, becoming watery, and lose a good portion of their nutrients.)
½ lb. of crispy cooked bacon, crumbled by hand into bite-size portions
6 hard-cooked eggs, sliced into portions that will hold up while tossing the salad
1 small red onion, finely sliced
5 slices of dill pickles, finely diced
1 cup of mayo
Salt and black pepper to taste
White vinegar to taste
Optional: I dislike mentioning this, but at times I have coated the potatoes with a bit of the fat dripping from the bacon; use at your own discretion.

If you like mustard, whip a few teaspoons into the mayo before adding to the potatoes.
Place the cooked potato chunks into a large bowl; add a bit (I mean a bit) of the bacon drippings, and toss well. Add half of the mayo, tossing well. Add the onion, pickles, and eggs; gently toss. Sprinkle with salt and pepper, add the rest of the mayo, drizzle vinegar on top, and gently toss.

Sprinkle in the bacon bits, toss all ingredients together, and tell your husband if he develops a heart condition not to blame you. My husband really enjoys this potato salad with a grilled rib eye steak; I feel guilty every time I prepare this meal.

"You're So Mediterranean" Potato Salad

This is Peter's second favorite type of potato salad and the one my mother made for us; it's this heart-healthy type that I usually prepare. When I'm serving this salad, Peter pats me on the butt, telling me, "Jesus, Phil, you're still so Mediterranean."

Ingredients:

3 lb. of cooked potatoes cut into chunks
1 medium-size red onion, thinly sliced
An assortment of pitted olives (whatever type you prefer, but not the jarred green olives with the pimentos in them)
A handful of salted capers
½ cup of olive oil
½ cup of white vinegar
Salt and black pepper to taste
Optional: thinly sliced roasted red peppers, steamed cut green beans, or if you prefer a spicy salad, thinly sliced jarred hot banana peppers (a combination of all three can be used)

Place cooked potatoes in a large bowl, sprinkle a bit of salt, add half the oil and vinegar, and toss well. Add the remaining ingredients; pour in the remaining oil and vinegar, tossing well. Serve at room temperature.

My Lil Boy's Favorite Lemon Chicken

1½ stick of butter or butter substitute
2½ lb. of chicken cutlets
Juice of 2 freshly squeezed lemons
¼ to ½ cup of hot chicken stock
Flour for dredging
Salt and black pepper to taste

Salt and pepper the chicken cutlets on both sides. Melt one stick of butter in a large skillet over a medium-low flame. Dredge the chicken into flour, shaking off the excess, and brown both sides in the melted butter. Remove from the skillet, and set aside on the platter.

Add the lemon juice to the hot butter, stirring and incorporating all the browning bits into the sauce. Add the hot chicken stock into the lemon butter, stirring well to mix all ingredients into a sauce. Add the remaining butter to the sauce, letting it melt slowly into the sauce. Place chicken back into the skillet, turning over once to coat each side well with sauce; cover and cook over a low flame for about ten to fifteen minutes or until chicken is cooked thoroughly. This makes a great meal served with mashed potatoes or cooked rice. Of course, have plenty of crusty Italian bread on hand for dunking. Lime juice also works well in this recipe.

Nicole's I Love Pasta with Pesto

I have failed to mention that I mostly use whole wheat pasta in my cooking; there has always been a strong debate between myself and my mother about which tastes better. My husband and children enjoy whole wheat pasta, breads, and crackers, and that is all I use. During the summertime months and especially in the fall when I need to use up all the basil from my garden before the first frost, I prepare large batches of this pesto and freeze it in plastic containers for later use. This is my daughter's favorite, and she enjoys picking the basil leaves apart while watching me prepare this sauce. Please understand that I don't have exact amounts for this recipe as I eyeball all the ingredients.

Ingredients:

1½ cup of olive oil
At least 4 cloves of garlic
Plenty of fresh basil leaves, at least 4 cups (please don't use the stems)
A good portion of fresh Italian parsley leaves, at least 1 cup (do not use stems)
At least ½ cup of pine nuts (you may also use walnut or almonds)
A generous amount of grated Parmesan cheese, about ½ cup
Salt to taste

In a blender or food processor, add half the oil, the garlic, half the basil, half the parsley, and half the nuts. Blend together until a sauce is formed. Add the remaining oil, basil, parsley, and nuts; blend again, making sure all ingredients form a smooth sauce. Place into a bowl, add cheese, mix well, taste, and add salt if needed. Toss half of this sauce into your favorite cooked pasta (it's best to use spaghetti or linguine). If you think it needs more sauce, add as much as you like, tossing well and sprinkling more grated Parmesan cheese on top of the pasta.

I have changed this recipe often to incorporate vegetables from my garden, using small zucchinis, adding one or two, and puréeing them with the other ingredients. Cherry or grape tomatoes also work well with this recipe, and all you need to do is place them in the blender with the other ingredients.

Serve over cooked spaghetti. My daughter, Nicole, loves this meal, commenting, "Mommy, it tastes really, really fresh." She even scoops a spoonful of the sauce onto crusty Italian bread for a snack, which makes me very happy she's eating healthy.

You can use this sauce to dress a turkey patty, a fried chicken cutlet, or even a breaded baked pork chop. Use your imagination; the possibilities are many.

Filomena's Favorite Pasta Dish

Although I was raised on pasta with red sauce, I can't say it's my favorite meal. I only prepare it often because my very diplomatic Irish American husband needs his red sauce fix and threatens to report me to my mother if I don't comply. My favorite pasta meal is the following:

Ingredients:

5 large portabella mushrooms, cleaned and cut into bite-size portions
4 to 6 slices of diced bacon or pancetta
4 cloves of crushed garlic
6 tbs. of vegetable oil
Red pepper flakes to taste
Salt to taste
Olive oil for drizzling over the cooked pasta
16 oz. of cooked whole wheat spaghetti

Place vegetable oil in a large skillet over a medium flame; when oil is hot, add bacon, cooking until almost crispy. Add red pepper flakes and garlic, toss well, and cook for a minute. Add mushrooms, mix well into the bacon; cook uncovered until mushrooms are tender and a bit crispy.

Add the cooked spaghetti to the skillet, tossing well with the bacon and mushrooms; if you like, you may add a bit of the pasta water, tossing well. Serve pasta with spoonfuls of the bacon and mushrooms on top; drizzle with a bit of olive oil and grated Parmesan cheese.

Finally an American

Peter was driving us home from Manhattan, where we had been working on a home-remodeling project for a very wealthy client. As we passed the Third Avenue Bridge on our way to the New York State Thruway, Peter turned to me, asking, "Phil, do you remember this place?" Smiling at him, I said, "I remember it very well." "Come on, Phil, let's take a look at where you started." He quickly turned the car before I could utter a word of protest.

He drove to the Mott Haven projects, parked the car near a fried chicken fast-food takeout place, casually stepped out of the car, walked over to the passenger side, and waited for me to get out. I hesitated, not wanting to leave the safety of the car. He opened the door and, almost laughing, said, "Come on, show me the building you lived in." "Pete, this is silly. I don't think it's a good idea for us to roam around here."

Peter leaned into the car, offering his hand in help. I stared at him for a second and then took his hand. He must have felt my nervousness and tried to put me at ease by saying, "Phil, you're with me. I'm not going to let anything happen to you." I thought, *Everyone thinks they're so tough until their ass is being pounded by someone tougher.* He held my hand as we crossed the street and walked toward the building I had lived in for twelve years. "Pete, this is it." I stood looking up at the second-floor kitchen window, wondering what had happened to the innocent young girl that had spent so much time staring out, wanting to fly away. She didn't exist anymore.

I pointed to the kitchen and living room windows for Peter. He asked me, "Phil, how did that bastard get in?"

"He climbed through the open living room window. He must have stepped on the bricks jutting out on the front of the building and pulled himself onto the ledge and into the window. But it's different now. The bricks are gone." The bricks under the kitchen and living room windows had been paved over to a smooth surface.

Peter looked around and found behind us a portion of the building with the same red bricks I recalled. Pointing to the brickwork, he asked, "Phil, was it like this?" "Yes, just like that. Maybe the bricks were removed from under the windows so that no one could climb them. The next morning, after the attack, I looked out of the window and saw muddy footprints on the ledge of our window." I thought to myself, *What a crappy job the police did on our case. They never took fingerprints or footprints.* I guess, for the police, it was just another case, part of the daily routine.

We walked around the bend of the building, and I pointed to my bedroom window, my brother's window, and my parents' window, telling Pete, "We were the first family to move in to this building when it opened. It was really very nice, everything brand new. The whole area was fairly safe and clean for a time. Then I guess the drug dealers found an open market, and everything changed."

I noticed a black man watching us, probably wondering what these outsiders were doing here. He walked past us too close and stared too often; I became very uncomfortable. Peter noticed, "Phil, don't worry, that poor bastard is so strung out on drugs that if you spit on him, he'll fall over."

The whole place was eerily quiet, and as I turned, looking toward the park that once held so much life, I recalled the pounding sounds of basketballs, the sound of music, and the never-ending blaring of fire engines. Why was it so quiet now?

I turned and walked under the vestibule toward the side hall stairs, with my husband right behind me. "Pete, those are the stairs I ran up to our apartment. First, I'd stand under the kitchen window, calling up to my mother, and then after checking no one was hanging out in the stairs, I'd run up to my mother, who had opened the upstairs door that lead to our apartment." I noticed a steel plate now firmly held that door closed. Peter, with a sad expression, just nodded and listened.

I stood there for no more than a few minutes, and the only recollection that flooded my mind was that of fear. I heard the echoes of my own screams as drug addicts came down those stairs, taunting me with a needle, the forever lingering smell of stale urine, and the crazed look in the rapist's eyes as he pulled me up those same stairs. Those memories made me feel vulnerable, even with my husband standing right next to me. "Come on, let's get out of here. I've had enough of this place."

Peter held my hand as we walked back to the car, asking me, "Which way did you walk to school?" I pointed. "This way." I think he was more curious than I was and started driving in that direction. The car ride was less than five minutes, and I was surprised at how quiet the neighborhood was, not at all the noisy place I remembered. He parked the car across from the Catholic school I had attended for eight years. Near the brownstones that had been there forever. We both got out, and he stood with one elbow on the car, listening to the flood of memories that spontaneously poured out of me.

"Pete, you see on the corner where that new school building stands? That's where the bad building stood. It was so full of drug addicts and dealers that the nuns didn't allow us to pass by it. We had to walk across the street and avoid the sights, but we could still see addicts staggering out and deals being made. Well, at least the smell of burning wood is gone, and I haven't heard a fire engine yet." Peter snickered. "Phil, in the sixties, when you got here, the South Bronx was like a war zone, not the best place to start a new life." "Yeah, you're telling me."

I walked away from him toward the front of the school doors that I had entered through so many times. The school that had once held so much life was now dark and lonely. A Hispanic man came out of the brownstone behind me and watched me staring at the school. I spoke to him, telling him that I had gone to this school. He stared at me almost in disbelief, and I continued to tell him that it was a long time ago. He nodded, telling me that the school had closed a few years ago, local children now attended the charter school, and parents didn't need to pay tuition. I thought, *At least now that corner of the block is put to good use.* I said good-bye as the man walked away.

I stood in front of those doors, asking myself, *Why did I still feel so connected to this place? What had I carried away inside myself that made me understand the soul of this neighborhood?* I stood motionless for a few minutes, and then I felt it more than understood it—the vibration of the struggle, not only my struggle, but that of countless others that had gone through this place. The vibration of the struggle to reach the prize of America, the struggle that made the prize so much sweeter.

I turned to walk back to my husband, smiling. Peter asked, "Brings back memories?" "Yes, it does. Many memories." We got in the car and drove around the corner to the church; it looked like a derelict building more than a church. The sight broke my heart. I asked Peter to drive away; the memories invoked feelings of sadness and happiness all at once. "Pete, let's go. I want to go home."

Jokingly, he asked, "Ms. Abys, shall I drop you off at the projects?" I turned to him, staring into his deep blue Irish eyes; we smiled at each other in complete understanding. "No, Mr. Smith, I don't think so." "OK, my little immigrant wife, then I'll just take you home with me." I pushed back the seat and closed my eyes, feeling so fortunate to finally be an American.

> To my readers, may you always have a passion
> for good food and great sex.
> May you always have passion to live your life to the fullest.
>
> May you always live life with a deep determination
> to reach the American Dream.
> With a strong resolve to uphold the principles of this great nation I'm
> so proud to call my home—life, liberty, and the pursuit of happiness.

On September 8, 2012, as I tried to write the final thoughts to this memoir, I became frustrated, slamming the laptop closed, and turned on the desktop to entertain myself with Facebook. I recently joined this worldwide phenomenon and really did not know what I was doing, just clicking different posts sent to me by a variety of members. My cousins in Naples had sent me a slew of comments in Italian that I could hardly read, and I just scrolled past them.

As the reader of this memoir, you may have become disillusioned with the concept of those outer forces that control our lives, possibly thinking that "she's just plain nuts." During the many years of writing, I have often called myself, "a head case," until, for no apparent reason, I clicked on the translation link to this quote, which was among dozens in Italian on my Facebook page, and it reaffirmed that indeed outer forces beyond oneself control our lives. The quote reads as follows:

"Each of us is the sum of all the moments we lived with all the people we met; and these moments become our story."

Single chick having fun on Vacation in Italy

Pete as young buck starting in the advertisement film business

Peter as a young stud in a Miller beer commercial

Pete filming Nagano Winter Olympic games 1998

Love is better the second time around

Love is stronger the second time around

Wedding Day with Mom

Taking our vows

First kiss after our vows

Wedding day celebration kiss

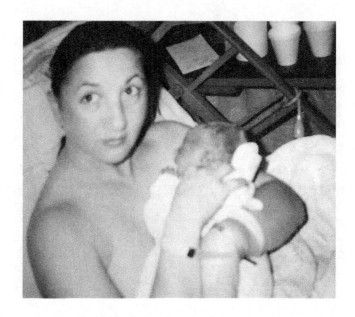

Jamie and mom, wow that was easy

Newly arrived Jamie with his very exhausted Dad

James' Baptismal Party

Mom and Dad holding their pride and Joy on Christening Day

James on his Christening Day being held by his aunt Paola,
with long time friends Nanette and her sister Jackie

New mom enjoying the sunshine

New Dad snoozing with his little boy Jamie

Zia Titina holding Jamie

Jamie my earthy angel

Jamie's Halloween Fun

Jamie our little slugger

Me and my little boy ready for nursery school graduation

Peter at Jamies' nursery school graduation

Nicole - Our tiny angel

A late in life blessing

A Christmas Blessing

Nicole's second birthday on Easter Sunday

Nicole ready for Pre K

Nicole Halloween Fun

Nicoles' kindergarten graduation—what an angel

Nicole ready for third grade

James and Nicole helping mom in the kitchen

Nonna Fortuna with grandchildren,
Christian, James, Nicole and Alex

My mom Fortuna with my Puerto Rican Mom Liz -two hot babes

Two very American Chicks

My two Neapolitan—American Angels

Family Fun in Rome

Back in Italy with James

My 55th Birthday Cake enjoyed in Bagnoli on a terrace top celebration

My 55th Birthday Celebration in Bagnoli

2010 in Bagnoli having family fun

Back in Bagnoli with Zia Anna—Do we look alike

In Bagnoli with Zia Pina

Back on the Beach in Bagnoli with my cousin
Monica- my 55th Birthday Celebration

My little boy James working as an intern
at Marlowe & Company in Washington DC

Nicole my teenage Angel

Filomena, Older, Wiser and so thankful to be living a life full of passion

My Father's Family Tree

Ugo Abys

This is the website where you can find our family history dating back to the sixteenth century; the site was started by my cousin Luca Abys of Naples, Italy, and I'm forever grateful for his hard work and love of family. I know my father would be so proud of this site that connects Abyses living in different continents.

http://www.myheritage.it/site-family-tree-54585091/abys-family-site

Il mio nome è Luca Abys e sono l'amministratore di questo sito.

Questa è l'origine della mia famiglia,

Abys

Famiglia menzionata per la prima volta a Coira nella persona di Johann, originario di Piuro (Valtellina), che acquisì la cittadinanza nel 1609. Incerti sono i rapporti con gli Abys che nel tardo Medioevo risiedevano nei Grigioni centrali. Proprietari di estesi beni fondiari, i membri della famiglia erano attivi come spedizionieri e commercianti. Per tradizione gli Abys erano inoltre militari al servizio di potenze straniere e della città di Coira (capitani). La famiglia ebbe in Andreas (XVII sec.) e Johann (1614-1697) due fra i primi medici grigionesi. Ad eccezione di Raget, i suoi rappresentanti nel Consiglio grigione furono sempre di secondo piano.

Fonte: Churer Stadtgeschichte, 2 voll., 1993
Autore: Jürg Simonett/ebo

in Dizionario storico della Svizzera (DSS), URL: http://www. hlsdhs-dss.ch/textes/i/I13660.php, versione del 03.02.2006

My name is Luca Abys. I am the administrator of this site.

This is the origin of my family,

Abys

The family was mentioned for the first time in Chur, Switzerland, in the person of Johann, a native of Piuro (Valtellina), who acquired citizenship in 1609. Uncertain is the relationship in the late Middle Ages that Abyses resided in the central Grisons. Owners of large land property, the family members were active as merchants and shippers. Traditionally, the Abyses were also soldiers in the service of foreign powers and the City of Chur (captains). The family had in Andreas (XVII sec.) and Johann (1614-1697) two of the first physicians in Grisons. Raget, was a representatives in the Council of Grisons.

Source: Churer Stadtgeschichte, 2 vols., 1993
Author: Jürg Simonetta/Ebo

In Historical Dictionary of Switzerland (DSS), URL: http://www. hlsdhs-dss.ch/textes/i/I13660.php, version of 03.02.2006

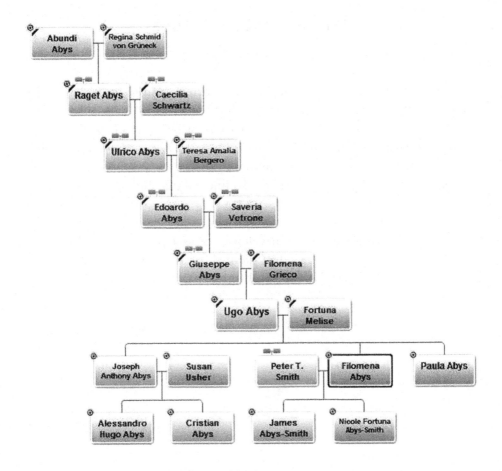

My Mothers' Family Tree

Fortuna Melise Abys

Mother—Carmela Sannino Melise—born in Crotone, Calabria, in August 1894, moved to Naples at age nineteen.

Father—Pasquale Melise—born in 1893; as far as we know, his family has always lived in Naples.

They married and had nine children: Luisa, Francesco, Anna, Fortuna (my mother), Giuseppina, Salvatore, Tonino, Maria, and Aldo.

> I'm so grateful to my mother for having the foresight to always
> speak Neapolitan to us; it has allowed me to remain connected
> not only to her family that I dearly love but to my culture,
> which I know will always be part of me.

Read on for an excerpt from Filomena's sequel to *A Bit of Myself.*

A Bit of Herself: A Conversation with Mom

Writing is a lonely process; it's just me and my thoughts as they swirl around in a maze of confusion. I pluck at them, one by one trying to organize and categorize them into a meaningful life. In front of me, I have bits of scrap paper written many years ago. Most are barely legible; faded and frail, they beckon at me to tell a story. A story that was told from mother to daughter through spontaneous conversation. While the daughter listened, the mother cleansed her soul and revealed a bit of herself.

The conversation, always in Neapolitan, was interpreted in English by the daughter, who for unknown reasons felt external forces guiding her hand to tell her mother's story and give meaning to a well-lived life.

She, my mother, stands near the stove; it seems to me that she has always stood in front of a stove preparing countless meals for her family. Fortuna, my mom, seems most content while cooking, and as I watch her, it gives me a sense of certainty, a feeling of forever. I understand that it's a false certainty but enjoy the feeling of permanency it gives.

I watch her now-aged body struggling to perform tasks that once were effortless as she begins to speak. "What can I say? Life has never been easy for me, always a struggle. Don't complain. You had it good in this country. You don't understand what hard work really is. You don't understand hunger and the humility of being taken out of school in second grade to work as a housemaid for the padrone."

I sense her bitterness, her great sorrow at not being given the opportunity of fulfilling her hidden potential, and I start to write.

Dear Reader,

I hope you have enjoyed reading my first memoir, I would truly appreciate any feedback; please feel free to send any comments to *fabys2@ aol.com*. Always live with passion.

Filomena

Index

R

S

Seamus, 191, 195-97, 201-2

shrimp, 226, 236, 290, 293

Signora Sparagna, 24-27, 29, 31, 37, 45, 66, 72

Signor Sparagna, 26-27, 37, 41

Smith, Peter, 156, 214, 246

South Bronx, 40, 50-53, 57-58, 79, 101, 169-70, 202, 216, 225, 276, 310, 322

Southold, 159, 193, 267, 271

Susan, 78-79, 84

T

tomatoes, 61, 157-58, 163-64, 221-22, 243

U

United States, 20, 42, 50-51, 162, 203

V

vegetables, 16, 63-64, 85, 102, 110-11, 171, 191, 220, 227, 231, 242-43, 255, 261-62, 306, 319

vinegar, 28, 110, 198, 238, 317

voyage, 37-38, 72, 162

W

wedding, 30, 98-101, 103, 105, 144, 175, 193, 229, 235, 239-40, 329

William, 138-44, 158, 166, 168, 174-77, 179-80, 182-89, 191-203, 206-8, 210-13, 216, 224, 240-42, 244

window, 29, 50, 52, 56, 89-90, 116, 125-26, 128, 130, 188-89, 215, 278, 321

witnesses, 91-92, 235

work, 31-32, 41, 44, 57, 92, 95, 100, 104-5, 108-9, 112-13, 118, 122, 127-28, 133-34, 138-39, 155-58, 160-61, 164, 167-69, 172, 174, 181-83, 186, 188, 190, 199-200, 203, 213-14, 218, 223-26, 231-33, 241-42, 245, 248, 256, 259, 265, 267-69, 275, 277, 280-81, 283, 287, 290, 292, 295, 297-98, 300-301, 308, 319, 353

Z

Zeppole di San Giuseppe, 33

zucchinis, 85, 106, 111, 238, 270

CPSIA information can be obtained
at www.ICGtesting.com
Printed in the USA
BVOW08s1914300817
493578BV00001B/1/P